Advance Praise for *Building from the Ground Up*

"A lot of what we think we know about the housing crash and the great recession is wrong. In *Building from the Ground Up*, Kevin Erdmann patiently helps us unlearn false lessons that are still doing our economy serious damage."

—RAMESH PONNURU, Senior Editor, *National Review*

"Erdmann is a rare combination of charming and disagreeable, which makes him a perfect challenger for poorly-supported conventional wisdom. In these pages he tells the untold story of the 2008 financial crisis—how the homebuilding industry took the fall for policy mistakes. Our problem was too little housing, not too much. Erdmann is an unabashed advocate for an industry that got framed. Erdmann's contemporaries may bristle at his provocative ideas, but like many of the best challengers of conventional wisdom, I expect he will be vindicated in the long run."

—ALAN COLE, Full Stack Economics, former Senior
Economist at the Joint Economic Committee

"Forget everything you think you know about the 2008 global financial crisis (GFC). Kevin Erdmann has the courage and insight to question the conventional GFC narrative. The policy implications of his exhaustive research are clear. In short, we need more homes and more homeowners. We are already seeing the social and economic costs of policies which make home ownership unreasonably difficult. Every policymaker should read this book."

—JOHN WELBORN, Lecturer in Economics at the
Political Economy Project, Dartmouth

BUILDING
FROM THE
GROUND UP

RECLAIMING
THE AMERICAN
HOUSING
BOOM

KEVIN ERDMANN

Post Hill
PRESS

A POST HILL PRESS BOOK
ISBN: 978-1-63758-161-2
ISBN (eBook): 978-1-63758-162-9

Building from the Ground Up:
Reclaiming the American Housing Boom
© 2022 by Kevin Erdmann

Post Hill Press
New York • Nashville
posthillpress.com

Published in the United States of America
1 2 3 4 5 6 7 8 9 10

TABLE OF CONTENTS

INTRODUCTION

The recovery from the Covid-19 recession may serve as a profound turning point in American economic development. This was a disruption that was thrust upon us. Nobody deserved to get sick. No hotel owner or restauranteur deserved bankruptcy. No maids, waiters, or flight attendants deserved to be unemployed.

This has led to public support for attempts to allay these discomforts. Of course, there are debates about the details. Every policy has tradeoffs, winners, and losers. As we come out of this, we will learn more about whether those tradeoffs were good or bad, on net. There will undoubtedly be some of both. However that falls out, it is clear that forbearance and a pro-growth tilt have become popular in ways they weren't during the 2008 recession.

In 2009, CNBC's Rick Santelli was credited with starting the Tea Party Movement from the floor of the Chicago Mercantile Exchange. He fumed, "Why don't you put up a website to have people vote on the internet as a referendum to see if we really want to subsidize the losers' mortgages?" and "How many of you people want to pay for your neighbor's mortgage that has an extra bathroom and can't pay their bills? Raise their hand."[1]

In 2020, millions of American homeowners were given a chance to miss some mortgage payments to help them get through the pandemic. This has not led to the ad hoc creation of a new political movement.

During the pandemic, much of the financial support has come in the form of subsidies and cash transfers. As we escape the pandemic, prosperity will depend more, again, on Americans helping ourselves, working together, and finding new ways to engage with one another economically.

The US economy has an incredible amount of pent-up potential. I mean this in a real sense. I don't mean that stock prices can go up more or that incomes will rise. Those things can happen. But if they happen, it will be the result of Americans being productive, taking risks, and innovating.

The American economy has become tied up in knots because in many ways we have simply made it illegal to…well, to just do stuff. Most people my age likely remember people who, decades ago, might have watched several children at their home, or say, cut hair in a makeshift one-chair salon in their garage so they could earn some cash while staying home with their kids. So much of that type of economic activity has disappeared today because the state requires onerous occupational licensing. Or the state, or city, or homeowners' association may forbid some types of home-operated businesses. Or countless other rules meant to make things more orderly.

These sorts of rules usually have pros and cons, but it is possible for the pendulum to swing too far in one direction. In the book *Shut Out*, I highlighted how entire metropolitan areas have become inaccessible to millions of families by making it very difficult to build new housing. Those difficulties sometimes start with good intentions—making sure the local infrastructure can handle more people, making sure displacement of locals is minimized, managing environmental impacts, and keeping units with historical importance. But the tools for applying these sorts of oversight are now routinely abused. For instance, proposed buildings in San Francisco are opposed because they might throw a shadow on a park early in the morning a few days a year. It's going to be very hard for San Francisco to be a world-class center of innovation, and to be affordable, if buildings can be opposed for casting shadows.

These obstructions have made metropolitan success synonymous with high costs. It wasn't always this way. It doesn't have to be this way. One reason nineteenth century and twentieth century America were beacons of hope and prosperity is that people moved to places that offered opportunity. Back then, metropolitan success was synonymous with population growth.

We have created a sort of reverse-flow Oregon Trail of Americans migrating to new places not because of hope for a new life but, instead, because of desperation for an affordable life. Americans frequently move to cities that legally allow more housing rather than to where housing would be more valuable to them.

We have a tremendous amount of potential to heal from the wounds of the pandemic and its recession simply by giving ourselves permission to do stuff again. Specifically, the story I have to tell you is about the economic fetters we have fitted on each other that are associated with the calamities of the Great Recession and the global financial crisis.

By 2005, the country appeared to have been overtaken by a housing bubble. It seemed there was too much money, too much credit, too many speculators, too many bankers, and eventually, too many houses at prices that were too high. Forbearance and a pro-growth tilt certainly wouldn't be prudent ways to handle all of those things. So, policymakers tried to pull back on economic growth and bank credit to kill the bubble. Americans reacted angrily wherever policymakers tried to lessen the pain and bail out various interests. Unlike the pandemic, we seemed to have brought this on ourselves, and we deserved our correctional fate. Or at least somebody did.

There had been a lot of newfangled mortgage products and speculators in selected housing markets. Certainly. But it turns out, fundamentally, the housing bubble was being driven by that perverse reverse-flow Oregon Trail. A handful of metropolitan areas had become unaffordable, not just to newcomers, but also to many of their own families, who now had to pick up and move. Those cities had become unwelcoming because building a home in metropolitan areas like Los Angeles is just one of the normal, regular things that Americans just weren't allowed to do any more.... Oh, you can build one. But just like the garage stylist or the stay-at-home babysitter, you have to get permission first, and the permission frequently ends up being the hardest part of the task. In cities like Los Angeles, the permission takes much more effort and is more costly than simply building the house.

It is natural to be angry that your home is becoming unaffordable to you. It is also natural to be angry at the family that replaced you, or worse, a speculator, and to be angry at their banker or at policymakers that seem to favor them over you. And a year later, if that family, or worse, speculator, is in default and the home you couldn't afford is in foreclosure, you bet it's natural to be angry.

The source of all these indignities was a lack of adequate housing, especially in a few places where it has become a big problem. The increasing amount of home construction before the Great Recession was a second-best solution for tackling that problem. We *needed* houses, but the houses had to be built in different places than where they were most needed. This meant that meeting our growing need for housing created displacement. People had to move to the cities where homes could be built. They were a step toward the cure for this artificial scarcity we had created. We can't just…do stuff. And one thing we aren't allowed to do anymore is move to a place like Los Angeles without making somebody else somewhere in that city move away to make room for us.

My challenge to you is to consider that maybe a predisposition toward growth and production would have been helpful in 2008. The financial shenanigans in mortgage markets weren't funding homes we didn't need. We needed homes. The financial shenanigans were the result of making it so difficult to build them in some places. Maybe when we gave into our anger about the symptoms of an economy embroiled in a pathology of artificial scarcity, we only worsened the underlying disease.

It's like the old cliché where you find a cigarette in your child's room and to teach them a lesson, you make them smoke a whole pack so that they get so sick they never want to touch a cigarette again. That's what we did to the American economy in 2008. We ended up in the financial emergency room. I'm here to break the news that it wasn't even our kid's cigarette. Not only was the result of our discipline worse than we had intended it to be and unfair for many Americans who lost jobs or homes because of it, it was an attempt to address a problem that we hadn't really understood well.

So, this is a story about the pent-up potential of the American economy today. It's about the ways that our economy is poised to grow and create opportunity as we escape Covid-19. It's also about the new damage we have been imposing on the economy since the 2008 financial crisis. And it's about the long-standing damage that urban housing regulations have been creating for decades now.

In order to tell this story about our potential today, I need to back up and detail the twenty-first century history of choices that got us here. The histories you have read have been focused on the symptoms without understanding the disease. What if, in 2007 and 2008, we had embraced growth and creation instead of financial chasteness and discipline? If that was true of 2008, just think what we can do today if we give ourselves the chance.

There has been a frustrating sense of inequity and stagnation in our economy. We can break away from that problem, but the first step must be to give ourselves permission. We are tied up in knots. The first task going forward is to untie them. This is a story about how some of those knots were tied.

PART 1

A New History of the Great Recession

CHAPTER 1

WHAT REALLY HAPPENED

The following chapters reflect a new history of the housing bubble, the Great Recession, and the global financial crisis. In many ways, conventional wisdom should be turned on its head.

How has conventional wisdom been wrong? It has been built on the presumption that a housing bubble led to the construction of too many overpriced homes. To the contrary, the United States has never had too many homes. If anything, we have been suffering from a distressing shortage of homes—even in 2005.

What is the most obvious reason why a product or service might become very expensive? Because there isn't enough of it to go around! The reason some homes became very expensive in 2005 is that there weren't enough of them. That should be obvious. Right?

Even though the basic story really is that simple, it is so at odds with the conventional wisdom that it reasonably requires a lot of evidence. My previous book, *Shut Out*, contains many details and evidence about this problem. If you need to be convinced about those details, *Shut Out* is a handy background to this book. But those details mostly just add up to this simple preliminary point: Home prices have been high because there aren't enough of them.[2]

Practically any media you have seen or read about the housing bubble probably has described the housing bubble as the final hurrah in a decades-long housing mania. Americans were massively overinvesting in McMansions. Keeping up with the Joneses. Bankers were like the devil on our shoulders, pushing us in over our heads until it all finally toppled of its own unsustainable weight.

The funny thing is government data doesn't really back up that story. In the late 1940s, residential investment jumped up to meet the pent-up demand for better housing after the Great Depression. As a percentage of GDP, it has been declining ever since then. By 1980, Americans were regularly increasing our incomes and our consumption of other goods and services at a faster pace than new housing was being built. At the height of the housing bubble, the growth in the size and quality of American homes was only just beginning to catch up with real income growth for the first time in decades.[3] It has been at least forty years since this country has been truly engaged in a residential building boom. Table 1 compares the growth of total personal spending adjusted for inflation to the growth of spending on housing.[4]

	1960-1980	1980-2000	2000-2006	2006-2018
Average Annual Growth in Total Real Personal Expenditures	3.7%	3.6%	3.1%	1.8%
Average Annual Growth in Real Personal Expenditures on Housing	4.4%	2.7%	2.5%	1.3%

Table 1 tracks real values—size, quality, amenities, etc. This doesn't mean we spend less of our incomes on housing than we used to. It just means we aren't getting larger or better homes for that spending. That is especially the case since the financial crisis. Residential investment over the past decade has returned to Great Depression levels, so that the growth in the real value of our homes has only averaged 1.3 percent annually since 2006. Yet, according to the US Bureau of Economic Analysis (the BEA), we are spending more of our incomes on rent than at any time *since* the Great Depression.[5]

That is one of the notions about the housing bubble where our intuition fails us. It seems obvious that if we are investing more in new housing, then we will be spending more to live in that housing. To the contrary, increasing the supply of housing leads to *lower* rents. This is especially true where the problem is most acute. If cities like New York and Los Angeles allowed as much residential investment as cities like Atlanta, rents there would plummet. An underappreciated perversity of the twenty-first-century American economy is that our leading economic metropolitan areas—New York City, Los Angeles, San Francisco, and Boston—have much higher housing costs than the rest of the country, and the main reason is that they allow far less home building than other cities.[6]

That is a strong reason to support an active home building market. The value of new marginal investment in the housing stock is generally claimed by tenants, mostly because rents on the existing stock of homes decline.[7] Rising rents have been a major component in the rising cost of living over the past few decades, and the lack of residential investment is the main reason.

Imagine a world where doctors encouraged smoking, where marriage counselors encouraged secretive philandering, where business consultants encouraged procrastination, or where schoolteachers encouraged the popular children to taunt and bully kids with special needs. Regarding the housing bubble and the recession, economists and policymakers have been making a mistake of similar proportions. Almost all respectable economists and policymakers have agreed that the pivotal issue with the American economy as we entered the Great Recession was that we had built too many homes—we had tricked ourselves into unsustainable residential investment. Our collective reaction to the accumulating financial crisis was deeply affected by the presumption that a housing boom had led to unsustainably high residential investment. We must cure ourselves of that myth. In 2005, we could have used more homes, not fewer.

I realize that this may seem like an incredible assertion to make. It isn't an assertion I ever planned on making or expected to make. I certainly never expected to spend years of my life developing it. And, certainly, there is never a shortage of half-baked theories about how economists are wrong about things. Yet the evidence for this assertion is overwhelming. I have been overwhelmed by it. I have been surprised by it. And I am left with little else to do but share with you the conclusions that the overwhelming evidence should compel us to reach. The health of the American economy depends on getting over our fear of housing.

A BRIEF OVERVIEW OF CONVENTIONAL WISDOM

Debates continue about the causes of the Great Recession, but they largely share some basic presumptions. First, an inevitable housing bust that began around 2007 was the result of a housing bubble that had developed in the previous years. The excesses of the bubble were underestimated, so policymakers were surprised by the extent of the bust, and eventually that bust grew into a financial crisis and the Great Recession. If the bust was inevitable, then the answer to "How could we have avoided the financial crisis and the recession?" seems like it is obviously, "We should have avoided the housing bubble to begin with."

How would we describe the housing bubble? Among the conventional answers are as follows:

» A flood of new mortgages to unqualified borrowers that led to an unsustainable increase in home ownership.

» Speculative buying that drove prices far above historical norms with no relation to rental value or ability to pay.

» A rise in newfangled financial securities that drew capital into a bloated housing market.

» Foreign savings that flowed into the US, also flooding the housing market with capital.

» Low interest rates created by the Federal Reserve.

» A massive oversupply of housing as a result of all that excess capital.

There is an undeniable core of truth in some of these observations, or at least some basic observable fact that seems to have confirmed that they were correct and momentous. Yet, there is still unresolved debate about some of those claims and others that are wrong.

There were pockets of speculation toward the end of the housing boom, but there really wasn't a shift downward in average homeowner income or in measures like home buyers' credit scores.[8] Prices certainly were very high in some cities, but rising rents really were the most important reason for that. In most cities where prices have shot up far higher than household incomes, it is because rents in those cities are eating up more of their incomes and will continue to.[9]

Activity in the private mortgage-backed securitization (MBS) market did surge from mid-2003 until 2007, but that activity was a relative latecomer. Home ownership had peaked by 2004. That lending activity increasingly facilitated investor and speculator activity rather than financially marginal home buyers.

The more complex securities like the more exotic types of collateralized debt obligations (CDOs) were especially latecomers, really only becoming popular when construction, home ownership, and sales were all near their peak levels or declining. That decline lasted for nearly two years before the official beginning of the recession. Those complex securities are frequently the focus of retrospectives about the financial crisis. CDOs, and especially the more exotic types with names like CDO-squared and synthetic CDO, were important factors in how the financial crisis played out, but they really had very little to do with the relentless upward march of housing costs in the most expensive cities like Los Angeles and New York City.[10]

Has the lack of active private MBS and CDO markets since the crisis caused housing in New York City and Los Angeles to become more affordable? Are American working-class families now flooding into those cities because, by taming the out-of-control mortgage market, we now live in an unprecedented era of affordable urban housing? To the contrary, the high rents that were the primary driver of rising home prices have only continued to soar.

Limited housing supply in a few prospering cities (New York City, Los Angeles, San Francisco, and Boston, primarily, which I refer to as the "Closed

Access" cities) drove up local rents and prices. Those rising costs induced hundreds of thousands of households to move away from those cities in search of a lower cost of living. The places associated most directly with a housing bubble (cities in Arizona, Florida, Nevada, and inland California, which I refer to as the "Contagion" cities) were overwhelmed by this wave of migration.

We might truly call the housing markets in the Contagion cities, between 2004 to 2006, bubbles. Yet, even there, the real story of what happened is not a story of booming excess. Those areas were overwhelmed by a migration wave because they were less expensive. The new households flooding into those cities were coming in search of compromise. For many of them, these were second-best substitutions for cities they could no longer afford to live in.

Certainly, in the midst of this housing refugee event, there was speculative and fraudulent activity. A homeowner, a developer, or a housing investor who watched the entire string of events from within a Contagion city could be forgiven for viewing it simply as a speculative bubble. Yet a boom in cheap substitutes is not the sign of a thriving or overstimulated economy. It is the sign of an economy deprived of better goods and services. The bubble that was busted was already a bubble in compromise and exclusion. It was a bubble that should have been busted with *more* supply—more homes in California and the Atlantic Northeast—not busted with a crackdown on the growth of money and credit.

Americans were investing in new homes in 2005 at a sustainable, relatively neutral pace in line with rising incomes. But our most prosperous cities now fail to allow even a normal amount of housing or population growth, so normal growth leads to upheaval in those cities. What looked like a country with a bubble was really a country that has become incapable of supporting reasonable levels of residential investment. A country tied up in knots.

If you live in a Closed Access city, in order to increase the size and quality of your home, some other poor sap will need to be nudged out of the city to make more room for you. That is the story of the great housing bubble.

The Closed Access cities will only allow a limited amount of residential shelter. When our economy grows faster than the Closed Access cities are willing to grow, then an ugly process of segregation into and out of those cities takes place. So, ironically, at the height of the so-called housing boom, the population of the Closed Access metropolitan areas was declining.

In short, fundamentally, the housing bubble was triggered by a localized housing shortage, not a national oversupply. All of the apparent excesses and cataclysms were side effects of that central problem. At its core, this was a drama caused by deprivation rather than profligacy.

Rents are a key point where the conventional wisdom has been thoroughly and explicitly wrong, which demands a wholesale reinterpretation of the financial crisis. The key assertions underpinning the conventional story of the housing bubble are that (1) prices were rising with no connection to rents and (2) supply was being created with no connection to demand for shelter.[11] This is simply false. As wisdom grows with hindsight, the point is obvious. Clearly, the places where home prices were and are the highest are the places where rents are the highest.

Before the mid-1990s, rents didn't differ as much between metropolitan areas, and so before then, prices among different metropolitan areas weren't nearly as different as they are today. The Herculean irony is that this period that led to a moral panic about irrational home prices was based on a rational, systematic reaction to that problem. Every year, as housing supply in the Closed Access cities has fallen further and further behind the demand for it, rents have risen to levels previously unheard of, *systematically* driving up prices.

The Financial Crisis Inquiry Commission (FCIC) was the massive governmental project meant to get to the bottom of the financial crisis. In their report, numbering hundreds of pages, they spent one paragraph on rents, and in that paragraph, they dismissed rising rents as a cause of the bubble, citing rising price/rent ratios. Now, it is *plausible* that a financial bubble could lead to irrationally rising price/rent ratios. It just so happens that in this case, for the most part, it hadn't. The places where price/rent ratios had risen the most were places where *rents* had risen the most! Buyers were driving up prices because they could see that rents were going to continue to rise.

This problem has gotten so bad that locals now get angry at plans to bring in corporate headquarters or to expand facilities with highly paid workers because higher pay will just cause local rents to rise. When angry local activists throw rocks at Google commuter busses, they aren't angry that the riders in those busses are overpaying for homes they can't afford. They are angry because the riders in those busses *can* afford to pay more for housing. Whether they know it or not, they are angry because whenever anything economically good happens, their cities' strict housing policies turn that progress into a nasty process of economic sorting and segregation—a game of economic musical chairs.[12]

The FCIC recognized that this was an important empirical point to make because if rising prices were mostly related to rising rents, then the entire project would be turned on its head. Rather than an irrational bubble, rising rents would suggest that the housing boom was driven by a basic demand for shelter. That is, in fact, what was happening and financial markets, at most, were facilitating this fundamental demand. The FCIC and most others got this small but incredibly important fact very, very wrong. Just on this single point, the entire literature on the housing boom and the financial crisis requires a reassessment.

The Contagion cities were the only places where prices did rise and fall without such a strong systematic influence from rising rents. By 2004 and 2005, the migration out of the expensive Closed Access cities was getting large enough to be disruptive. That migration consisted of (1) households with lower incomes who had mainly been renters, and who were forced out of the Closed Access cities by rising costs, and (2) homeowners with higher incomes who decided to realize windfall capital gains from selling their Closed Access homes. These migrants spread out through the country, but they especially ended up in certain popular landing spots for Closed Access refugees—the Contagion cities. In 2005, the populations of Arizona and Nevada increased by more than 1 percent, just from the net inflow of migrants from California.[13] The FCIC report does not contain a single word about migration.

The FCIC entirely missed the core components of the story.

Both rising construction activity and rising prices tended to occur in the same cities. The Contagion cities and the Closed Access cities were the main locations for that activity. The housing boom was, in fact, inducing new construction where it was desperately needed. The more desperately it was needed, the higher local prices were driven.[14] There really wasn't a building boom in the rest of the country.

There were places that couldn't build homes fast enough because they were tied up in knots. There were places that couldn't build homes fast enough because they were flooded with people escaping those places. And there were a lot of places where construction was just normal. That's it. That describes just about everywhere. The statements you see in a thousand books and articles that we were building too many homes don't describe any actual place.[15]

We have made ourselves poorer by tying ourselves up in regulatory knots. When you are poorer, basic necessities become more expensive. You could say that our collective mistake was to notice this problem—that basic necessities were more expensive—and to conclude the reason things were more expensive was that other people had too many dollars. We blamed the Fed, the bankers, and government subsidies. The problem, instead, was that we didn't have enough, regardless of how many dollars everyone had. We were so lacking in housing that families were literally crossing state lines in search of it.

This is how we came to embrace failure and crisis. These exclusionary cities have become a tumor ballooning in the belly of our economy, and we shamed ourselves for our swelling obesity. We aimed to starve ourselves to cure it.

CHAPTER 2

AMERICAN EXCEPTIONALISM SINCE 2007

Global forces have collided to create these intense pressures for housing in select urban centers. The information age has made some cities important centers for innovation and economic activity. In the past, those cities would have grown as a result of that. But over the course of the twentieth century, many cities have accumulated a dense web of local regulations that make it very hard to build a lot of homes. So, the owners of the metro area's real estate effectively become an accidental cartel in control of a limited resource—the OPEC of urban shelter. The de facto production caps are created through countless objections and delays to new urban housing, facilitated by municipal planning departments.

In this regard, the United States is not unusual. Many developed economies face similar problems. London in Great Britain. Sydney in Australia. Toronto in Canada. There are also countries that have not been as captured by this problem—for example, Germany, Japan, and South Korea. The United States has a foot in both worlds. We have the Closed Access cities, but we also have economically dynamic cities where housing is not constrained and where home prices remained moderate—for example, Dallas, Houston, and Atlanta.

The common explanations for the housing bubble are oddly America-centric: Fannie Mae and Freddie Mac, subprime mortgages and bank dereg-ulation, loose Federal Reserve policy, federal housing subsidies, and home ownership programs. But the expansion of the American housing market before 2007 was not particularly unusual internationally, either in terms of prices or of construction activity. All of those explanations should be suspect.

On the other hand, compared to other large, developed economies, our housing market *has been unusual* since 2007. Across the board, housing prices and starts collapsed for years. Construction employment has collapsed com-pared to other countries. Prices in Closed Access cities have declined com-pared to places like London and Sydney. Prices in cities like Atlanta and Houston have declined compared to places like Germany and Japan.

Prices weren't unusually high in the United States before 2007 compared to our international peers, but US prices after 2007 have been unusually low. According to the Organisation for Economic Co-operation and Development (OECD), home prices adjusted for inflation in the US were about 38 percent higher in 2019 than they had been in 2000. In other anglosphere countries (the United Kingdom, Canada, Australia, and New Zealand) they were up from 86 to 178 percent. The postindustrial urban housing problem is hitting all of these countries. The thing that has made us different has been that our home prices have been very much *lower* since 2007 compared to the other countries.[16]

The same can be said of construction employment. On the eve of the Covid-19 pandemic, the total number of workers in the construction sector in the US was about 15 percent higher than it had been in 2000. Construction employment in the UK has grown slightly more than in the US—about 20 percent. In the other countries, construction employment has grown any-where from 72 to 112 percent.[17]

What if construction employment in the US could have followed along with employment trends in Australia and Canada? There were about ten million construction workers in the US in 2000. The difference between the American economy and other anglosphere economies amounts to mil-lions of jobs.

The hard truth is that there was no overarching reason why millions of workers in the construction sector had to be thrust into long-term unemployment. The bust was the result of a mania that developed in the United States that came to *see* the bust as inevitable. Credit markets began to tighten. Expectations of falling home prices mounted. And the broad national reaction was, "It's about time." We treated the bust as medicine that needed to be taken.

That medicine cured nothing and only created disastrous side effects because it was based on false premises. Measures that might have created broad stability were delayed or avoided because those measures would "bail out" speculators and lenders, and when the Federal Reserve and the Treasury finally did implement some measures aimed at stabilization, they were widely criticized. They are still widely criticized today for bailing out Wall Street.

In the vast expanse of the country where home prices had remained moderate during the boom—places like Oklahoma City; Raleigh, North Carolina; and Birmingham, Alabama (the list is long)—a mortgaged home was about as affordable as it had been for many years. By 2012, those houses were more affordable than they had been for decades.[18] This affordability was mostly achieved by denying mortgage credit to large segments of the population, which destroyed demand in the most affordable markets. And households who already owned homes in affordable neighborhoods had their life savings sucked out from under them as their home values collapsed.

Most of the collapse in the affordable markets happened after the financial crisis of late 2008. Most of the defaults happened after that, also. The collapse engineered by public policy was not the mirror image of the boom. There was some snapback in the Contagion cities, which mirrored the previous run-up in prices. But collapsing home values in affordable cities like Oklahoma City, Raleigh, and Birmingham weren't reversing anything. The collapse also wasn't a mirror image of the boom within metropolitan areas. In most cities, home prices had risen by similar amounts in both expensive and affordable neighborhoods. Yet, after the financial crisis, in every kind of city, whether home prices had been high or not, the damage was usually the greatest in the most affordable neighborhoods.

Patterns in homeowner characteristics also don't match the boom-and-bust picture. Between 1995 and 2007, characteristics like income and education were becoming *more* important factors in who owned homes, not less. And contracting mortgage markets after 2007 have only reinforced that shift. Compared to 1995, there are fewer low-income homeowners with less than a college degree. By contrast, there are more high-income or college-educated homeowners.[19] On net, the buyers during the boom were college-educated professionals, but it has been less-educated borrowers with lower incomes who have been blocked from getting mortgages in the fallout.

The rotten fate of those homeowners in Oklahoma City and Birmingham became inevitable because we collectively insisted on it. Public reactions to the events and policy choices of 2006 onward were deeply influenced by the false idea that Americans had been overinvesting in housing to an extreme.

What happens to an economy when a very important asset that is in short supply is treated as if it is in an unsustainable surplus that must be "worked off?" In a word, a crisis is what happens, and a crisis is what did happen. We must look again at those public reactions and policy decisions with clear eyes.

CHAPTER 3

KICKING THE TIRES
ON THE EVIDENCE

Before I get into the details of the chronology of events, I want to take a moment to think about how collective understanding requires a canonized base of knowledge: a set of facts and concepts that can be asserted with little or no proof. There has to be a canon, even if it isn't right. It certainly never is completely right.

This is obvious when we look back in history. For most of history, the idea that invisible organisms caused sickness was not part of the canon. The idea that species evolved from previous forms of species was not part of the canon. The idea that the earth orbits the sun was not part of the canon. And so on. Their absence left voids that were filled with other conjectures, sometimes with disastrous results. Those conjectures were believed just as fervently as we believe in our own received canon.

In 1847, a Hungarian physician named Ignaz Philipp Semmelweis discovered that a fever which frequently killed mothers in birthing wards could be greatly reduced if physicians washed their hands before dealing with patients. He faced significant opposition, and the practice wasn't fully accepted until after he had suffered a nervous breakdown and died in an insane asylum.

From our point of view, European doctors must have been an outrageously stubborn group. They were literally killing many of the expectant mothers that sought their care. But they had their own explanations that made sense to them for the fever. It might seem easy enough to wash your hands before dealing with patients, but if we all agreed to take easy precautions against every oddball warning we heard, we would spend our entire day taking easy precautions against things that would turn out to mostly be crackpot theories. The canon should be hard to change.

During the housing boom, American builders kept putting up more homes. Prices kept climbing in spite of all the new units. Lenders kept creating new mortgage products in order to keep the whole racket going. It seemed obvious what was happening. And the air was filled with damning, if circumstantial, evidence.

Forecasters had been predicting a decline in housing starts since back in the mid-1990s.[20] Yet housing starts continued to rise for a decade along with prices. With each passing year, the forces that were causing the bubble appeared more powerful and dastardly.

Case, Shiller, and Thompson documented the unrealistic expectations of home buyers who thought prices would continue to rise at an unsustainable pace.[21] In 2010, *The Washington Post* included the idea that housing prices always rise in a series of the ten worst ideas of the decade. "Countless delusions and mistakes brought on our financial crisis, but none did as much damage as the belief that home prices never go down...[A]t the start of this decade, this belief became the lynchpin of an entire investment philosophy."[22] Chuck Prince, the CEO of Citigroup, famously said, "As long as the music is playing, you've got to get up and dance."

These are all images of lemmings heading for the cliffs. Could those attitudes move trillions of dollars of capital into unneeded and inflated assets? It's plausible, but hard to prove. Yet there was so much evidence. What further proof did we need? There are countless papers quantifying the effect of lending standards or bank deregulation on home prices. It really would be ludicrous to completely deny the connection.

Some combination of speculation, reckless lending and borrowing, or of federal fiscal or monetary over-stimulus seemed to be fueling a bubble. A bubble is bound to eventually bust. The debate continues about exactly which source of overstimulation created the bubble. Yet the consensus formed early that some form of overstimulation had occurred. And, disastrously, that meant that there was a consensus that bad things were bound to happen in the American economy even before bad things happened.[23]

Unfortunately, the consensus—the canon—was wrong. But the canon doesn't change easily for a reason. That makes the task I have set out here, at once, both difficult and easy. It is difficult because changing the canon *should* be difficult. It is easy because the canon is supported by shadows of apparent evidence that have never been stringently vetted. The housing bubble filled a void when we needed an explanation for the developing economic contraction. Once that happened, we were satisfied with corroborating evidence that was merely plausible. Contradictory evidence, on the other hand, was suspect.

Of the countless histories of the housing bust and the crisis, how many have paid notice to construction employment and home prices in countries like Australia and Canada that have generally just kept climbing? If the trigger for a US contraction was that we had too many homes at prices that were too high in 2005, why didn't the same tragedy befall Canada and Australia?

One of the factors commonly implicated in the housing boom-and-bust is a wave of global capital that fueled rising home prices. Spain and Ireland are frequently cited as other examples of countries with housing bubbles that busted.[24] Isn't that weird? How many other conversations about global finance skip over Germany, Australia, Japan, and Canada and focus on Spain and Ireland? The problem is that none of the other major economies had a boom-and-bust like the US did. Some had booms that didn't bust. Others didn't have housing booms at all. The difference between "cherry picking" and "removing outliers" is hard to discern in practice. The difference is frequently determined by our sense of acceptable premises, especially if those premises are strongly held.

Semmelweis didn't need to be a genius to see that his patients were living when he washed his hands. It was obvious when he decided to pay attention to it. Nobody had bothered to notice before.

THE IDEAS THAT I AM NOT CHALLENGING

First, rest assured. There is a lot of evidence that I am not challenging. Many of the purported causes of the housing bubble I listed in chapter 1 have a nugget of truth:

» In the years leading up to 2007, lenders were increasingly providing loans with more flexible, and sometimes ill-advised, terms.

» The privately securitized subprime and Alt-A loans were traded in markets that were vulnerable to a systematic breakdown when investors lost faith in housing markets.

» The more exotic versions of those securities, like CDOs, CDOs-squared, and synthetic CDOs, which became more popular in 2006 and 2007, were especially vulnerable to systematic breakdown.[25]

» Especially in 2006 and 2007, an increasing proportion of home buyers in volatile housing markets were investors and speculators, and since they were more likely to default when home prices began to decline, they were eventually an important factor that led to a cascade of rising mortgage defaults and homes for sale.

» Regulations that encouraged some financial firms to hold securities that became unstable during the downturn concentrated losses from those securities in the banking and financial sector.[26]

» If banks had been designed to be safer, with more of a capital cushion for instance, they would have been capable of taking on more losses without becoming insolvent or illiquid and triggering a crisis.[27]

Those were all important developments that affected *how* the housing bust and the financial crisis played out. But a prerequisite for these developments to have *caused* a crisis is that they first caused an unsustainable bubble.

My point isn't that these developments were harmless or that they couldn't, hypothetically, create unsustainable activity in housing markets. My point is that, in hindsight, the mechanism through which they were supposed to have created an inevitable collapse—excessive investment in real estate—didn't happen. Homes were being built where homes were in high demand—as shelter, not just as investments. In other areas (the majority of the country) building activity and prices were moderate and could be easily explained with fundamentals like rental value and long-term real interest rates.

As we walk through the series of events that led to the crisis, these are the sort of questions you should ask yourself: "What policy choices would have maintained stable construction employment in Kansas City? Would there have been a financial crisis in 2008 if those policies had been enacted? What would have been so bad about such policies? Why were policies that would have accomplished that so unpopular?"

For this reason, I won't dwell too much on the specific qualities of the mortgage products that became popular from 2004 to 2007. At this point, you may want to reply that research from well-regarded economists in prestigious journals shows that loose lending can systematically push up demand that leads to higher prices and more building. That reply is reasonable. But empirically, in most of the country, neither of those things happened. It doesn't matter if they can happen or if they did happen in a few places. There were many places where they didn't happen, and yet, when each of those places was subsumed by economic calamity, a thing that didn't happen there was blamed for it.

It could very well be the case that by 2007, the optimal outcome would have led to a brief decline in building and double-digit price contractions in cities like Phoenix or Orlando. Those newfangled mortgage products were undoubtedly a part of that story.

Today, the common narrative of the crisis has places like Phoenix and Orlando as poster children. But construction dissipated, and prices fell in Kansas City and a hundred other cities, too. There has been remarkably little curiosity about why that happened and whether we should have aimed to prevent it. If we're looking at lost jobs, a wealth shock, and lower incomes, the bulk of the damage came from the multitude of cities like Kansas City.

It is one thing to observe that Phoenix is susceptible to speculative over-reach and that the remedy for that might only be achieved through some painful short-term consequences in Phoenix. It is quite another to observe those things in Phoenix and to accept a 30 percent decline in construction employment in Kansas City as a consequence. There has been a dearth of introspection about the disconnect between those consequences.

Furthermore, *prices* may have been doomed for a correction in Phoenix. Yet, the evidence that construction employment needed to decline, even in Phoenix, let alone in Kansas City, is surprisingly weak. The *idea* that there was a vast overinvestment in housing by 2005 was an important cause of the painful events of 2008. That idea was wrong.

IT AIN'T WHAT YOU DON'T KNOW THAT GETS YOU INTO TROUBLE.

Popular literature covering the dramatic events from 2006 onward generally gets the facts right. Those events happened. There is little to disagree about. Many, many books have been written about the financial crisis. The films *The Big Short* and *Inside Job* both won Oscars for examining the financial crisis. They generally contain many details about events from 2006 onward and few details from before 2006. *The Big Short* is a good example. The stories told in the last two hours of the movie adaptation of *The Big Short* are dramatized with precise and generally accurate detail. But those accurate details are built upon a canonized presumption about what caused those events.

The Big Short opens by zipping through the preceding twenty-five years in three minutes. It begins with the development of mortgage-backed securities in the early 1980s. Time-lapse footage of rising skyscrapers and scenes of bankers throwing cash at strippers crescendos with, "And America barely noticed as its number one industry became boring old banking. And then one day...almost thirty years later...in 2008...it all came crashing down."

Out of two hours and ten minutes, I am only asking you to question three minutes of material. The three minutes that avoid detail. That foundation is what all of the precise details of the rest of the movie got built on top of—the idea that 2008 was just the final, inevitable act in a twenty-five-year-long drama. The canon determines which details we track and which details we ignore. The time-lapse footage of skyscrapers is a fitting metaphor for the divergent way that canonized knowledge directs our attention. *The Big Short* didn't need to spend two hours convincing the audience that its setup was true, because the audience supposed that they already knew it was.

In truth, those time-lapsed skyscrapers were facing more and more legal obstructions. After 1980, Americans were investing less of their growing incomes each year into larger, nicer homes, not more. In some places, those homes were getting more expensive because it had become largely illegal to develop new housing nearby. The idea that bankers in the early 1980s created a monster that led to a thirty-year housing binge is simply backward. The late 1980s and 1990s saw, by just about any measure, the lowest rate of new housing production since the Great Depression.

The opening image of the movie is ironically set behind a quote from Mark Twain. "It ain't what you don't know that gets you into trouble. It's what you know for sure that just ain't so."

DEMANDING MORE THAN PLAUSIBILITY FROM THE CANON

Midway through the movie, one of the characters travels to Florida to check on a bubble market on the ground. He finds many homes for sale, mortgage brokers who brag about originating mortgages recklessly to people that can't afford them, homeowners down on their luck, neighborhoods full of vacant homes, real estate agents convinced the market will recover from a brief decline, and an erotic dancer who owns six highly leveraged investment properties.

The meeting with the erotic dancer cuts immediately to a call back to the office: "Hey, there's a bubble."

Those scenes describe the market in early 2007. The image projected by the movie is a stark and accurate portrayal of the time. His phone call makes perfect sense if that was just the next step in a twenty-five-year story of reckless lending.

But what he really should have said into the phone is "Hey, there's a bust." And instead of seeing that bust as an inevitable comeuppance for everyone involved in a twenty-five-year-long drama of excess, he should have seen it as a terrifying new development that should have been stopped.

Some contradictions the characters in *The Big Short* didn't consider: If mortgage brokers were so busy handing out mortgages, why were there so many empty homes? If so many naïve speculators suddenly owned multiple properties, why were there so many listed homes that hadn't found buyers?

There are possible answers to those questions. Maybe there were so many extra homes because builders were adding supply at an unquenchable pace, or because previous owners were losing their homes faster than new suckers could be rounded up.

Those ideas seem plausible. Fortunately, data is available to check those questions. We don't need to settle for plausibility.

In early 2007, foreclosures had just started to rise, but not to the extreme levels they eventually would. Eventually, quarterly foreclosures per ten thousand borrowers would reach about twenty nationwide (compared to about seven in better times) and reach as high as forty to eighty in the worst states. But that wasn't really the case until 2008 through 2010.[28] Foreclosures can't explain those stark images in early 2007.

How about builders? Builders had begun to sharply *cut back* on housing starts in early 2006. At the end of 2005, sales had been pretty brisk. Suddenly, sales started to plummet. Builders reacted quickly to falling sales, and new home inventory peaked by July 2006 at 572,000 units. After that, builders were putting up fewer homes than they were selling. The reason there were still nearly that many new homes for sale a year later is that by June 2007, sales had fallen by 43 percent from the 2005 peak.

Brokers really were handing out a lot of mortgages. Mortgages outstanding were still growing at the time, both in terms of rising dollars and the number of accounts. All the factual observations in the movie were happening. But the unexamined plausible explanations for why they were all happening, upon examination, aren't so plausible after all. Builders weren't flooding the market with new homes, foreclosures on existing owners weren't particularly high yet, and home sales were plummeting in spite of the lending.

So, why *were* there neighborhoods full of empty homes for sale? Why were sales so low if mortgage brokers were so busy?

MORTGAGES, MORTGAGES EVERYWHERE, NOR ANY OFFER TO BUY

The empty neighborhoods were new neighborhoods. The reason they were empty was that since early 2006, new home buyers had begun cancelling their orders. Homebuilders are generally quite generous about this. They demand a small deposit up front when they begin construction on a new home. Over the six months or so it takes to build that home, things happen. Frequently, the buyers need to sell their existing home. Things don't always work out, so builders generally let customers cancel, and at most, they keep the small deposit as payment.

Normally, cancellations are under 20 percent. The largest homebuilder in the US, D.R. Horton, reported cancellations at over 40 percent by the end of 2006. Cancellations continued to be high in 2007. By 2007, D.R. Horton began to cite difficulty getting mortgages as a reason for cancellations. But in 2006, they cited decreased home buyer confidence and the inability of customers to sell their existing homes.[29]

Those empty neighborhoods in *The Big Short* had little or nothing to do with borrowers who defaulted on their mortgages. Those neighborhoods were empty because those who had ordered homes there were choosing not to accept the homes when they were finished.

This shift in sentiment was happening in general. The number of first-time home buyers was in decline by 2006, and the number of homeowners selling and switching to renting was increasing.[30] Prolific research partners

Atif Mian from Princeton University and Amir Sufi from the University of Chicago found that during the same time that private MBS markets were increasing funding for a small group of investors and speculators, more traditional borrowers were becoming more pessimistic about housing investments and less active as buyers.[31]

According to the Census Bureau, from the end of 2005 to the end of 2007, America grew by about two million households. They were almost all renters.[32] (That continued to be the case until 2015!)

The explanation for empty homes in 2007 that seemed plausible to the characters in *The Big Short* was that Wall Street ran out of suckers to sell bad mortgages to. Yet, in 2007, the portion of working-age households who owned their homes wasn't particularly high by historical standards. For the better part of two years, an unusually high proportion of potential homeowners had been opting out. By mid-2007, the mortgage industry was beginning to feel a desperation for new borrowers, but it clearly wasn't because of market saturation. If there was a lack of qualified borrowers, it wasn't because all of the potential qualified buyers were already homeowners. Qualified buyers had soured on the housing market long before foreclosures became unusually high.[33]

"HEY, THERE'S A BUST."

So, it seems, even though the Florida mortgage brokers in *The Big Short* were busier than ever, they weren't busy enough to counteract other Americans who were fleeing the housing market. And by 2007, many of the mortgages they were originating were cash-out refinancing rather than for purchase. All of these trends were at their extremes in places like Nevada, Arizona, and Florida—the places that were the epicenter of the American housing refugee wave.

This shows up starkly in long-term population trends in Florida, Arizona, and Nevada. They had been growing at high rates since World War II, mostly because of people moving there. Population growth for the US before the financial crisis was hovering at around 1 percent per year.

Annual population growth for Nevada, Arizona, and Florida, collectively, averaged over 2 percent per year. In 2005, it popped up a bit to about 2.8 percent. But suddenly it reversed. By 2007, population growth in those states was down to 1.6 percent. By 2009, it bottomed out at 0.8 percent.

The shortage of housing in the Closed Access cities was the source of this migratory roller coaster. Even though that shortage was never resolved—Closed Access vacancies have remained very low and rents very high—migration out of the Closed Access cities suddenly dropped. In the Contagion cities, decades-long migration trends had briefly inflated and then suddenly stopped.

Researchers at the Federal Reserve Bank of New York found that after the end of 2005, inventory of existing homes for sale started to stack up in some cities. In those cities, home prices collapsed. But it wasn't from a sudden surge of new supply or new listings. It was from a sudden disappearance of buyers.[34]

It is important to keep those migratory shocks in mind when thinking about housing vacancies. Vacancies are one of those measures that seems to plausibly support the conventional story but doesn't upon closer review. There was never overbuilding anywhere. Vacancies were lowest where building was booming.

Where vacancies have risen in major American metropolitan areas since the turn of the century, they have been associated with sharp, unexpected declines in population growth.[35] In the cities where migration suddenly dissipated, home prices collapsed, construction withered, incomes took a hit, and employment cratered. Collapsing employment and rising vacancies happened where *long-term* construction activity had been strong, not where construction in 2004 and 2005 had increased. The amount of construction that was happening in a state in the 1990s was a much better predictor of its unemployment rate in 2010 than the amount of construction that was happening there in 2005.[36] In other words, the housing bust and the Great Recession weren't the reversal of a building boom. They were the reversal of decades-long-established migration patterns because in our misplaced effort to kill a housing bubble, we killed the economy.

Migration out of the Closed Access cities declined because optimism, incomes, and eventually access to mortgage funding all declined. That is why home building cancellations spiked in 2006, long before prices were declining and mortgage defaults were stacking up. The initial shift was discretionary. The country had been spreading its elbows a bit and building new homes in the only places where we legally could. But by 2007, like a turtle retracting into its shell, Americans reverted back to squeezing into the limited supply of homes in the Closed Access cities.

The places that were really hurt, and where vacancies now started to accumulate, were the Contagion cities who had simply been trying to meet the demand for housing that came from the new arrivals, as they had been for decades. When the collapse in migration led to a collapse in demand in those cities, builders were suddenly stuck with thousands of homes that had been built to meet real demand for shelter. And it was precisely because construction had such a long and established history as a dominant part of the economies of the Contagion cities that the downshift in migration hit hard.

In 2006, per capita personal income grew in Florida, Arizona, and Nevada by 6.7 percent compared to the national growth rate of 6.3 percent. By 2008, the year of the financial crisis, US per capita personal income growth dropped to 2.7 percent and then declined by 4.0 percent in 2009. The Contagion states were basically a year ahead of the rest of the country in that decline. In those states, by 2007, income growth was already down to 2.8 percent. Then per capita income declined by 1.1 percent in 2008, and it declined further in 2009 by 6.6 percent.[37]

Those states were in economic distress by 2007. Our attention was focused only on evidence of excess. The sideshow of subprime-funded investment properties distracted us from noticing that something was terribly wrong and should be fixed. When the protagonists in *The Big Short* saw it happening, they thought, "See! We were right!"

That reaction has little to do with the observations of facts on the ground in 2007. That reaction is the result of the canonized assumptions that the film casually tossed out in its first three minutes. That reaction is due to the things everyone knows that just ain't so.

What if it turns out that the bankers partying and throwing money around at the beginning of *The Big Short* had little to do with relentlessly rising home prices, and the protagonists weren't really as right as they thought they were?

Take Arizona. At the end of 2003, the median home in Arizona cost about the same as the median home in the US—just over $154,000. Then, over the next year, the price of the median home in Arizona jumped by about $30,000—about double the change for the US. Over that same year, borrowers in Arizona increased their outstanding debt by just a few hundred dollars per capita compared to other Americans.

Then it happened again in 2005. The price of the median home in Arizona gained a whopping $74,000 compared to an $18,000 gain for the median US home. Again, there was little difference in the debt taken out by Arizonans versus other Americans. In 2005, Arizonans added about $2,000 more in per capita debt outstanding than other Americans did, and most of that difference was in the fourth quarter of 2005 when home prices had just about reached their peak.

In 2006, home prices started to level out, especially in Arizona. But in 2006, per capita debt in Arizona increased by $10,000—more than twice as much as the rest of the country. Then, in 2007, the median home price in Arizona *collapsed* by $28,000, yet Arizonans added another $8,000 in debt. In 2008, the median Arizona home lost a heartbreaking $44,000 in value, and by then, faith in real estate collateral had been so rattled, mortgage markets broke down, and Arizonans didn't increase their debt load at all.[38]

The housing boom in Arizona was a boom in equity. Rising debt generally came after rising home prices. That same basic pattern played out in all of the states with Closed Access or Contagion cities. Home prices jumped up to extremely high levels first. In New York, New Jersey, Florida, Nevada, and California, when prices initially boomed compared to the rest of the country, there was not a concurrent rise in debt.[39]

The housing bubble in Nevada and Arizona didn't happen because they had been descended on by bankers. They were descended on by Californians.[40]

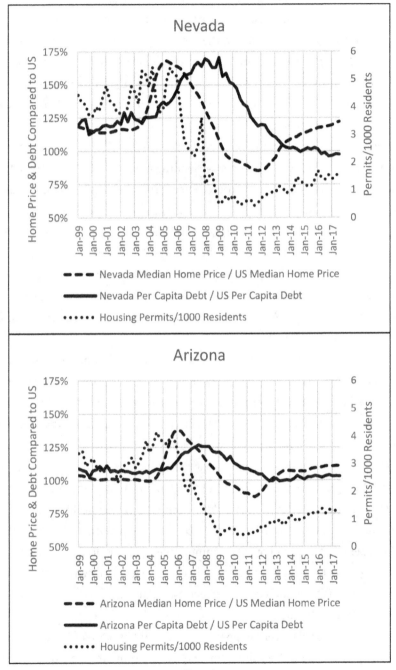

Figure 1

When Californians suddenly stopped coming, their economies started to collapse from the shock. They were now in a position where their incomes were lacking, but they had substantial home equity to borrow from. Per capita personal income in 2007 in Arizona was about $36,000 and that was after the effect that $8,000 in per capita borrowing had on local spending. Imagine the economic depression they would have been hit with by 2007 without that debt-funded spending.[41]

Figure 1[42] shows how backward the thinking has been about this. Supposedly, the story goes, aggressive lending pushed up home prices, which led to a building boom. The chain of events in Nevada and Arizona was in exactly the opposite order. Figure 1 shows the rate of new home building in each state and also the price of homes and the amount of debt outstanding per capita, relative to the rest of the country. In other words, where debt per capita is equal to 100 percent, that means it was the same in Nevada or Arizona as the national average. If it rises to 120 percent, that means that residents in Nevada or Arizona increased their total debt by 20 percent more than residents in other states.

The first thing that happened was that home building increased. This was a response to the inflow of new families. The increase wasn't that high compared to the long-term rate because both states already had very high rates of home building. Then, after building had been somewhat elevated for a while, prices shot up. Then, at about the time that construction and home prices both peaked and started to decline precipitously, finally, per capita debt began to rise. By the time the subprime mortgage panic happened in the summer of 2007, the cumulative amount of any building above the long-term trend was already reversed. By the time the broader financial crisis happened in September 2008, cumulative construction was well below the long-term trend and the previous boom in prices had generally reversed. Today, there is still much less construction in these areas than had been typical in previous decades.

Did the financial crisis happen the way it did because of lending activities in 2006 and 2007? Certainly. But the scenes from 2007 and 2008 weren't the closing act of a twenty-five-year drama. They were the opening scenes of a tragic sequel, though they didn't need to be. This was a new era where Americans suddenly stopped moving to these cities that had been growing for decades.

By 2007, the mortgages that were being originated by those reckless brokers in *The Big Short* and packaged eventually into CDOs weren't funding a housing bubble. They were originated during a collapse. Rising prices came first. Rising debts came after.

"In 2008...it all came crashing down." Who dared to stand athwart Act Three and stop it? Who would dare to bail out twenty-five years of excess?

It is common to see pundits or analysts singled out because they were wise enough to "call the bubble" as early as, say, 2002. And the question is posed, "Why were economists and policymakers so surprised by the collapse?"

That question assumes that the collapse was inevitable. It is time to ask the questioner some questions.

Why did real estate prices and construction in Toronto and Sydney just keep marching upward? Why doesn't "calling the bubble" apply to them?

In the most expensive American cities (the Closed Access cities) where vacancy rates remained below 4 percent throughout the crisis, why did construction collapse for several years?[43] Was there research in 2002 that warned housing starts needed to collapse in cities with less than 4 percent vacancy rates and exorbitant rents?

Was there research in 2002 warning that sixty-year-old migration and population trends would soon need to stop in their tracks?

Are there papers from 2002 that explain how the mortgage on the median home in Birmingham should only require 11 percent of the median household's income, and that monetary and credit austerity would be necessary until that happened? If the Birmingham homeowner in 2002 assumed that the value of a home with a mortgage payment that required about 16 percent of their income would be pretty stable, were they being naïve?[44] Were they clinging to the "lynchpin of an entire investment philosophy" that was destined to ruin them?

The answer that ties all these questions together is that those American markets—the Closed Access cities, the Contagion cities, and the countless cities that never really experienced anything that looked like a bubble—all experienced a negative shock in demand for housing that had nothing to do with any previous excessive investment into housing.

We *could* have implemented policies that would have maintained more stable housing markets, more stable national income growth, and more stable labor markets. The broad reaction I see to that idea, even after all we have gone through: But then we wouldn't have learned our lesson. Speculators would be even more reckless today if we had bailed them out.

Fortunately, in recent years, more economists have been realizing that the Federal Reserve had become too focused on what was perceived as a housing bubble, and they let nominal economic activity slow down far too much in 2007 and 2008. The economist Scott Sumner has been a key proponent of this view since early in the Great Recession. The Joint Economic Committee (JEC), which is the economic advisory group to Congress, issued a report in September 2020 that summarized well this developing view of the recession. The report reviewed the depth and the slow recovery from the Great Recession and noted that, "Both of these problems were attributable in part to the Federal Reserve's too-tight monetary policy, a decade-long series of errors. These errors all ran in the same direction, curbing spending too much. This helped cause, deepen, and lengthen the output gap. It is, of course, easier to identify these errors with the benefit of a dozen extra years of hindsight that contemporary decision-makers did not have. Indeed, many of the[se] points...have already been acknowledged by past or current Federal Open Market Committee (FOMC) members."[45]

Conventional wisdom is slowly beginning to change, but in real time, it was unified behind the expectation that housing starts and prices needed to drop significantly, and eventually the consensus was that lenders and speculators needed to be disciplined by failure. The problem was that there were never too many homes being built anywhere. There was never malinvestment into real estate that had to be "worked off." So, to enforce the outcomes that seemed necessary, the Federal Reserve and federal mortgage regulators had to implement demand shocks so severe that they created a whole host of other tragic outcomes.

In 1850s Europe, it seemed inconceivable that simple handwashing was an important part of a safe healthcare regimen. In 2007 America, it seemed inconceivable that simply continuing to build more urban homes was an important part of a healthy economy. The fact that rising Closed Access urban rents were the primary cause of rising home prices was not part of the canon. Its absence left a void that was filled with other conjectures with disastrous results.

The decisions institutions made and the judgments we made about them were largely based on the presumption that before 2006 there were too many houses, and so after 2006, we had to experience an economic shock in order to "work them off."

There was an understandable backlash about the excesses that developed in lending markets from 2003 to 2007, but we threw the baby out with the bathwater. In 2007, the construction workers who were starting to lose their jobs could have built apartment buildings in San Francisco for the thousands of families that would have preferred to live there. Positive economic expectations for middle-class newcomers who had been moving to the Contagion states for decades could have helped the businesses there who suddenly lacked revenue. A reasonably generous mortgage market in Birmingham could have reinvigorated a sustainable market for middle-class home ownership.

To suggest any of those things in 2007 would have been derided as just continuing to pump up a bubble. A brief lending boom had been tacked onto a larger story that it really had little to do with. Both the obstruction of new supply and the infusion of new capital can cause prices to rise. So, a decade-long story of deprivation that had increased housing costs became universally and passionately connected to a temporary story of excess. The result is that a decade later, hardly any new affordable homes are being built because it is too hard for families who would buy them to get mortgages. Newspapers are littered with stories of "Wall Street" landlords who keep raising rents, yet those tenants would get rejected if they applied for mortgages that frequently would have monthly payments that are a fraction of their rents.

The point of this new history is not to cast blame nor to absolve villains. That is no more helpful than it would be to shame nineteenth century doctors who didn't know about germs. The point is to have the correct canon so when the next economic turning point comes, it is easier to get the important stuff right. When you have the right canon, saving lives can be as easy as washing your hands.

One can accept that the United States did not have a destabilizing, excessive number of homes in 2005 while still demanding appropriate mortgage underwriting, prudent bank regulation, and so forth. A clear-eyed and transformative view of the financial crisis requires a willingness to disentangle these issues. As we proceeded through the crisis, the damage from the myth that we had too many houses accumulated. Those ill-advised financial activities were taking place in a context that had been created by inadequate housing, rising rents, and sudden migration shifts. This has never been accounted for. Taking these issues into account will radically change your perspective about what happened, and what should have happened. I am asking you to sharpen your scrutiny of these events, not relinquish it.

PART 2

Demand During the Housing Boom

 CHAPTER 4

FANNIE, FREDDIE, AND GINNIE

Were rising levels of debt and changing mortgage terms a cause or a result of rising home prices? If rising prices were primarily a result of limited supply and rising rents, then how does that change the way we think about sources of demand for housing, like mortgage access?

There are four main conduits for mortgage financing in the US. Ginnie Mae mainly guarantees mortgages issued by the Federal Housing Administration (FHA) and Veterans Affairs (VA), and that guarantee is fully backed by the federal government. Fannie Mae and Freddie Mac were government-sponsored enterprises (the GSEs) that held or guaranteed privately issued mortgages. They have been taken into conservatorship by the federal government since September 2008. Banks and other financial institutions issue mortgages and sometimes retain them in their own portfolios. And finally, privately issued mortgages were combined into private pools funded with bonds sold to private investors that were not guaranteed by any of the public agencies. They are frequently called subprime and Alt-A loans if they have some characteristics that are considered riskier than loans that go through the Fannie and Freddie channel. This conduit claimed a significant share of mortgages briefly during the housing boom.

The willingness of underwriters and investors to take risks for those various types of mortgages is undoubtably a factor that affects the price and construction of homes. There are plenty of poor lending practices or borrower misconduct that can, and have, caused market disruptions. That doesn't mean that all lending or all financial innovations are bad.

Even if a financial innovation boosts home prices, it isn't necessarily bad. If builders discover a better form of insulation or a more durable roof, homes will be worth more, and buyers may be willing to pay more. That means that the invention is good! The same can sometimes be said of financial innovation. A product that makes it easier for tenants to responsibly own their homes, or a product that makes it easier to buy or sell a home makes that home more valuable.

This is easy to see in the extreme. If mortgages were illegal, those with preexisting wealth would be able to earn high returns renting to families that lacked the cash savings needed to buy a home. That would not be great. Some innovations in financing make the economy a more functional and equitable system—even when they are associated with higher prices or more spending on housing.[46] The question is where that line should be drawn.

When conventional wisdom settled on the idea that American housing markets were in a bubble, it made these difficult distinctions seem easy. Every innovation seemed reckless. Every increase in price and quantity seemed unsustainable.

To understand how important urban supply problems have been versus financial and public inducements and subsidies, we need to carefully consider scale and timing.

The main housing subsidy comes through income tax benefits, which mostly accrue to rich households with valuable homes and large mortgages. The total amount of subsidies provided to homeowners through income taxes adds up to about $288 billion annually.[47] On the other hand, the BEA estimates that Americans pay about $264 billion annually in residential property taxes.[48] These roughly even out.

In normal markets, Fannie Mae and Freddie Mac probably lower the interest rate on conforming loans by an average of about 0.25 percent, which amounts to about $13 billion in savings, annually. Fannie and Freddie, along with programs through the FHA and the VA, facilitate some access to home ownership and standardization of mortgage contracts. But in the broad scheme of things, as far as their effect on home prices goes, they just aren't that big of a deal.[49]

All of this is a preface for thinking about the various shifts and changes that happened in mortgage markets before 2007. We should not interpret every development as benign or as malignant. Conventional wisdom has focused our attention on the malignant. Federal lending programs are one target of criticism. The GSEs have become totems of the unsustainable bubble because, in September 2008, the government took them over and taxpayers took on the risk of future losses on their mortgages. Yet not only are the federally supported conduits for mortgages a relatively small factor compared to other subsidies and taxes on housing, they also all lost a tremendous amount of market share during the boom.

Ginnie Mae and the FHA had been losing market share for years. Ginnie Mae had guaranteed more than 15 percent of outstanding mortgages in the early 1990s, and that decreased to 3.6 percent by 2007.

Beginning in 2003, Fannie Mae and Freddie Mac suddenly experienced a sharp decline in originations. During the housing boom, in just two years, the portion of mortgages outstanding that were guaranteed by the GSEs (Fannie Mae and Freddie Mac) declined from 44 to 36 percent.[50]

The decline of the GSEs coincided with pressure from Congress, the White House, regulators, and the Federal Reserve, which came in two separate rounds. Freddie was the first to come under pressure, culminating in the resignation of CEO Leland Brendsel in June 2003. Pressure on Fannie followed, leading to the resignation of CEO Franklin Raines in December 2004.[51]

Among those applying pressure on them was Alan Greenspan, who, by then, was being blamed for feeding the housing bubble with low interest rates. During congressional discussions about the GSEs in 2004, Greenspan testified that they posed "very serious risks" to the US financial system and that Congress should strengthen their regulator, limit their growth, and raise their capital requirements.[52]

In the case of Freddie Mac, some of the pressure came from the Securities and Exchange Commission (SEC) and led to penalties and settlements of several hundred million dollars, along with a tightening of capital requirements.[53]

The allegations were based on accounting regulations that are tremendously complicated, and there is not always agreement even among experts. The SEC was enforcing new rules that required Freddie to report fluctuating earnings because the estimated value of certain assets fluctuate with volatile measures, such as short-term interest rates and expected credit losses.

Here is an excerpt from the SEC press release, "Freddie Mac, Four Former Executives Settle SEC Action Relating to Multi-Billion Dollar Accounting Fraud:"

> The SEC's complaint alleges that Freddie Mac engaged in a fraudulent scheme that deceived investors about its true performance, profitability, and growth trends. According to the complaint, Freddie Mac misreported its net income in 2000, 2001 and 2002 by 30.5 percent, 23.9 percent and 42.9 percent, respectively. Furthermore, Freddie Mac's senior management exerted consistent pressure to have the company report smooth and dependable earnings growth in order to present investors with the image of a company that would continue to generate predictable and growing earnings

> 'As has been seen in so many cases, Freddie Mac's departure from proper accounting practices was the result of a corporate culture that sought stable earnings growth at any cost,' said Linda Chatman Thomsen, the SEC's Director of Enforcement. 'Investors do not benefit when good corporate governance takes a back seat to a single-minded drive to achieve earnings targets.'[54]

Would anyone reading this without prior knowledge guess that the charge against Freddie was that they had *understated* income and stockholders' equity by $5 billion by maintaining allowances for potential future losses?

In his November 2007 settlement, former Freddie Mac CEO Brendsel said that even though he didn't admit guilt, he agreed to return some of his salary because according to his attorney, "it requires that most of the money paid will be used to assist families who are threatened with the loss of their homes."[55]

Fannie was next. Eventually, it would also have to restate its earnings. The net effect of the restatement, as with Freddie Mac, was an increase in stockholders' equity (the total estimated value of the firm's net worth) by $4.1 billion.[56] Again, the central issue was applying complicated accounting methods that reduced fluctuations in quarterly earnings.

Yet again, the regulators came with gusto. The SEC's chief accountant, Donald Nicolaisen, surprised Fannie Mae executives at a December 2004 meeting. He held up a piece of paper and said that if the paper represented the four corners of the accounting rules they were supposed to follow, "you were not even on the page." Raines was forced to resign.[57]

As with Freddie, nine-figure fines followed, along with sharply worded SEC press releases. Eventually like Brendsel, without admitting guilt, Raines donated $1.8 million in Fannie stock to help families dealing with a drop in home prices and a recession.[58]

Years later, in depositions associated with a class-action shareholder lawsuit, Nicolaisen admitted that Fannie's "not even on the page" accounting methods were actually a fairly common interpretation of the rule among firms and accountants at the time.[59]

Conventional wisdom had come to a point where any sign of excess seemed salient, even if they were contradictory signs of excess. In 2007, just as the GSEs were beginning to take on excessive credit losses that pushed them into conservatorship, the former leadership were being punished for *overfunding* reserves set aside for potential losses. The new CEOs would, themselves, be accused of the opposite sin—*underestimating* potential losses from future defaults. Isn't it funny how the allegations against these executives, which are the binary opposites of each other, can both seem to be evidence of reckless CEOs fueling a housing bubble? Both can be described as executives engaged in short-term, quarter-to-quarter thinking. Brendsel and Raines were accused of keeping a sort of slush fund of paper losses so they could reverse them when they needed to keep a nice level growth of quarterly earnings. Later, GSE executives were accused of not keeping a large enough reserve of paper losses. (Eventually, many of those losses were reversed again after the GSEs performed better than expected.[60])

Furthermore, isn't it a coincidence that two institutions with different executive teams committed the same types of alleged fraud in the early 2000s, then they both committed the opposite alleged errors several years later, again at the same time? Then, isn't it another coincidence that when they eventually were declared insolvent by the federal government and taken over, they managed to fail on exactly the same day—September 7, 2008?[61]

Most accounts of the history of Fannie and Freddie describe them as powerful lobbying machines pushing Congress to do their bidding. This reversal in their fortunes was a product of the mistaken belief that the rise in home prices was from excessive lending, speculating, and federal subsidies. With that premise, it is natural that the most powerful institutions in the market who benefitted from federal support would lose their favor among voters and policymakers. With home prices seeming to rise to unsustainable levels, who would dare come to their defense? In fact, those that were seen as supportive of Fannie and Freddie, such as Congressman Barney Frank and Nobel Prize winning economist Joe Stiglitz, have taken hits to their reputations as a result. Even in their own defense, both Stiglitz and Frank accept the presumption that, in the end, Fannie and Freddie were reckless, and their recklessness was partially responsible for a bubble followed by an inevitable crash.[62]

The pressures on Fannie and Freddie did little to quell the ballooning housing market. The home ownership rate stopped rising once Fannie and Freddie were pulled back in 2004. Yet, in spite of that, 2004 and 2005 would be the years with the strongest construction activity and price appreciation.

The drop in market share for each one coincided with the federal investigations into their earnings. First, Freddie Mac cut its activity in 2002 and 2003 as investigations heated up, then Fannie Mae did because of investigations there in 2004.[63] Donald Bisenius, an executive vice president at Freddie Mac, told the FCIC that "the accounting issues distracted management from the mortgage business, taking 'a tremendous amount of management's time and attention and probably led to us being less aggressive or less competitive in the marketplace [than] we otherwise might have been.'"[64] Fannie Mae stated in their 2004 annual report that new calls for additional capital coverage led to "significantly reducing the size of our mortgage portfolio."[65]

Another sign that there was a retraction in GSE competitiveness is the spread between jumbo loans and conventional loans. Jumbo loans are prime loans that are larger than the legislated maximum size allowed for Fannie and Freddie. The difference between rates on jumbo loans and conventional loans sold to Fannie and Freddie is a measure of the advantage Fannie and Freddie have in the marketplace.

From December 2002 to December 2004 the spread between jumbo-loan rates and conventional rates dropped from thirty-seven basis points to nineteen basis points.[66] In other words, the rates on *non*-GSE jumbo loans dropped compared to the rates on GSE-qualified loans. The GSEs had become less competitive in the market for more expensive homes in the less risky parts of the mortgage market.[67] From 2002 to 2006, conventional thirty-year mortgage rates were also rising compared to AAA corporate rates.[68] A shrinking spread between subprime and conventional rates was, in part, due to rising rates at Fannie and Freddie rather than declining subprime spreads.

Much of their former market share flowed into the newly ascendant, privately securitized mortgages. But mortgages held on bank balance sheets also grew to fill the gap left from declining GSE activity. Securitization is frequently blamed as a cause of the housing bubble because mortgage originators could pawn off poorly underwritten loans to investors who did not know how bad they were. Yet, contrary to the idea that the period was characterized by reckless securitization, retained bank assets were increasingly devoted to real estate lending—both residential and commercial. Nonsecuritized real estate loans held by banks rose from about 25 percent of their total assets to about 34 percent between 1998 and 2006.[69] The rise in real estate values and the associated rise in mortgages outstanding meant that mortgages were becoming a larger portion of domestic aggregate financial assets. Commercial banks were becoming more exposed to real estate risk because the Closed Access housing cartel was creating bloated real estate prices.

From 2003 to 2006, all the other conduits rose to fill the gap left by the GSEs.[70] If the motivation for the decline in GSE market share after 2003 had been aggressive lending through the private securitization channel, then we might expect to see the extreme market share gains of the private pools to come at the expense of most or all of the other lending sources. But, instead, from 2003 to 2006, Fannie and Freddie lost market share, and trends in market share of every other category—private securitizations, banks, and other non-securitized mortgage investors—turned up.

These are examples of how perception is guided by our assumptions. In national numbers, total mortgages outstanding tends to rise and fall along with rising and falling home prices. Much of the popular literature is built on the implication that rising prices are a result of rising mortgage debt. As I pointed out in chapter 3, this is, at best, a partial reason for rising prices, and, in fact, it might be more accurate to say that rising home prices lead to rising debt, more than the other way around. Certainly, in 2019, differences in home prices were largely responsible for per capita debt of $73,000 in California compared to $40,000 in Ohio.[71] No amount of aggressive lending standards would drive debt levels and home prices in Ohio today up to the levels California has.

If increasingly available debt is driving up prices, then the temptation is to obstruct conduits for lending. However, if real estate debt is high because home prices have been driven higher by local supply constraints, then the prudent action may be to help banks find ways to funnel ownership of that debt to the most stable conduits that match investors and borrowers.

At first glance, the SEC announcements about settlements on the Fannie and Freddie accounting scandals seem to project the image of reckless lenders who had created a housing bubble and were being tamed by regulators. Yet, what the SEC had really done was make the most stable conduit for mortgage lending a less competitive option for borrowers during the pivotal years from 2003 to 2007.

OTHER NEGATIVE SHOCKS FOR GSES

Some of the decline in GSE activity was also related to weakness that came from declining interest rates and large-scale refinancing from 2001 to 2003. That decreased the rate of income on their loans and put additional competitive pressure on them.[72]

There was also another regulatory headwind with Fannie and Freddie. While prices were rising, regulators had to decide the top loan limit for government-sponsored loans. Loans above a certain size cannot be purchased by the GSEs and are generally held by banks or are securitized as jumbo loans. In 2004, regulators chose to increase the government-sponsored loan size limit at a rate below prevailing market conditions. In 2003, loans at Fannie and Freddie could be up to $322,700. In 2005, the limit was set at $359,650, a rise of about 11.5 percent over two years, while the average home price had increased by nearly 30 percent across the country.

Under the premise that too much demand and too many federal subsidies were the cause of rising prices, regulatory pressures against the GSEs and a tighter limit on GSE loan size seems like an obvious solution. Yet when prices continued to rise anyway, this just nudged mortgage markets even more in favor of the new, less stable forms of borrowing.

The change in the loan size limit had a clear effect on GSE lending. Through 2003, the average house receiving a Fannie Mae mortgage had a market value that was close to the average house in the country, give or take 5 percent—and was at the low end of that range in 2003. In 2004, it was 15 percent lower. In 2006, it was 20 percent lower.[73] These regulatory barriers shifted mortgage activity to the new private lending markets.

These policy choices, made during the run-up in the boom, were early examples of how important it is to have the right canon. If reckless lending was producing an unsustainable bubble, then any pressures to reduce lending seemed like they must be helpful. But, since much of the pressure pushing up home prices was coming from a lack of supply in key cities, reducing the competitiveness of some forms of lending increased the demand for other forms of lending. There are principled arguments both for and against the federal mortgage programs, but one of the arguments in favor of them is that they create a standard for mortgage terms and a pool of mortgage securities that are more systematically stable during market upheavals. That was one of the reasons for their development after the Great Depression.

The irony, which played out again and again through the crisis, is that regulatory actions, which were based on the presumption that lending was creating instability, ended up creating instability *themselves*.

At the same time, there were also pressures on the GSEs to expand affordable lending. Since the mid-1990s, there were programs focused on pressing the GSEs into originating more loans for underserved and marginal communities. The lenders did respond to this pressure, yet aggregate measures show little effect on total borrowing. The reason appears to be that these programs mainly led the GSEs to poach market share from the FHA/Ginnie Mae conduit that had been the traditional source of mortgages for marginal borrowers. In fact, the affordable housing programs at the GSEs may have had an ironic effect. According to research by Xudong An and Raphael W. Bostic at the USC Lusk Center for Real Estate, "More aggressive GSE pursuit of targeted borrowers under the affordable housing goals induces potential FHA borrowers with the best credit quality to use the conventional market and obtain conforming conventional loans instead. In response, the FHA has to apply more strict underwriting standards to keep its risk profile within an acceptable level and consequently reduces its loan volume."[74]

In his extensive dissenting statement to the FCIC report, Peter Wallison argued that pressure to meet the Department of Housing and Urban Development (HUD) goals for lending to low-income and underserved borrowers also led the GSEs to be less competitive in more conventional lending, since they were lending into underserved markets at a loss and had to subsidize those losses with their more conventional business.[75]

These pressures led to a shift from FHA to GSE market share. The combined market share of the GSEs and FHA had been about 50 percent of mortgages outstanding in 1994, and it was still about 50 percent at the end of 2003. By 2007, their combined market share was about 39 percent.[76] Wallison documents the concerns GSE personnel had about the risks created by the HUD goals. Yet, GSE filings also show relatively stable borrower credit scores until standards tightened dramatically in 2008 and after. The shift in lending quality at the GSEs and among lenders in general appears to have been more in the terms of loans rather than in the quality of borrowers.[77]

Many explanations of the bubble also point to the Community Reinvestment Act (CRA), but that explanation also has similar complications and simply cannot explain the scale and character of the price boom.

In a widely cited paper titled "Explaining the Housing Bubble," Adam Levitin from Georgetown University Law Center and Susan Wachter from the Wharton School of the University of Pennsylvania, do a superb job of outlining the various demand-side explanations for the housing boom. Both the affordability programs at the GSEs and other programs aimed at expanded home ownership, like the CRA, have parallels regarding their place in the boom and bust. Many critics claim that these programs pushed up demand for home ownership, fueling a bubble. Levitan and Wachter dismiss the home ownership programs at Fannie and Freddie as important factors pushing up home prices. They argue that the only period showing price behavior that can be described as a bubble was the brief period between 2004 and 2007. They limit blame for any bubble activity to private securitizations. Regarding the CRA, they argue:

> [T]he residential-housing bubble was mirrored almost exactly by a commercial real-estate (CRE) bubble. Although there is some interlinkage between residential and commercial real-estate prices, the CRE bubble cannot be attributed to the residential bubble. As the CRA does not apply to commercial real-estate lending, it cannot explain the existence of the CRE bubble. Yet, the synchronous growth and collapse of the residential and commercial real-estate bubbles cannot be coincidental. In sum, the case that the CRA drove banks to improvident lending is not tenable.[78]

(Although Levitin and Wachter didn't apply the same reasoning to dismiss the causal importance of private securitizations in creating a housing bubble, this same point would be reasonable grounds for doing so.)[79]

It is true that the GSEs engaged in some shifts in underwriting and in loan terms, allowing some interest only amortization, etc. toward the end of the housing boom. Yet, GSE mortgages performed better than both privately securitized mortgages and mortgages held at banks. If demand generated from financial engineering caused home prices to be high, the GSEs are just another chapter in the roll call of demons whispering over our shoulders. However, if prices are high because of high urban rents, then the GSEs and the FHA were remarkably countercyclical—losing market share when markets were hot and then expanding when markets collapsed. They were doing pretty much what they were intended to do until the government took the GSEs over in September 2008. It might even be said that more competitive GSEs in 2006 and early 2007 would have helped to reinvigorate the conventional buyer's market that was drying up, steering activity away from the private securitizations that became so toxic.[80]

CHAPTER 5

UNCONVENTIONAL MORTGAGES, HOME PRICES, AND CONSTRUCTION EMPLOYMENT

Among the factors pushing up home prices, what was the relative scale of the effect of new forms of mortgage financing? Did this financing push up prices willy-nilly and irrationally, or was it systematically facilitating real estate transactions in locations where prices were high because of a lack of supply? This is especially difficult to figure out because home prices can only really rise in places with both inelastic supply and sources of funding for buyers at market prices. It is necessarily a dual causation. Home prices only rose moderately where new homes could be built fast enough to match new buyers, and they can't rise above the level that financing mechanisms are designed to fund.

There are some reasons why private markets might have taken some market share from the GSEs in 2004, even if the GSEs hadn't been under outside pressure. Regulations loosened in 2004 regarding predatory lending. The federal Office of the Comptroller enacted a preemption rule, exempting national banks from local rules that forbade certain rates, fees, and penalties and required regulatory oversight of the ability to repay the mortgage. This allowed non-conventional mortgages to expand, especially in the Closed Access cities where the cost of housing made mortgage financing risky and inaccessible to many households.

Amendments to the Basel Accords, a set of rules banks are supposed to follow, were implemented in 2001 and 2002. Those changes put private securitizations on more equal footing with GSE securities and may also have facilitated this shift.[81]

Private securitizations probably changed the relative distribution of buyers in various ways. Many of these loans were facilitating the purchase of properties by households that were prime or near prime borrowers with high incomes, but they lived in areas where home values were too high to be purchased with conventional loan terms.[82] They were also more likely to be used by investors and speculators.

There is a lot of anecdotal evidence about unqualified borrowers, especially as the subprime boom aged, but empirical evidence is surprisingly mixed about aggregate changes in borrower character. In recent research that utilizes longitudinal data on individual borrowers, Stefania Albanesi, Giacomo De Giorgi, and Jaromir Nosal have shown that in zip codes with large concentrations of subprime credit scores, the new borrowing was from buyers with credit scores that were high, young buyers with rising incomes, and investors.[83] Their findings suggest that underwriters had become more capable of finding borrowers with improving economic prospects, and that the collapse of those mortgage markets had little to do with a surge of borrowers with poor economic prospects. As researchers with the Federal Reserve Bank of Boston put it, "[A]s a quantitative explanation for the massive increase in mortgage debt in the early 2000s, any theory that rests on a broad extensive-margin credit expansion for low-income individuals will fail to fit the facts... [R]apid growth of subprime loans did not *cause* a reallocation of mortgage debt toward low-income borrowers, but rather *prevented* a reallocation of debt toward the wealthy."[84]

Researchers working with the Federal Housing Finance Agency (FHFA) have produced a comprehensive review of mortgages originated for purchase since 1990. Their findings also suggest that the terms of mortgages changed, and investors were more active, but there wasn't much of a change in the credit quality of traditional borrowers. They found that there was a rise in loans with less documentation and with terms like interest-only payment periods, negative amortization, or balloon payments. Interestingly, those terms became more common both for mortgages sold to the private securitization markets and those kept by the banks that originated them. The banks making those loans were willing to take the risk of holding them.[85]

In research on borrowers in Massachusetts, Connecticutt, and Rhode Island, the percentage of subprime borrowers with credit scores above 620 *rose* as a proportion of the total from under 40 percent in 2000 to 70 percent in 2005, but over that same time, loan-to-value ratios and debt to income ratios rose while income documentation declined. Many were near-prime borrowers taking on riskier terms. And, often, they received near-prime interest rates.[86]

John Griffin at the University of Texas and Gonzalo Maturana at Emory University found evidence that the rise of dubious mortgage lenders contributed to rising home prices from 2002 to 2005. Yet they also found that the mortgage lenders making the riskiest loans understood borrower risk better and priced it more accurately than more conventional lenders.[87]

This collection of evidence is generally what we would expect to find if a lack of supply was pushing up prices: borrowers with stable or rising credit quality seeking to stretch the terms and constraints of mortgages in order to deal with rising prices. It could still be the case that those stretched terms were ill advised and destabilizing. The deeper question I am raising is: Did those mortgages arise in a vacuum, as a fundamental causal force dictating the direction of American housing markets? Or was this more of a side effect of rising prices caused by the urban supply problem?

In areas not characterized by a shortage of housing, credit markets just don't have that much power to move prices. Places like Texas are examples of a housing market characterized by expanding credit where supply is ample. Subprime mortgages were used extensively there.[88] Defaults during the housing boom were somewhat high in Texas, but not nearly as high as the spikes seen in Contagion markets during the crisis. And prices remained much lower in places like Texas than they were in places where home building is more difficult. So, if loose lending was correlated with rising prices, and prices rose much more in Los Angeles than they did in Austin, was the "cause" of rising prices a lack of building in LA or loose lending in LA?

The literature on this question has been framed as if the causation can be placed onto loose lending: loose lending caused prices to rise, and it especially caused them to rise where supply was lacking. The way that framing has loaded all the causality onto credit markets is not an empirical conclusion. It was a rhetorical choice. It was a choice that *seemed* acceptable when rents were wrongly ignored as a strong factor creating high prices.

DID PRIVATELY SECURITIZED MORTGAGES PUMP UP A HOUSING BUBBLE?

There have been many attempts at quantifying the effect of loose lending on the housing boom. Marco DiMaggio at Harvard Business School and Amir Kermani at the University of California, Berkeley estimated that from 2004 to 2006, the preemption of state anti-predatory lending laws facilitated an 11 percent increase in annual lending, a 3.3 percent increase in annual home prices, and a 2.2 percent expansion of employment in the non-tradable sectors (things like local services). All of those gains reversed in subsequent years.[89]

Mian and Sufi measured the effect of privately securitized mortgages from mid-2003 to 2007 on housing markets.[90] They found that from 2003 through 2006, home prices increased by 12.1 percent more in the quarter of zip codes that had the most active private securitization lending than they did in the quarter of zip codes with the least active private securitization markets. Construction also increased in metropolitan areas with more privately securitized lending. Then, both prices and construction reversed. By 2009, both prices and construction in places where private securitizations had been more active were below the levels of places where they had not been as active. It seemed as if unconventional lending led to excessive activity that inevitably reversed.

In both cases, researchers found that these effects were strongest where housing supply was more constrained.

By treating the urban housing shortage as a fixed factor—just a state of nature that changing credit conditions act on—the way that the results are communicated is that credit access caused rising prices, more construction, and rising employment, and its effects were especially strong where housing supply is inelastic (where it is hard to build new homes).

But we could just as easily treat different credit regimes as the fixed factor and conclude that in any given type of lending market, inelastic housing supply raises home prices and *lowers* employment (by reducing construction and limiting population growth). When credit conditions are looser, home prices will rise more where supply is limited, but on the bright side, employment will benefit (because high prices will induce more home building and construction employment) and more homes will get built.

Isn't that a more appropriate way to look at it? Since researchers have universally treated supply elasticity as a given, they have been led to these awkward conclusions that rising employment is dangerous and that building more homes where they are needed is unsustainable and disruptive.

Let's compare the scale of the effect of changing credit markets to the relative importance of high rents in cities that have long-term housing supply problems. Figure 2[91] provides a number of helpful clues. The dots to the right are cities with high rents. The higher the rents are in a metro area, the further that metro area is to the right on the graph. (Generally, where I mention rents, I am talking about the rental value of all homes, both owned and rented. Thanks to sources like Zillow, we now have good real-time estimates of those values, so we can think about the value of the service of shelter that each home provides, which serves as the fundamental driver of its market price. When I mention rent, throughout this book, I am not referring strictly to the renter/landlord market. I am referring to the rental value of all homes, so that an apples-to-apples comparison can be made between rent and price.)

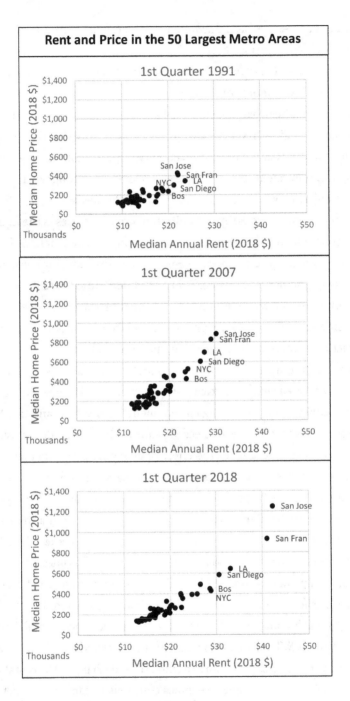

Figure 2

The higher dots in the figure are cities with high prices. The higher the home prices are in a metro area, the farther up on the graph its dot will move. In 1991, cities with higher rents tended to have higher prices, but there wasn't an extreme difference between cities. By 2007, and more so by 2018, the main development has been that rents in a handful of cities have become very high. The cities with extremely high rents are the California cities and the northeastern cities that allow very few homes to be built compared to other cities. They have both high rents and high prices as a result.

During the period where credit markets were looser, the main effect was to increase prices where rents are higher. For many cities, prices and rents adjusted for inflation have not changed much over time: not in 1991 before the rise of the Closed Access city problem, not in early 2007 near the peak of the subprime boom, and not in 2018 when the subprime boom was long dead and its effects had long since been reversed. In all scenarios, rents and prices were about the same in those cities. Or, at least the changes were so thoroughly dwarfed by the problem of high Closed Access rents that they are barely noticeable in the chart.

After 2007, the private securitization markets collapsed, and so 2018 and 2007 show the difference between a market with looser credit and a market without it. Compared to 2007, prices in 2018 were lower for any given rent level in the expensive cities. In other words, before accounting for changing rents, the dots have generally moved down. But the increase in rents has generally made up for it, causing prices to be as high or higher than they were in 2007 in the most expensive cities.

This is not natural. The only way that rents can remain so strikingly high across entire metropolitan areas is through an overbearing set of governing institutions whose prime function is to obstruct all the forces that would naturally coordinate to build more homes and reduce rents back to a normal level. A lot of hard work goes into doing that.

It is also interesting to compare 2018 to 1991. In 1991, in relatively expensive cities where the annual rent on the median unit was about $20,000, the price for that unit was about $300,000. In 2018, you could say the same thing. Where the typical unit might've required annual rental payments of about

$20,000, it was likely to cost about $300,000. The main difference between 2018 and 1991 is that in 2018 there were cities where the median annual rent was above $40,000. (All figures are adjusted for inflation.)

In 2007, the median home price in an affordable city with active sub-prime markets and low interest rates may have been $200,000 instead of $190,000. Or, in San Francisco, it might have been $800,000 instead of $660,000. On the other hand, high rents maintained with political obstructions made the median price in San Francisco $800,000 instead of $250,000. The brief mortgage boom was a mole hill on the side of the mountain of our housing supply problem.

The mortgage boom also was not haphazard. Prices rose the most where constrained supply had pushed up rents. In 2007, rent was a stronger explanatory variable determining prices than it had been in 1991. The market had become more determined by fundamentals—more rational, as it were—not less.

If high prices in San Francisco were jointly caused by a lack of adequate building and by loose lending, why did prices need to be brought down? And why did they need to be brought down by changing lending standards (which led to a temporary *decline* in construction in housing-starved cities) rather than by building more homes?

The mortgage boom accelerated the demand from Americans for housing in highly valued locations. There is no reason to automatically equate rising construction and rising prices with unsustainability or excess. There are some cases where prices had likely become unsustainably high, but the data on construction, population flows, and vacancies is clear. Securitized mortgages were associated with more construction, and that was good! We needed more homes!

High rental values, migration surges, and low vacancies are frequently not mentioned in academic papers that attempt to quantify the effect of lending markets on home prices during the boom. Because of those omissions, the literature focused on credit presumes that more credit led to overbuilding and empty homes. The growth in construction employment seemed to lead to a necessary subsequent decline. On this point, the traditional litera-ture isn't simply rhetorically misdirected. It's frequently empirically wrong. Growth in construction was significantly correlated with lower vacancies—in both rental and owned properties—during the building boom. In other words, construction was increasing where homes were in high demand and few were empty.[92]

To highlight these trends, Figure 3[93] compares changing levels of con-struction employment for the US as well as for Los Angeles (a Closed Access city), Phoenix (a Contagion city), Atlanta (a growing city), and Detroit (a rust belt city).

Figure 3 shows the percentage of the employed labor force engaged in construction. From the mid-1990s to the peak of the housing boom, the percentage of employees engaged in construction work in the US increased from less than 4.5 percent to more than 5.5 percent of the labor force.

National numbers seem to tell the "too many homes for too much money" story. But, as this chart makes clear, changes in those national trends are miniscule compared to variation between cities. The rate of building in cities is highly correlated to population growth—both in the short term and in the long term—and the difference between cities is huge.

Let's compare these metro areas.

Detroit had below-average construction activity, which was declining during the housing boom. Of these four, Detroit was the metropolitan area with the sharpest rise in vacancies. In the US, the percentage of empty hous-ing units for sale or for rent ran about 4 percent or 5 percent. By 2006, vacan-cies in Detroit were up to 9 percent. Vacancies there weren't the product of a building boom.[94]

Atlanta was a growing city. It had slightly higher than average construc-tion activity, but there was little increase in construction activity during the mortgage boom. Vacancies there had risen to about 8 percent from 2000 to 2003, before the peak building boom years, and remained somewhat ele-vated as recession hit. Again, as in Detroit, those vacancies weren't related to a building bonanza.

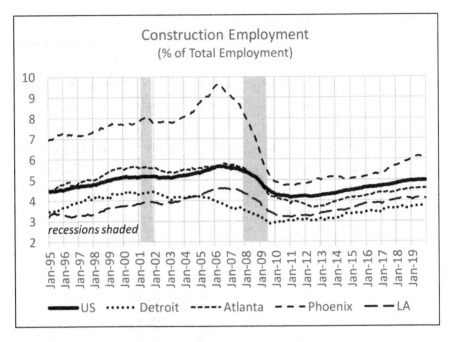

Figure 3

Phoenix had a very active construction sector, which had a significant increase in activity during the mortgage boom. Its vacancy rate was about average until 2008, when vacancies moved up to a level similar to Atlanta and Detroit. But construction activity had been declining since 2006. Rising vacancies don't align with high construction activity in Phoenix. High vacancies in Phoenix were caused by the *collapse* in lending and in household migration. As Mian and Sufi noted, excess building and prices associated with the growth in privately securitized mortgages had reversed by then. Their research doesn't address the migration whiplash that accompanied those changes in cities like Phoenix. By the time vacancies peaked in Phoenix in 2009 and 2010, the decline in building after 2005 had more than countered any rise in building that had happened before. Vacancies only increased after in-migration had sharply declined.

In all three cases—Atlanta, Detroit, and Phoenix—rising vacancies were associated with unforseen downshifts in trend population growth, for various reasons. In my research, this is the pattern I have found across the country throughout this period.[95]

When the housing bust arrived, the Contagion cities were hit with a double whammy because when the dissipation of the Closed Access migration surge caused population growth to significantly slow down in those cities, the market for home purchases in general was also collapsing. By 2008, Phoenix was lacking in both families that were seeking shelter and families that could get a mortgage in the collapsing market.

Los Angeles had very low construction activity. Construction employment increased there during the mortgage boom, rising to just above the level of construction employment in Detroit by 2005. Vacancies and construction employment there have been well below the national average continuously since 1999.

These patterns are emblematic of patterns among the largest metropolitan areas of each type of city. They are all very different. Very large differences in construction employment are mostly related to long-term trends in population growth. But these cities have one thing in common. The subprime lending boom from 2003 to 2007 didn't create an oversupply of homes or excessive construction employment in any of them. Those mortgages induced construction activity that was meeting pent up demand. Where there wasn't pent up demand, construction activity didn't increase. The new homes and the jobs that were created to build them were unadulterated positives. Construction employment wasn't behind some sort of fake unsustainable boom that was masking employment losses in other sectors like manufacturing. Where construction employment was strong, people desperately needed homes. Those jobs were sustainable. They should not have gone away.

The problem wasn't that securitized mortgages were pushing up construction in LA. That's not a problem. That's the solution to a problem. The fact that prices have to soar well above a half million dollars per unit in order to induce an increase in construction is the problem. That isn't the fault of lenders. That's the fault of local governments in the LA region who relentlessly block new buildings so that prices have to rise that far in order to justify the hassle of getting permission.

Prominent analysis such as the FCIC report and much of the academic and popular literature has presumed that blunt-force demand drove the housing bubble. A blunt-force increase in demand means more spending, and either that means higher quantities or higher prices. When home buying demand collapsed and it led to both declining prices and collapsing construction in cities all over the country, that presumption has been universally applied as an explanation. The collapse in demand had seemed inevitable and the reason it led to a collapse in construction and prices everywhere is that every city must have either experienced rising prices or rising construction during the boom. In either case, whether homes were overvalued or had been overbuilt, a price collapse would follow.[96]

The empirical evidence is the polar opposite of this. There is no evidence in the housing supply data that metropolitan areas with more moderate prices were associated with rising construction. There is no coherent explanation for why construction activity from 2003 to 2006 required millions of construction jobs to be lost from 2007 to 2010 in every major metropolitan area. Construction jobs disappeared from 2007 to 2010 because of things that happened from 2007 to 2010. Those jobs didn't disappear because there were suddenly, simultaneously, too many homes in every single city. There was no supply-side reason for the decline in housing production and construction employment that the literature associates with the reversal of the mortgage boom.

The subprime boom was associated with a proportional rise in construction employment in LA. But construction in LA had become such a puny force that the proportional rise was not nearly enough in absolute terms to adequately house Angelenos. Therefore, much of the rise in construction employment had to happen in Phoenix. Construction employment in LA could double before anybody even needed to wonder about whether it was sustainable. If it *had* doubled, there wouldn't have been such a disruptive housing boom in Phoenix.

As the country ran headlong toward crisis, it is well worth wondering, as we revisit each step along the way, why construction collapsed so deeply in all of those cities well before the September 2008 financial crisis. It is worth wondering if it was wise of policymakers to accept that and even to encourage it.

Lending markets weren't unimportant. They played some role in the development of the boom and definitely in the bust. The scale of that role is still up for debate. But here's the thing. Regardless of how important lending was, there was never any reason for two million construction jobs to disappear. Instead of seeing the decline of banking and the decline of construction as twin predestinies, declining construction should have been seen as a sign that we had pushed too far against the lending boom. And since construction had declined substantially before most foreclosures happened and before the 2008 financial crisis developed, one must further ponder if those lending activities would have been associated with so much economic upheaval if we had proceeded with more of a goal of stability.

Because of the subprime lending boom, construction employment in Los Angeles, where the median home rents for more than $2,500, managed to push ahead of construction employment in Detroit, where the median home rents for less than $1,200. I hope that someday soon, economists and policymakers minds' will boggle when they think back to how this was treated as an unsustainable development that was a step toward an unavoidable tragic financial crisis.

Severe reductions in economic activity and in lending became the consensus tool for cooling housing markets. But that doesn't follow from the evidence. It follows from the *choice* of treating inadequate local housing supply as a state of nature and credit markets as a malleable effect. What if we had reversed that? What if, in 2008, instead of making it effectively illegal for many people to get mortgages, we had instead insisted on making it legal for them to build homes in Los Angeles? Not only would that bring home prices down much more effectively, it would have had the most pleasant side effect of putting people *to* work instead of putting them *out of* work.

CHAPTER 6

LOW INTEREST RATES

In addition to an increase in nonconventional mortgage lending, the other primary potential source of new demand for housing during the boom was low interest rates. As with mortgage standards, if we presume that there was an unsustainable housing bubble, then our conclusions about what caused it seem relatively easy. Lower interest rates induce more demand for buying and building homes, and so it seems they must have made the problem worse. But if burdens on the supply of homes are the pivotal problem, the effects of interest rates aren't so straightforward. A number of questions must be satisfied:

» What effect do interest rates have on home prices and construction activities?

» Which interest rates are important and what causes them to decline?

» Are low interest rates naturally stabilizing or destabilizing?

The short answer to these questions: low interest rates only had a moderate influence on prices. The Federal Reserve doesn't have that much control over the interest rates that are important to home prices. And low interest rates can be stabilizing and beneficial in places where adequate housing can be built.

WHAT EFFECT DO INTEREST RATES HAVE ON HOME PRICES AND CONSTRUCTION ACTIVITIES?

The global economy is integrated enough that interest rates in various countries tend to move together. Interest rates in Canada and Australia have generally moved in line with interest rates in the United States, and home prices have been elevated there.[97]

Is there is an international counterexample of a country with low interest rates that doesn't have an urban supply problem? Yes. One example is Japan. Japanese interest rates were lower than in the US during the housing boom. Japan didn't have a housing bubble in 2005, and home prices there are moderate.

But we don't really need to go that far. The US has plenty of examples of cities where low interest rates didn't cause prices to skyrocket—Dallas, Charlotte, Atlanta, etc.

It is true that low interest rates can put upward pressure on prices. The monthly payment on a thirty-year mortgage is about 12 percent higher at a 6 percent interest rate than a 5 percent interest rate. For a potential borrower who might either rent or own, the lower interest rate makes the decision to own easier, even at higher prices.[98]

In chapter 5, Figure 2 showed how important rising rents have been. If low interest rates were the main reason for rising prices, then price/rent ratios would increase in all types of cities. Since the urban supply crisis is the main cause of rising prices, price/rent ratios have increased the most in cities where rents are high.

Some pressure on urban rents comes from access to high paying jobs in some cities. Cities with high and rising rents also have high and rising incomes. If low interest rates were the main reason for rising prices, then price/income ratios would increase in all types of cities. But a peculiar pattern has arisen. In metropolitan areas where families tend to have higher incomes, they tend to have to spend more of those higher incomes on housing.

Before 2001, thirty-year mortgage rates were over 7 percent, and in cities where incomes were lower, price/income ratios tended to be around 2.0–2.2. In other words, if the typical family earned $60,000 annually, the typical house sold for a little more than $120,000. Then, mortgage rates declined to a range between 5.5 percent and 6.5 percent, and price/income ratios in cities where incomes were lower increased to about 2.6–2.8. That's about a 25 percent increase roughly equal to the savings on a thirty-year fixed rate mortgage payment. That is the change in home prices that might have been facilitated by a combination of loosening mortgage credit markets and declining interest rates in cities with lower incomes.

The price/income ratio in typical cities with the highest incomes reached above 5.5 by the end of 2005. The difference between a city with a median price/income ratio of 2.8 and one with a ratio of 5.5 was short supply.[99]

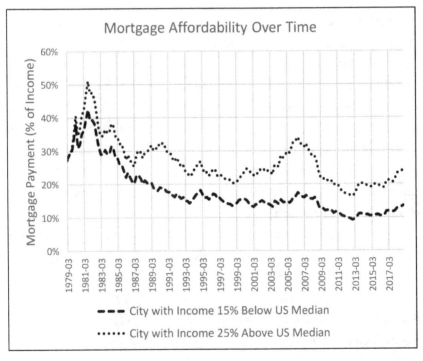

Figure 4

Figure 4 compares the portion of the median household's income required to make the mortgage payment on a conventional loan in cities with lower incomes and cities with higher incomes. During the housing boom in cities where incomes are lower, the typical mortgage payment took about the same portion of family incomes as it had for twenty years. In cities with higher incomes, mortgage payments took more.

As with credit standards, interest rates can move prices, and they did, but the shape of the American housing market during the boom is not the shape of a market dominated by low interest rates and loose lending. In 1979, the portion of the median household's income required to pay the mortgage on the median home was about the same in both poor and rich cities. By the peak of the housing boom, the typical mortgage payment in rich cities took twice as much of household income as the typical mortgage payment in poorer cities. The difference remains nearly that high today.

Low interest rates were associated with reasonable, typical moderate changes in home values in cities where home building was ample. In cities where home building is obstructed, it takes a higher and higher income to get in, and it takes more of that high income to pay the mortgage.

WHICH INTEREST RATES ARE IMPORTANT AND WHAT CAUSES THEM TO DECLINE?

Many critics blame the Federal Reserve for low interest rates....

As I write that, I realize again how powerful the premises are in creating the conclusions. Critics *blame* the Fed for low interest rates. But there is no "correct" interest rate. Rates are a price. They are what they are. Why should we be put off any more by a 3 percent mortgage rate than we are by a 7 percent mortgage rate? A misunderstanding about the unnatural forces that are pushing up home prices (local political opposition to building) has led to misplaced antipathy about neutral, natural forces that affect home prices. There is nothing inherently bad about any given level of interest rates. The idea that low rates are bad comes from the premise that anything which encouraged residential investment was part of the problem. Once that myth is exorcised from your mind, there is little reason to have an opinion about an interest rate.

That criticism is also misplaced because the long-term real[100] low-risk interest rates that factor into home values have little relation to the short-term fed funds rate, which is the policy rate that the Federal Reserve manages.[101] The rates don't reliably move in the same direction in the short term. Nominal long-term rates tend to reflect market expectations of future inflation plus expectations of future economic growth and numerous other factors.[102]

The Federal Reserve is frequently assigned a strong role in feeding a housing bubble, even by its own members.[103] Outside of home prices and high mortgage debt levels, however, there is little reason to even view pre-2007 monetary policy as particularly stimulative. The mania about the housing bubble has been so strong that the consensus view of a recklessly loose monetary policy has developed based on little else. Compared to previous periods of economic expansion, 2002 to 2007 saw moderate inflation rates, moderate nominal income growth, and moderate gains in the stock market.

The lack of a better explanation for high home prices has led to an ad hoc association of loose monetary policy with the housing bubble. Except for the housing boom, the single piece of evidence that monetary policy was loose is that the target interest rate was low during that time. Short-term interest rates were below 2 percent from the end of 2001 to the end of 2004. Cheap credit is seen as stimulative—leading to rising home prices, bank deposits, and consumption. The Federal Reserve itself creates confusion here by communicating their policy stance in terms of interest rates. At any single meeting, the signal of looser (more inflationary) policy is to lower the policy rate. But that is only in the short term. Over the long term, low interest rates are the product of *past, tight* monetary policy decisions that lowered inflation. In the 1970s, for instance, when money was easy and inflation was hitting double digits, interest rates were very high.

An analogy I like to use here is that monetary policy is like backing up a truck with a trailer attached. If you want the trailer to go to the right, you have to first turn the steering wheel so that the back of your truck starts to move to the left, then you start to turn to the right. When the Federal Reserve wants more inflation, they are actually aiming for higher interest rates in the long term, because inflation makes interest rates go up. So, when they say, "We are lowering the target rate by a half percent to loosen policy," they are really just briefly turning to the left in order to get the trailer moving to the right. Just like with the trailer, if the Fed has to keep turning to the left, that means that it hadn't turned sharply enough to begin with. The reason the target interest rate collapsed from 5.25 percent to near 0 percent in 2008 was because the Fed wasn't turning sharply enough. The policy stance was too tight. And by late 2008, we ended up having a disastrous deflationary shock.

In this analogy, you can think of long-term interest rates as the trailer. For instance, in 1998, the Fed lowered their target rate from 5.5 percent to 4.8 percent. After briefly declining along with it to 4.4 percent, the rate on ten-year treasuries jumped back up over 6 percent, and the Fed raised their target rate back up in 1999. That was an example of lowering the rate enough to avoid an economic contraction. They turned the wheel enough to get the trailer moving in the other direction. Long-term interest rates increased, and when they did, short-term rates also went back up.

This is especially true over the long-term. You might be able to claim that temporarily low interest rates are due to a loose monetary policy that will create future inflation, but if those rates are still low years later, then that doesn't mean that the Fed is being even more stimulative than you thought. It means they weren't being stimulative to begin with. It means you were wrong. This is a common mistake, and it is common, in part, because the Fed uses interest rates as a confusing communication device. Understanding Fed communications is as difficult as backing up a truck with a trailer attached.

Interest rates reflect both inflation and the real return savers demand on safe securities. Low interest rates after the year 2000 were the result of an extended period of tight monetary policy that lowered inflation, which also lowered interest rates. They were also the result of savers who were willing to accept lower returns on assets that seemed safe.

The Federal Reserve started to raise the fed funds rate in 2004 in an attempt to slow down growth. But long-term rates (such as thirty-year mortgage rates) didn't rise along with it. They remained at their already low levels. The thirty-year mortgage rate was about 6.3 percent when the Fed's target overnight rate was still at 1 percent in June 2004. By March 2006, the Fed's target overnight rate was up to 4.5 percent. The thirty-year mortgage rate was still 6.3 percent. (A great example of how little power the Fed has over most market interest rates.) That is because investors didn't expect inflation to rise, and they also didn't want to take more risks, so they continued to invest in things like mortgage securities even though the interest yields on them remained low. Alan Greenspan called this a "conundrum."[104]

This is the opposite of the Fed's late 1990s moves. Remember, in 1998, the Fed lowered the short-term target rate enough that inflation caused long-term rates to increase. In 2004 and 2005, they were raising their target rate to lower inflation. Long-term interest rates stayed low. Those low long-term rates were a dangerous sign—a sign that they were pushing too hard. Eventually they pushed hard enough to create a recession and a deflationary shock in 2008. While this is not widely understood, this view on the matter is not unique.[105] Others have pointed to Fed decisions in late 2007 and 2008 as unnecessarily contractionary.[106]

Interest rates are such a common focal point of conversations about monetary policy that my description may sound strange. But this really has been a long-standing debate among macroeconomists. Some economists known as market monetarists have been making strides to change this confusing framework. *The Money Illusion*, a new book from economist Scott Sumner presents a technical discussion on these issues and the 2008 recession.[107] Some of this can get complicated, but really, if you hear others equate low interest rates with loose, inflationary monetary policy, ask yourself one simple question: When inflation was running above 5 percent annually in the 1970s, was monetary policy tight or loose, and were interest rates low or high?

Later, I will outline how little control the Federal Reserve can have even over short-term interest rates, and the role that played in the crisis.

ARE LOW INTEREST RATES NATURALLY STABILIZING OR DESTABILIZING?

One important way that monetary policy and the housing bubble seemed to be related was that homeowners were using their newly inflated home equity to fund new consumption. Since those high home values were presumed to be a temporary result of loose lending and money, that new consumption was also presumed to be unsustainable. When home prices returned to what was considered normal, not only would Americans have to cut back on consumption, but they would be indebted due to the unsustainable consumption they had indulged in. We were not as wealthy as we thought we were, and eventually the bills would come due.

Mian and Sufi have estimated the scale of consumption funded with mortgage debt. "The entire effect of housing wealth on spending is through borrowing, and, under certain assumptions, this spending represents 0.8% of GDP in 2004 and 1.3% of GDP in 2005 and 2006. Households that borrow and spend out of housing gains between 2002 and 2006 experience significantly lower income and spending growth after 2006."[108]

If that consumption was funded by fake, temporary increases in wealth created by loose money and credit, then naturally, the proper policy response is to tighten credit and monetary policy as soon as possible before the debts that fund that consumption get more bloated. This is the usual criticism leveled against the Federal Reserve in hindsight. They should have stopped the bubble earlier.[109]

It seems as though the borrowing identified by Mian and Sufi is destabilizing. Consumption for those borrowers was too high from 2002 to 2006, and then it had to be reduced after 2006.

Whether their wealth is permanent or temporary, the effects of housing wealth on consumption during the boom would have been the same. Either way, there would be an increase in borrowing among new home buyers and among homeowners who could make up for shortfalls of cash by borrowing. Either way, there would still be a wealth effect on consumption.

But if high prices are the result of inadequate housing, then in the Closed Access cities, wealth wasn't temporary. As long as urban housing is obstructed, that wealth will remain. The *collapse* in wealth *after* the crisis was temporary. A decade after the crisis, Closed Access rents—the source of that wealth—have continued to rise, and home prices will continue to rise above previous highs as long as they do.

(The rise of remote working and the related rush out of some cities has temporarily reduced urban rents and allayed this problem for now. It remains to be seen how permanent this will be. Unless there are tectonic shifts in the way Americans work, this will be a speed bump on the road toward long-term rising costs. Unless population growth in cities like Los Angeles permanently grinds to nearly zero, then each year there will continue to be more people who want in or who simply want to stay than there will be houses for them, and the demented musical chairs routine will continue.)

The debt-fueled consumption wasn't due to Americans spending beyond their means. It was due to some Americans having the means to spend without being productive by owning homes with inflated rental value. They got that wealth by making sure that if you wanted to build a home near them then the local government would stop you. The debt wasn't building up because some Americans were profligate spendthrifts. It's worse than that. We're becoming a country of petty oligarchs.

As I pointed out in chapter 3, the borrowing in the Contagion cities in 2006 and 2007 was different. In those cities, home prices weren't necessarily permanently higher, and the borrowing was more cyclical. There, much of the debt was taken out when local incomes were suddenly in peril and the debt was being used to level out local consumption when the decline of migration flows caused local economies to contract. They were already having local economic crises, and they were borrowing to cover their expenditures while they waited for a recovery.

In both cases, families weren't borrowing to fund unusual, unsustainable spending. They were engaged in what economists call consumption smoothing. They have some idea of what their future incomes will be.

Families make spending decisions based on both how much money they have today and how much they think they will have in the future. During the boom, the Closed Access borrowers were going to be richer in the future when they sold their homes, so they spent more today. (In fact, many of them banked their gains by selling their homes and moving away.) After the boom, Contagion city borrowers suddenly had a shortage of income, which they reasonably expected to recover in the future when the economy would recover, and they happened to have equity in their homes with which to smooth their spending in the meantime. By the way, those Contagion city mortgages taken out in 2006 and 2007, which ended up being the mortgages that had really high default rates, were taken out after the Fed had already hiked up its target interest rate. The mortgages with high default rates weren't taken out in a low-rate environment.

In a recent paper, economist J. W. Mason found that for households at the top and bottom of the income distribution, over the past two decades, consumption has grown parallel with incomes. Neither group caused an unsustainable growth in consumption.[110] Higher debt has not been the result of spending by poor households. They are reducing their spending rather than increasing their borrowing. Poor households cannot easily access large amounts of credit. The rise of debt is mostly associated with the rise of Closed Access cities—upper middle-class households taking out mortgages to buy expensive Closed Access homes.

Whether debt-fueled spending was sustainable or not, the new current consumption would be inflationary in either case. Using Mian and Sufi's numbers, there was 1.3 percent of new consumption that wasn't matched by a rise in current production. That new debt-fueled consumption would either push up consumer prices until others were driven to consume less, or it would draw in imports.

This consumption did lead to a sharp rise in imports. Imports net of exports reached more than 5 percent of GDP at the peak of the housing boom. But it didn't lead to more inflation. Inflation remained near 2 percent during the housing boom.

This is because the additional debt-fueled consumption wasn't a monetary phenomenon. The Fed creates inflation by printing money. The Fed wasn't creating that much money at the time. The Fed was already slowing the growth of currency in order to counteract this wealth-fueled spending. They were able to keep inflation near their target rate, but there was little that a functional monetary policy could do to counteract the pressure on increased imports. Those homeowners were increasing their consumption, but they weren't producing more, so the things they consumed had to come from somewhere else.

The only *functional* way to stop this consumption smoothing from happening would be to prevent the real estate properties from capturing monopolistic rents in the future. The only *sustainable* way to do that would be to encourage more building in Closed Access cities so that future rents will be lower. That hasn't happened. Closed Access homes sold (and again today, sell) for such high prices because their high rental value means they are worth that much. If future rental values have not changed, then the only way that monetary policy could make wealthy housing oligarchs poorer would be to push home prices down in spite of their elevated rental values—to suck enough cash out of the economy that those homes couldn't fetch the prices that they were worth. In other words, once the country was committed to countering wealth-funded consumption with tight monetary policy, it was pragmatically *committed to creating a financial crisis in real estate.*

But what about the rest of the country? Low interest rates aren't naturally destabilizing. In cities where homes can be built easily, the dollar value of a new house is mostly based on the cost of building one. In the long run, lower interest rates will tend to lower rents rather than raise prices.

While that is a textbook description of what would happen in a market with no limits to new supply, it isn't just a hypothetical. The Bureau of Labor Statistics tracks rent inflation for some metropolitan areas. From 1995 to 2000, both the Closed Access cities and high demand cities that weren't Closed Access or Contagion cities averaged more than 3.5 percent rent inflation annually. From 2000 to 2005, rent inflation in the Closed Access cities moved up to 4.5 percent but rent inflation in the other cities declined to 2 percent. After the crisis, home building in many cities has been very low. As a result, from 2013 to 2018, rent inflation was back up above 3.5 percent for both types of cities.[111] Where homes can be built, new construction brings down rents. Where an inadequate number of homes are built, rents rise. As I mentioned in chapter 1, one way that building new homes makes us all better off is that it causes rents to be lower for everyone.

In the Closed Access cities, rent doesn't just pay for lumber. That is a small part of what rent pays for. Most of what rent pays for is monopolistic profit to homeowners where developers are prevented from creating more homes. So when factors like lower interest rates or higher incomes allow some households to buy more houses, it doesn't push rents down like it does in other cities. It pushes out enough of the existing tenants to make room for the extra housing that some households can now purchase. It is no accident that the housing boom coincided with a mass migration of hundreds of thousands of families out of the Closed Access cities. When conditions allow people to have more houses, the Closed Access cities have room for fewer people.

The problem of how to frame the question affects analysis of monetary policy just like it affects analysis of the effect of credit on home prices and construction.

There are those who emphasize interest rates. They conclude that low interest rates can have more of an effect on prices when supply is inelastic.[112]

There are researchers who see other sources of demand as more important. There are those who see it as an issue of consumption. They argue that an increasing number of households with high incomes prefer to live in "superstar cities." Inelastic supply makes prices there rise.[113]

There are those who find that workers can be more productive in some cities and that causes homes to be more expensive where workers have high incomes and housing supply is inelastic.[114]

If inelastic housing supply is just a state of the world we have to accept—if home prices will always be expensive and unpredictable in Los Angeles because builders aren't allowed to produce more of them—then all of these different types of research point to different ways to get rid of volatility in housing markets. Tighter lending standards, higher interest rates, lower incomes, or limits on migration can all reduce the pressure on rising prices.

Yet none of those factors caused home prices to be unusually volatile in Austin, Texas or Raleigh, North Carolina, where home building is active.[115] Elastic supply makes housing markets less volatile regardless of what factors are pushing demand up or down. Where houses can be built, the housing boom was reducing rents. Where supply is elastic, low interest rates aren't destabilizing.[116]

Criticism of "rational expectations" models of the housing market has been based on the idea that it was the "rational" part of the model that failed—that home buyers became irrational. But it was the "expectations" that became erratic. It is harder for prices to remain stable when high prices can't trigger the new supply that would bring them back down.

All of these various studies about volatile housing markets point to a single solution: make housing supply elastic again. Build more houses.

Instead of enacting that unifying solution, public policymakers instead ended up changing all of the other variables, directly or indirectly. They tamed aggressive lenders. They tried to raise interest rates. They lowered incomes. They caused migration to decline. Those disparate solutions didn't get at the core problem. They ended up creating new dislocations rather than solving the existing ones.

PART 3

From Soft Landing to Suicide Pact

CHAPTER 7

THE BACK-DOOR EXODUS

In many ways, Americans in general had soured on housing before policy-makers did. Some of the signs of this shift were quite acute. Years of shifting sentiment had built up by the time market panics were developing in late 2007.

In 2004 and 2005, the home ownership rate had leveled off. At first, there were still about the same number of new homeowners as there had been in recent years, but there were more homeowners selling out and becoming renters.[117] The decline in housing markets and in home ownership rates associated with the financial crisis happened first through the back door—owners exiting ownership voluntarily.

Much has been said about the infamous housing ATM—households tapping inflated home equity for consumption. There is a flip side to that. Before prices started to fall, many households were using their homes as ATMs by *selling* them rather than borrowing from their home equity.

Some research has aimed at estimating the effect of home equity borrowing on rising spending. Mian and Sufi tracked existing homeowners and found that they extracted about 25 percent to 30 percent of unrealized capital gains by borrowing from their growing home equity.[118]

On the other hand, home sellers would be more likely to save the proceeds from selling their former homes. Where an existing owner sold and exited the homeowner market, the mortgage payment taken on by the new home buyer was likely larger than the payment that the old owner had been paying, if they had been paying one at all. A sale like that would increase mortgages outstanding, but it likely had the opposite effect on spending that home equity borrowing did.

A significant amount of home equity had been lost by mid-2007, when home prices were still relatively stable. Some of that reduction in equity was from the "back door" flight out of ownership—the old owners, whose mortgages from years ago were small, selling to new owners whose mortgages had to be larger.

During the boom period, about 6 percent of homes were sold each year, and *net* out-migration of homeowners from the Closed Access cities reached an annual rate of nearly 2 percent.[119] So, out-migration of homeowners to less expensive cities plausibly accounted for a quarter or more of Closed Access home sales during this time. Homes were more expensive because there weren't enough of them in the Closed Access cities. Americans weren't blowing up a bubble. On net, they were trying to get out from under it. They were moving to other places where they didn't have the risk of a very expensive house.

At the end of 2005, average homeowner leverage was about the same as it had been for a decade. The average homeowner had a mortgage worth about 38 percent of their home's value. After 2005, growth in mortgages slowed, but not as much as the growth in home values. Between the end of 2005 and the middle of 2007, total owner-occupied home values rose by about $785 billion, but mortgages outstanding of homeowners grew by more than $1.4 trillion. That means that the equity owners had in those homes declined by $636 billion even though home values were generally holding steady.[120]

We might attribute a minimum of about $600 billion of the new borrowing to existing homeowners taking out equity, as estimated by Mian and Sufi.[121] However, some part of the new borrowing was the net increase in borrowing that was funding home purchases. By then, the number of new homeowners wasn't rising. Those purchases were replacing existing owners who were exiting home ownership. Increasingly, existing owners were also selling and being replaced by investors.

The mortgages taken out in 2006 and 2007 that had very high default rates were taken out during a time when home purchase activity was declining. By the middle of 2007, even though home values were still holding relatively steady, the mortgage on the average owner-occupied home had risen from 38 percent to 44 percent of the home's value. Some of that can be attributed to borrowing against equity in cities where home values were high, but some of it, ironically, was due to a flight from home ownership rather than a rush into it.[122]

Taking a broader view of supply and demand and of the various flows of capital and households in these markets, it makes sense to think of housing as being composed of two different asset classes—equity and debt. The rise in leverage coincided with a complex mixture of financial trends. The rise in homeowner leverage was due to two countervailing trends. Some of the higher leverage was fueled by investors willing to invest in the new private mortgages (the debt part), but some of it was due to a lack of households willing to take on the risk of long-term ownership of a home (the equity part). The evidence from this period has been treated as if it is on a one-way street. The preponderance of negative trends in home ownership and residential investment after 2005 calls for a less-absolutist view of the period.

THE STEALTH SUPPLY OF EMPTY HOMES

One way that the shift out of the housing market played out was in cancelled new home orders, which I mentioned briefly in chapter 3. Normally, when a customer has financing lined up, homebuilders will only require them to make a small deposit in order to begin construction on a new home. While construction is underway, many things can happen that prevent a customer from purchasing the finished new home. Maybe they couldn't find a buyer for their previous home. Maybe something happened to change their financial situation. So, homebuilders allow customers to cancel their orders, even if the builder has completed a new home to the customer's specifications. All the customer must sacrifice is the small deposit they had put into escrow, which usually amounts to just a few thousand dollars.

This is effectively like a default on a low-down payment mortgage for the buyer, except that homebuilders tend to be generous about cancellations. They are simply treated as a normal part of the business model. They don't carry the severity of a default or a foreclosure. Even in normal years, 15 percent or more of new home orders might end up getting cancelled. From 2005 to 2006, the rate of cancelled orders at major homebuilders doubled, rising to more than 30 percent, where it would remain until after 2008.[123]

In 2005, homebuilders had been having such a difficult time keeping up with demand that they were holding lotteries to allocate new lots to potential buyers in some cities.[124] In 2006, because of the surge of cancelled orders, the tide turned, and unsold inventory increased. These were homes built for qualified buyers who had signed contracts for specific homes. This was a real problem for the builders, and they responded by cutting back on new construction in order to focus on selling this newly vacant inventory.[125]

At a September 2007 Federal Reserve meeting, Ben Bernanke and other members finally were able to get the committee to start lowering interest rates after their decision to keep the target rate at 5.25 percent in August had rattled mortgage markets. Richard Fisher, the head of the Dallas Fed said, "I'm very concerned that we're leaning the tiller too far to the side to compensate risk-takers when we should be disciplining them." [126] For more than a year before that meeting, homebuilders had been cutting back on construction in order to try to sell the empty inventory left by cancelled orders. The market had already been disciplining the homebuilders for quite some time. Share prices for major homebuilders Pulte and D.R. Horton had already fallen from highs above forty dollars to the low teens.

Foreclosures eventually started to accumulate later in the crisis. Many foreclosures are caused by multiple factors. A homeowner who becomes unemployed might manage to hold onto their home for a while—maybe they can even borrow against it to help get through the rough patch. A homeowner whose home loses value so that they have negative equity will likely keep making payments anyway. But a homeowner with negative equity who becomes unemployed is more likely to default on their payments. One question in the debates about who to blame for rising defaults: Were the defaulting borrowers victims of circumstance or were they tactically leaving their devalued homes with the banks? Were they unable to make their payments, or did they stop making payments because they decided that it was worth it to get out from under their devalued house?

That debate isn't necessary. The new home buyers who began cancelling their orders in 2006 could get rid of their new homes without the personal and moral costs of a mortgage default. That offers a much clearer picture into the evolving market than defaults do. It happened much earlier. It wasn't caused by borrowers who realized over time that they weren't able to make their mortgage payments. The customers who cancelled their orders never made a mortgage payment.

The mortgage default crisis happened long after the collapsing market was stressing homebuilders. Privately securitized loan originations basically disappeared in the summer of 2007. The Closed Access and Contagion cities were beginning to see rising foreclosure rates. But more than 90 percent of excess foreclosures occurred nationwide after the private loan market collapsed. More than 70 percent happened after the broader economic collapse of September 2008 a year later.[127]

By late 2007 and 2008, when policymakers were looking for ways to stabilize the economy without bailing out the reckless lenders and speculators that were blamed for the bubble, the American housing market was well into a crisis already, both in terms of supply and demand. Americans had been dealing with a lack of well-placed supply for a decade already, and policymakers were resolved to reduce residential investment even further. The overwhelming public sentiment in 2007 (and still today) was that American housing investors were too complacent and that they needed to rediscover fear. To the contrary, Americans had been tactically disinvesting from home equity already for some time, but policymakers were resolved to increase the fear of investing in home equity.

CLUES FROM HOME PRICES

In *Shut Out*, I noted that the initial decline in mortgaged home ownership was among the homeowners with the highest incomes. Mortgaged home ownership rates started to decline in 2006 and 2007 among households with incomes in the top 20 percent. The mortgaged home ownership rate for households with incomes near the median were still about the same in 2009, as they had been in 2005, and declined after that.[128]

The shift in sentiment among different types of homeowners as the housing boom peaked left an imprint on housing markets. In most large metropolitan areas, sales turnover slowed down in more expensive areas first.[129] A similar pattern happened in home prices. Within metropolitan areas, prices in high-priced neighborhoods generally were the first to begin declining.[130]

Later, in 2008 and after, lending standards were severely tightened, more than they had previously been loosened. So, within metropolitan areas from 2008 until around 2011 or 2012, limits on lending really hit less expensive zip codes hard. I will discuss that more in later chapters, but the key issue here is that the evidence just doesn't line up well with the common story that the country had slowly filled up with unqualified homeowners who started to realize that they couldn't make their mortgage payments, triggering a market collapse. All the early indicators say that the market soured first among the buyers with more discretion, higher incomes, ample home equity, and so forth. The collapse in markets with lower incomes, lower home prices, and more dependence on credit markets happened later. Overburdened defaulting borrowers weren't the trigger of the crisis. They were the result of an accumulating crisis that policymakers were long unwilling to address.

Home prices compared to prices of commercial real estate also show a similar pattern. Owner-occupied housing mostly looks different because of the late bust, not because of a unique bubble. As shown in Figure 5,[131] single-family home prices tracked by the Case-Shiller index followed very closely with the prices of apartment buildings tracked by CoStar. Mortgage lending has been tightened sharply since 2008, so single-family home prices have been much lower than prices for apartment buildings since then.

In the period leading up to the crisis, prices of other categories of commercial real estate (offices, retail, and industrial) all continued to climb higher until mid-2007, after home prices had leveled off. Just like the comparisons with other countries, American single-family home prices look oddest after the boom when they are lower than prices in other types of real estate.

In short, single-family home prices didn't behave differently than prices of other real estate during the boom. The initial retreat from home ownership was tactical and discretionary, rather than distressed. The retreat from owner-occupied housing started well before the mortgage crisis, and in many ways, owner-occupied housing remains depressed today, both in prices and production.

Figure 5 Residential vs. Commercial Real Estate Prices

We can create a story here about "smart money" and "dumb money." The smart money got out early and the dumb money was left holding the bag. But at some point, creating bag holders is a choice. If we embrace the policy of a disciplining instability, and the predictably terrible results of that instability can be blamed on dumb money and its enablers, then we have a "get out of jail free" card for damaging economic policy choices. How do we judge business cycle management if our resolve to support the destabilizing, disciplining approach is reinforced when that approach leads to economic disaster? What if policymakers had started trying to make "smart money" more optimistic in 2006 and 2007 instead of making sure that "dumb money" learned its lesson? Are you sure that a more stable housing market and a more stable economy would have been all that bad, in comparison?

 CHAPTER 8

LOSING THE COMMITMENT
TO A SOFT LANDING

Eventually, as the housing bust deepened, the country accepted or cheered on instability. Yet, in some ways, the Closed Access problem is subtly supported by a preference for stability—whether it is real estate insiders worrying about "oversupply," local homeowners fretting over the aesthetics of new buildings or the hassles of new traffic, or urban activists fighting gentrification and renter dislocation. They all want stability.

On the other hand, what the Closed Access housing markets desperately need is much lower rents and prices. Affordability would require a deep change. Affordability would be destabilizing.

During the housing bubble, prices moved quickly enough to levels that were so unusual that it seemed that surely the spring needed to recoil. If it goes up quickly, surely that means it will come down. The preference for stability was weakened by the sense that things had moved too fast.[132] But even so, at the first signs of a peaking market, the hope was for the spring to recoil slowly. The talk in 2005 and 2006 was of a "soft landing."

At their June 2005 meeting, held when home prices were near their peak, the FOMC (the committee that makes decisions about monetary policy at the Federal Reserve) had an in-depth discussion of housing markets and their potential effects on monetary policy. It was a productive, level-headed meeting. Concerns were raised about overheated markets as well as the potential of even a 20 percent price collapse—both reasonable points to consider at the time.

Committee members noted the aberrations from historical price norms and the probability of price moderation or declines in coming years. But, for instance, senior FOMC economist Andreas Lehnert noted that homeowners generally had a decent equity cushion at the time and mortgage insurers seemed to be well capitalized.

Richard Peach noted that in the aggregate, price appreciation had been stronger among higher-priced homes that were purchased by households with higher incomes, suggesting that expanding credit to marginal owners was not the primary cause of rising prices.[133]

Janet Yellen noted that new credit products and improved efficiencies that increased liquidity of real estate holdings could have created some permanent increases in relative home values. She also recognized the parallels in valuation between residential and commercial properties, which suggested that new products in the residential mortgage market were not the primary cause of rising prices.

Jeffrey Lacker noted the local nature of rising home prices and the value of the new high-density, urban, high-skilled labor market—the markets I call "Closed Access." David Stockton expressed some reservations about the sustainability of high prices but noted that for a housing contraction to lead to a crisis, several negative trends would have to coincide, some of which, like interest rates, the Fed had some control over.[134] At that time, the Fed target rate was only up to 3 percent.

Ben Bernanke wrote about the June 2005 meeting, "To the extent that any mispricing existed, historical experience suggested that it would correct slowly, perhaps through an extended period of stagnant prices. And, the staff economists argued, if housing prices did fall, interest rate cuts by the Fed could cushion the blow to the broader economy."[135]

In the summer of 2005, the FOMC had a view of the housing boom that fit well with the description I laid out in Shut Out. But by the time Shut Out was published in 2019, that description had become contrary to conventional wisdom. So why did they change that position?

BABY STEPS TOWARD INSTABILITY

By March 2006, housing starts began to shift downward and real estate values leveled off. The Fed had raised its target short-term rate to 4.5 percent and was still raising it. Mortgages outstanding were still growing.

The personal consumption expenditure (PCE) inflation indicator was slightly above 2 percent for the entire period—not high enough to justify allowing a crisis, but high enough that it was reasonable for the Fed to try to moderate nominal growth according to its general price-level targets.

At the March 2006 meeting David Stockton noted, "As has been the case for some time, housing is central to our forecast of some modest deceleration of activity. Residential investment has been contributing about ½ percentage point to the growth of real GDP over the past few years. So a flattening out of activity in this sector would, by itself, be sufficient to bring about the necessary slowing in aggregate production."

Janet Yellen added "I did want to comment briefly on the risks associated with housing. This is the sector that obviously bears close watching because it can represent the leading edge of the effects of the monetary tightening." She noted that "tighter financing conditions are finally exacting a toll." This comment contains two important points. First, Yellen clearly identifies the well-understood connection between construction activity and monetary policy. Second, the expression of exasperation—"*finally* exacting a toll"—is a linguistic cue that the Fed had already pushed harder than it had thought it would need to in order to slow down construction. The reason they had to push so hard to get home sales to fall is that there was no overarching macroeconomic reason for home sales to fall. Home sales had been rising where vacancies were low, and housing was in relatively short supply.

Ben Bernanke said, "So except for housing—and that is, of course, a critical sector—it looks as though the economy is, if anything, growing more quickly than potential. Housing is the crucial issue. To get a soft landing, we need some cooling in housing. So far there is a good bit of evidence that there has been a peak, but we do not know a great deal more than that."

Later, Bernanke added,

"As I discussed, I see the economy as still being basically quite strong, and it needs to moderate to become consistent with its long-run potential. The vehicle by which that is going to happen is the slowing in the housing market. I think we ought to raise the rate today and not to signal an immediate end for several reasons. First, we could think of our policy in terms of the mortgage rate rather than the funds rate. The mortgage rate is currently about the same as it was when we began tightening in June 2004, and it is still providing support to the housing market. If we failed to act today or signaled that we are definitely done, we would create a rally in the long-term bond market and in the mortgage market. We would create, I think, some risk of re-igniting what is currently a cooling market. I think that would be a mistake."[136]

The Fed was purposefully slowing down housing construction, but they were still aiming for stability.[137] Bernanke expected this investment to be reallocated to other sectors. The Fed saw the housing boom as inflationary. But how exactly was a decline in construction going to reduce inflation? Was a decline in construction going to reduce inflation in San Francisco? The inflation there was largely due to a *shortage* of housing. Would it reduce inflation in Dallas? In Dallas, home prices weren't excessive, so home equity lines of credit weren't a sizable source of funds for household consumption, and residential investment there had been pushing *down* rent inflation. Economic growth did slow in 2006 as the Fed had intended, but it was a decline in real economic growth without much effect on inflation—mostly because rents increased as home building cooled off.

Second, the idea that stubbornly low mortgage interest rates were stimulating was also a perspective that pointed the FOMC in a dangerous direction. Long-term interest rates that remain low in the face of rising short-term rates can be a sign of low economic expectations and slowing growth.

The fact that home ownership and housing starts were turning down in the face of those low rates should have further worried the committee. The idea that housing was due for a decline reduced this concern.

Yet the Fed did manage to engineer a soft landing as good as anyone could have hoped. Having worried about a 10 percent or 20 percent price shock, they arrived in the middle of 2007 with housing starts back down to a level common in the late 1990s while home prices had barely declined at all.

At this point, policy was generally close enough to reasonable to avoid a major economic dislocation, and any errors would have been reversible. Taking their own goals at face value—that a decline in residential investment had been warranted—the Federal Reserve had achieved what, it turns out, was a most unsatisfying outcome: a truly soft landing.

THE FED'S CRITICS

The benign position of the Federal Reserve, even as late as the summer of 2007, was an important element in the development of the crisis. This has been one source of criticism against the Fed. Why didn't they see what was coming? In the summer of 2007, they expected both home prices and housing starts to just flatten out for a couple of years. Those forecasts ended up being strikingly optimistic.

On this point, it is useful to think about the difference between consumer prices and asset prices. Consumer prices reflect supply and demand for goods and services that are used today: food, gas, healthcare, utilities, and entertainment, for example. Asset prices are much more complicated. They are based on expectations of future sources of income and the willingness of current savers to pay for the right to that income: prices of stocks and bonds, for example. In housing, rent is the measure of consumer prices and home prices are a measure of asset prices.

The Fed is responsible for consumer price stability. Asset prices can frequently be harbingers of coming economic dislocations or recoveries, so the Fed pays attention to the prices of stocks, bonds, and homes. But they aren't tasked with *controlling* the prices of those things. They *are* tasked with controlling the prices of consumer goods.

This was a key distinction that informed Fed decisions during the crucial march toward crisis. When prices or consumption decline, the Fed acts to counter those trends. If inflation had been 2 percent and fell to 1 percent, or if unemployment had been at 5 percent and increased to 6 percent, or if national income growth had been 5 percent and fell to 3 percent, the Fed would normally treat those as signs of instability that it is supposed to reverse. It would stimulate the economy to try to move inflation and nominal income growth back up and move the unemployment rate back down. But since housing is an asset, the Fed doesn't treat it as something it is responsible for controlling. Generally, that is the correct position to take.

As home prices leveled out and started to decline, the Fed didn't reflexively forecast that home prices would rebound. They aren't in charge of asset prices. In late 2006, the Fed staff forecast slow growth.[138] By the middle of 2007, prices had remained flat since the peak, and they were forecast to remain flat for a couple of years. Then prices started to collapse. By the end of 2007, the forecast was now for the decline to continue at a rate of about 3 percent annually. By the middle of 2008, the forecast decline was about double that. Even in mid-2009, the forecast was for two more years of annual declines of 6 percent. The steeper the prices fell, the more the Fed shifted their forecasts of future price declines even lower.

Oddly, they took the same approach to housing starts, even though construction activity directly affects unemployment, which is one of the measures they try to control. And they had explicitly discussed their attempts to moderate construction activity in 2006. In early 2006, housing starts were still near their peak of about 2.1 million units per year, and Fed staff forecast that they would remain at that level for the foreseeable future. Each quarter, the annual rate of housing starts would decline by about a hundred thousand units, and Fed staff would move down their forecast. Until the summer of 2007, their forecast for the rate of housing starts that they expected at the end of 2008 generally matched the rate of starts in the quarter leading up to the meeting. By the end of 2006, starts had declined to about 1.6 million. By the end of 2007, starts were down to 1.2 million. By the end of 2008, starts were below 700 thousand. Starts would remain flat for several more years.

From the first quarter of 2006 to the first quarter of 2009, the Fed's estimate of the total number of homes that would be built from 2006 through 2011 declined by six million units. Building rates would continue at historically low levels for years afterward. Conventional wisdom accepted this as a necessary reaction to having built too many units in the boom. It is strange that it did so. There is absolutely no way to add up housing construction activity before 2006 and find extra units anywhere close to six million. That size of a decline is actually strong evidence that the problem was an extreme demand shock—a lack of funding for buying and building homes after 2006. That is the only remotely reasonable explanation for it. A contraction leading to a decline in the future rate of building of one or two million units could have been plausibly explained as a correction to overbuilding. The contraction in the Fed's forecast of housing starts was already that large by mid-2007 when prices started to collapse. I have argued that there was never systematic oversupply. Certainly, by the time home prices were collapsing, there was not. With each passing quarter, the expected construction implied by the Fed's continually declining forecasts moved down by about another half million units. Each quarter should have been further evidence that builders were being hit by a demand shock—a lack of money and credit required to build needed homes—rather than a supply correction, but it was interpreted as the opposite. The Fed had created a severe demand shock and they never were able to awaken from the trance they had stumbled into. Really, the trance everyone had stumbled into.

It is common for actual outcomes to be more volatile than forecasts and for forecasts to reflect recent trends. The point is that the Fed is a special sort of institution. It has some control over how many dollars Americans spend by creating inflation or deflation of those dollars. When the price of consumer goods declines, the Fed forecasts a reversal of that decline because it intends to *assert control* over those prices. When the price and construction of homes continued their long decline, the Fed forecast the continuation of that decline because it did not assert control over home prices and construction activity.

Most monetary policy experts would agree that this is entirely appropriate. The Fed controls consumer prices, not asset prices. That is all well and good as a principle. But did the Fed or its critics really follow that principle?

One of the common measures researchers use to estimate appropriate monetary policy is the Taylor Rule. It is a guideline for targeting short-term interest rates in a way that is intended to produce stable, low inflation and low unemployment. John Taylor, who that rule is named after, has been a critic of Fed policy in the years before the crisis. In his book, *Getting Off Track*, about the causes of the financial crisis, chapter 1 begins:

> The classic explanation of financial crises, going back hundreds of years, is that they are caused by excesses—frequently monetary excesses—that lead to a boom and an inevitable bust. In the recent crisis we had a housing boom and bust, which in turn led to financial turmoil in the United States and other countries. I begin by showing that monetary excesses were the main cause of that boom and the resulting bust.

In that chapter, he claims that the Fed should have raised interest rates earlier, and he argues that those higher rates would have led to lower home prices and fewer housing starts. He estimated that Fed stimulus had led to an oversupply of about one million homes. Later, Taylor writes that "the housing boom was the most noticeable effect of the monetary excesses." Clearly, it wasn't '70s-style consumer inflation that led to his criticisms. It was home prices. He was critical of the Fed because he *blamed them* for high *asset* prices, and he concluded that high prices must have led to overbuilding.[139]

Critics and commentators wonder how the Fed could have been so surprised by the collapse. Yet few argue that the Fed should have acted more forcefully to prevent the collapse. Boosting asset markets would've been inappropriate. Instead, they usually argue that the Fed should have specifically aimed to lower asset prices a few years earlier than they did. In the end, the critics aren't arguing that there is a principle against the Fed targeting asset prices. Critics commonly say that the Fed should have reacted *against* high home prices before 2006. They are arguing for a one-way principle: The Fed should explicitly push asset prices down when they are rising but should not support asset prices when they are declining, because that would be a bailout.

What sort of outcome should we expect from a system where the central bank is only supposed to try to directly affect asset prices in order to bring them down but never to stabilize them or bring them up? Eventually, inevitably, it will lead to the very outcome we got. Either ignoring asset prices or trying to control them both up and down would be better than this monetary masochism.

THE INEVITABLE, ACCIDENTAL MORAL PANIC

This is mostly a comment on the Fed's critics. The Federal Reserve has generally not committed to controlling asset prices, though certainly they loom large in the background. But by presuming that high prices were related to excessive construction, they ended up making the same mistakes.

In 2006, the Fed understood that tight monetary policy would lead to a contraction in housing markets. They tightened policy to create that contraction, understanding that they had the ability to stop the contraction. Then when the contraction happened, they didn't loosen policy to stop it as they had *promised* themselves they would in 2005. Instead of concluding that their current policy was tighter than they thought it had been, they concluded that their critics had been correct. Instead of reversing the collapse in construction and home prices, they accepted the collapse as evidence that housing supply and prices had been too high to begin with.

The irony is that if Fed forecasts in early 2006 had accurately predicted that home prices would decline by about 30 percent and housing starts by more than 70 percent before the crisis was over, the early 2006 FOMC would have adamantly concluded that they would have absolutely not let that happen. And they would have been correct to take that position! Where critics are wrong is to suppose that the Fed shouldn't have or couldn't have stopped it. The FOMC in 2005 had been explicitly committed to stopping that from happening.

As the housing market started falling apart, their reaction should have been, "Oh, it's good that the 2005 FOMC left us this handy playbook. It says we should lower interest rates until the slowdown we engineered in housing construction recovers." Instead they concluded, if only implicitly, that the 2005 FOMC had been wrong and their critics had been right.

The Fed didn't enter this period with a presumption that there were too many homes. In response to a question about whether there was an over-hang of housing supply at the March 2007 meeting, staff economist David Stockton said, "We have not taken that view...[W]hether the housing stock outran the long-run determinants is kind of hard to nail down. We see that as a risk, but it's not incorporated in this forecast," adding later, "In our fore-cast, we're not too far from the bottom." [140] He was correct. Or at least, he should have been correct.

With each passing quarter, when that bottom didn't come, their critics seemed increasingly more correct, and the 2005 playbook for a soft landing collected dust. So, a vicious cycle of pro-cyclical monetary policy became a vicious cycle in moral panic. With each passing quarter, it seemed like speculators and reckless lenders had saddled us with an even larger inevi-table crisis.

What a betrayal this was of the 2005 Federal Reserve plan! The 2005 Federal Reserve consoled themselves that if home prices started to decline enough to create economic dislocation, they could lower interest rates enough to stabilize them. They did eventually lower interest rates, but their own forecasts tell us that *they didn't think* they lowered interest rates enough to implement the plan that the 2005 Fed had intended to implement. Not only didn't home prices stabilize as the crisis deepened, but the Fed didn't even *expect* their tactics to stabilize home prices. The more prices collapsed, the greater the Fed's forecasts of even greater collapse became. Likewise with housing starts, the Fed continued to accept declining starts as the new normal. If they had thought they had lowered interest rates enough to stop their housing contraction from getting out of hand, their forecasts would have shown recovering housing starts.

Essentially, everyone has mistaken a demand shock for a supply overhang. Karl Case and Robert Shiller are somewhat famous for "calling the bubble." In Case and Shiller's 2004 paper "Is There a Bubble in the Housing Market?" they conclude:

> [J]udging from the historical record, a nationwide drop in real housing prices is unlikely, and the drops in different cities are not likely to be synchronous: some will probably not occur for a number of years. Such a lack of synchrony would blunt the impact on the aggregate economy of the bursting of housing bubbles.[141]

That's not what the bust looked like, yet they still get credit for calling the bubble. Interviewers today don't ask Professor Shiller about how the bust didn't look like the one he predicted. They interview him as an expert that predicted the bust. What Case and Shiller described is what you would expect to see if the trigger had been localized building booms. The bust that actually occurred, on the other hand, was in metropolitan areas nationwide, whether prices had been rising at 5 percent, 10 percent, or 30 percent at the peak of the bubble. By 2007, instead of each region's housing market moving based on its own character, the trends became synchronized, and prices started to decline everywhere.

Other bearish observers concentrated on the trade deficit and debt held by foreigners, complaining that we were overconsuming, overbuilding, and overspending with borrowed dollars. They predicted a contraction because these things were considered unsustainable.[142] Likewise, their doomsaying appeared to be accurate, yet the bust has not been associated with a falling dollar, declining public debt, or a reversal of foreign capital flows to the US or of the trade deficit.

The reason the crisis doesn't actually look like the crisis they predicted is that the crisis wasn't caused by any of those pre-crisis fears. The crisis was a self-imposed demand shock—a retraction in money and credit.

EMBRACING FAILURE: A KEY MOMENT

A key moment in the shift from soft landing to crisis was the Fed's annual meeting in Jackson Hole, Wyoming at the end of August 2007. This was a significant moment because it happened to come at a turning point in several economic measures, and because it signaled the direct connection between Fed perceptions about those measures and the loss of a commitment to recovery. Housing starts in the second quarter were down to a rate of 1.4 million, from the high of 2.1 million in early 2006. Prices had generally held firm, though. National indexes were near the record highs. Delinquencies and foreclosures were starting to rise.

Economist Ed Leamer made an extensive presentation to Federal Reserve officials about the history of housing markets and monetary policy. "[R]esidential investment consistently and substantially contributes to weakness before the recessions, but business investment in equipment and software does not. And the recovery for residences begins earlier and is complete earlier than the recovery for equipment and software."[143]

The message that his data was conveying was that the previous sixty years of economic experience suggested that the Fed should consider a reversal of collapsing housing starts to be an imminent goal. "The bottom line: Housing provides an extremely accurate alarm of oncoming recessions."[144] He made a strong case: Don't expect an economic recovery around the corner if housing starts are still declining.

Yet, he didn't recommend aiming for a recovery. After a thorough historical review where he argued that recovery had always followed rising housing starts (except in odd cases where something like a war interrupted normal cycle patterns), he argued that a massive oversupply of homes meant that recovery was not an option this time.

Take a look at Figure 6[145]. This is a graph of the number of housing starts over time, as a percentage of the total stock of homes.[146]

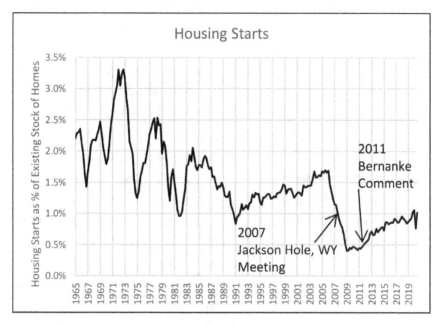

Figure 6

Population growth for the years 1985 to 2005 was not much different than the population growth rate from 1965 to 1985. The expansion of the housing stock had been slowing for decades in spite of that. There are two things we can say about the US housing market in the years leading up to the financial crisis, compared to earlier decades: (1) the rate of building was lower, in general, and (2) cyclical fluctuations in building (until 2006) were much *tamer* than they used to be.

From the early 1980s until 2008, the Federal Reserve had managed to tame inflation and to make business cycles both longer and shallower. This has been widely viewed as a success. The same trends happened in housing construction!

So, why do so many people act as if housing has been increasingly cyclical? One reason is that housing *is* an important cyclical sector, as Leamer pointed out. One can see this clearly before the 1990s in Figure 6. Before the 1990s, the cyclicality played out in construction. During expansions, we built a lot more homes, and during recessions, building contracted. As the country has gotten tied up in regulatory knots, it has become harder for construction to grow cyclically. So, today, the cyclicality plays out in volatile prices instead of in volatile construction.

But Leamer and so many others looked at the market leading up to 2007 and they saw cyclicality in both units and prices. Why? Ironically, one reason appears to be that since construction has been so muted, the measure of housing starts is rarely shown in the way I have shown it in Figure 6. Most economic measures are scaled over time. For instance, we compare GDP growth over time by discussing percentage growth. Vacancy *rates*, inflation *rates*, the unemployment *rate*.

There were about ten million unemployed workers in the spring of 2021, compared to about five million in 1971. That mostly just tells you that there are more workers today. The unemployment rate was about 6 percent at both times. But most of the time, when people analyze housing starts, they just talk about units. The reason they do so is that we have tied housing up in regulatory knots, making it harder to build more homes during economic expansions. So, almost every other measure of economic activity just keeps going higher and higher, but housing starts don't.

In 1972, housing starts peaked, briefly, at about 2.4 million units, compared to 2.1 million units in 2006. But that was in a country that only had seventy-three million units in 1972 compared to one-hundred twenty-five million in 2006. So, in percentage terms, housing starts peaked at 3.3 percent of the housing stock in 1972 and only 1.7 percent in 2006. In fact, as a percentage of the existing housing stock, housing starts in 2006 would have been considered recessionary in the 1970s.

By the time the Fed met at Jackson Hole, the collapse in housing starts was already a novel and striking cyclical downturn in a sector that hadn't seen significant cyclical movement in decades. Leamer presented the historical case for reversing the collapse in housing starts and then advised against it.

He wrote:

The inevitable effect of the low rates has been an acceleration of the home building clock, transferring building backward in time from 2006-2008 to 2003-2005. Our Fed thus implicitly made the decision: more in 2003-2005 at the cost of less in 2006-2008. That strikes me as a very risky choice. The historical record strongly suggests that in 2004 and 2005 we poured the foundation for a recession in 2007 or 2008 led by the collapse in housing we are currently experiencing.

And:

In 2007 the housing sector of the economy is now paying the Piper with very little possibility that a rate cut would make much of a difference. Once the wave has peaked and is crashing, there is not much that can be done to quiet the waters.[147]

We weren't officially in a recession yet. Housing starts had declined to a point in which Leamer's historical data pointed to a recession. They were already down to 1 percent of the housing stock by the third quarter of 2007. He threw up his hands, because "the low interest rates in 2002–2004 transferred sales *backward* in time, stealing sales that otherwise would have occurred in 2006–2009."[148] He even used the symbolism of crashing waves. The Fed saw dire times ahead and chose not to address it aggressively, because they became convinced that there were too many homes. There may be no other moment where this error rears its head more directly as the root of the economic crisis.

The effects of this thinking show up in Fed forecasts. As I noted above, until September 2007, Fed forecasts had just followed the market down. Whatever housing starts had been that quarter, Fed forecasts predicted the rate to stabilize there. In September, starts had come in at about 1.3 million units, and Fed forecasts pegged them at 1.3 million units at the end of 2008. Over the next several months, Fed staffers accelerated their downward expectations. By March 2008, they had moved their forecast down to 900 thousand units, predicting future housing starts to move even lower than they had been during the time of the meeting.[149]

Even in August 2008, staff continued to act like further cuts in supply were the key, reporting "We also have starts continuing to come down materially from their current level. So we think that the process will begin to get inventories into a more normal alignment."[150]

But don't mistake this as Fed bashing. The FOMC was bullish compared to most of its critics, and this notion that we just had more homes than we could handle was widespread. In the summer of 2008, Treasury Secretary Hank Paulson consulted with former Fed Chair Alan Greenspan about the coming takeover of Fannie Mae and Freddie Mac:

> Rattling off reams of housing data, Greenspan described how he considered the crisis in the markets to be a once-in-a-hundred-year event and how the government might have to take some extraordinary measures to stabilize it. The former Fed chairman had long been a critic of Fannie and Freddie but now realized that they needed to be shored up. He did have one suggestion about the housing crisis, but it was a rhetorical flourish befitting his supply-and-demand mind-set: He suggested that there was too much housing supply and that the only real way to really fix the problem would be for the government to buy up vacant homes and burn them.

After the call, Paulson, with a laugh, told his staff: "That's not a bad idea. But we're not going to buy up all the housing supply and destroy it."[151]

Paulson and his staff had a chuckle and moved on with other plans. What else could they do? It was actually a knuckle-headed idea, but they couldn't see that as long as the myth of overbuilding loomed so large. Greenspan was reflecting the consensus.

In his memoir Ben Bernanke later wrote, "Normally, a rapid rebound in home construction and related industries such as realty and home improvement helps fuel growth after a recession. Not this time. Builders would start construction on only about 600,000 private homes in 2011, compared with more than 2 million in 2005. To some extent, that drop represented the flip side of the pre-crisis boom. Too many houses had been built, and now the excess supply was being worked off."[152]

That couldn't be more wrong. The years 2009 and 2010 saw, by a wide margin, the lowest production of new housing units as a percentage of the existing stock of any previous two-year period since at least 1965. In fact, the same can be said for the three years leading up to 2010, four years, and so forth. For every period of any length of time since 1965, the period ending in 2010 was the period with the lowest production of housing as a percentage of the existing stock.[153] Of the previous forty-five years, 2011 was the least likely year to have supply to "work off."[154]

I have marked Figure 6 with both the Jackson Hole meeting and 2011, to bookend this period of time between the Leamer presentation and the Bernanke comment about slow growth. The perception of an oversupply of housing was key to both the crisis and the slow recovery. Housing construction hadn't been cyclical for at least twenty years until the Fed made it cyclical. If housing starts could have moved along that relatively flat line between 1 percent and 1.5 percent of the housing stock as it had been for some time, we might still be boasting of our great moderation rather than debating why it was interrupted.

At the end of August 2007, Ed Leamer warned Fed officials of a crashing wave and pointed to the primary historical process through which the crash could be avoided, and then concluded that this time was different. The crash was fated. Fed forecasts of housing construction after that warning suggest that Fed staff and governors agreed. They believed that they had already set in motion the crashing wave that had yet to come, and they would not dampen that wave by stimulating the economy enough to encourage more construction.

CHAPTER 9

THE PECULIAR EFFECTS OF CLOSED ACCESS HID EARLY SIGNS OF DECLINE

When housing markets were booming, the economy was moving along pretty well. Nominal GDP growth (real growth plus inflation) remained above 6 percent from 2004 through the first half of 2006. That was about where nominal growth had topped out in the 1990s, but it was lower than nominal growth had been in other post-World War II periods of economic growth. Real GDP growth (the actual increase in produced goods and services measured in dollars after adjusting for inflation) had peaked at the end of 2003. Nominal GDP growth held on longer, beginning a slow decline in the second quarter of 2006 because of the drop in residential investment. By the next quarter, GDP growth measures were not *exceptionally* low, but they were low and falling—at levels which had previously been associated with coming recessions in the post-World War II era. Let's compare various economic metrics from the first quarter of 2001 to the third quarter of 2006. The US economy was officially in a recession by the first quarter of 2001. The Federal Reserve had already begun lowering its target policy rate by then.

	Ending Unemployment Rate	1 Year Real GDP Growth	1 Year Nominal GDP Growth	Final Sales to Domestic Purchasers 1 Year Growth
1Q 2001	4.3%	2.3%	4.8%	5.4%
3Q 2006	4.5%	2.2%	5.3%	5.2%

The metrics are comparable. Without such concern about the housing bubble, forecasters would plausibly have been more worried about potential contraction than they were about potential overheating. Instead, the Federal Reserve had increased the fed funds rate at the end of June 2006 and then held it at 5.25 percent until September 2007.

What was different about these two points in time? One difference was that the sorts of dislocations that had led to a sharp decline in housing starts in early 2006 delayed some of the other normal signals of recession.

At least two factors mitigated or concealed recessionary trends in 2006 and 2007, which are related to the Closed Access housing supply problem.

1. During the expansion, there was a strong flow of migration out of the Closed Access cities, in spite of their strong economies. One of the early effects of a slowing economy was that the migration flows out of Closed Access cities slowed.

2. When construction started to decline, rents increased. The economic decline was associated with an inflationary supply shock similar to, say, the oil shocks of the 1970s, when a decline in oil production had led to high petroleum inflation.

THE CLOSED ACCESS MIGRATION PATTERN

In both 2005 and 2006, more than 1.5 percent of Closed Access city residents migrated to other places, net of in-migrants. This declined to less than three-fourths of a percent after the bust. In the Contagion cities, net in-migration in 2005 was at about 1.5 percent of the local population, but by the end of 2007, net domestic migration was negligible.

Thinking about these migration flows broadly, the US economy, in expansion, must be considered as two separate economies. In the Closed Access areas, the constraint isn't jobs, it's laborers. Employment growth is slow because employed workers can't afford to stay, and even though the cities provide ample opportunities for employment, workers move to other parts of the country to lower their cost of living.

In the rest of the country, labor opportunities are more likely to be a constraint. During the expansion, not only did their economies need to grow fast enough to provide job opportunities for local residents but also for the hundreds of thousands of workers moving in from Closed Access cities.

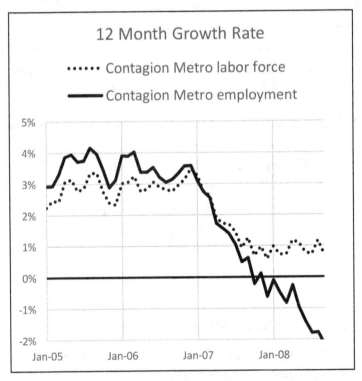

Figure 7 Employment and Labor Force Growth in Contagion Cities

In 2005 and 2006, the national labor force was growing faster than the typical 1 percent population growth, even with an aging workforce. This was a strong labor market. Then, at the beginning of 2007, the Contagion cities experienced a sharp drop in employment growth. As Figure 7 shows, in the Contagion cities, in the first half of 2007, labor force growth shrank along with waning employment growth.[155]

This was disruptive, but it only led, initially, to a small shift upward in local unemployment. Instead of raising unemployment in the Contagion cities, this first blow to labor markets was related to the decline in migration flows. In spite of this sharp and sudden collapse in employment growth, the collective unemployment rate in the Contagion cities was still a remarkably low 3.6 percent in May 2007. In other words, the drop in employment growth in the Contagion cities didn't happen because locals were becoming unemployed. It happened because households stopped moving there. Unemployment only spiked after migration dried up and labor force growth in the contagion cities settled at about 1 percent—roughly a zero net migration growth rate. Unemployment rises when there is a gap between labor force growth (people available for work) and employment growth. The separation between labor force growth and employment growth in late 2007 happened when net migration had zeroed out. Now, locals finally started losing jobs.

The decline in employment growth in the Contagion cities was both in construction and non-construction industries. In the previous recession, twelve-month employment growth in these same cities had briefly turned negative in early 2002. When that happened, the unemployment rate in these cities was about 6 percent. When twelve-month employment growth turned negative in October 2007, their collective unemployment rate was still only 4.5 percent. The reason for the difference is that in 2001 there wasn't this whipsaw shift in migration. The relationship between the migration pattern, labor force growth, and unemployment suggests that it was initially the drop in migration that triggered an economic contraction in the Contagion cities, and not the other way around. This delayed unemployment as a signal of economic contraction in the Contagion cities, which were really hurting by then.

Some researchers have pointed out that Closed Access housing has lowered American economic output because it prevents workers from living where they can be the most productive.[156] That means that migration into and out of the Closed Access cities has a countercyclical effect. When the economy is strong, people move out of those cities to economize on spending, which slows national economic growth a bit.

In 2007, when that migration flow suddenly stopped, those workers were choosing to remain in the Closed Access cities, which kept their spending elevated. In other words, the Closed Access migration acts as a speed governor on economic growth. If the accelerator has been pushed faster than the engine can go, the initial retraction doesn't slow the engine down. It just puts less pressure on the speed governor. The flow of workers out of the Closed Access cities slows down economic growth when growth is high. As potential growth slowed, the flow of workers out of those cities also slowed. As the recession intensified, labor force growth in the Closed Access cities increased in 2008.

Remember that important moment in Fed decision-making—the Jackson Hole meeting at the end of August 2007? Consider the timing of the shift in the Contagion cities from sort of manageable declines in labor force before about August 2007 to rising unemployment after. At that moment these cities were turning from downturn to recession. These cities needed growth. That truly was the last point before things started to turn much uglier. The reversal of recent migratory surges had quickly become a reversal of decades-long migration patterns into these cities. Builders in these cities had responded to that. Housing starts by August 2007 had dropped by about 35 percent nationwide, but in these cities, they had already dropped by well over 50 percent.

The problem these cities had was definitely not that "low interest rates in 2002–2004 transferred sales backward in time, stealing sales that otherwise would have occurred in 2006–2009."[157] What they lacked after 2006 was people. People needed money, credit, and faith in a stable economy. These are the places where streets full of vacant homes portray the aftermath of the housing bubble in the popular literature. The Contagion cities would have had many *fewer* vacant homes in 2010 if the Fed had aimed for *more* housing starts in 2007 because in a stable, growing economy, people move to the Contagion cities.

COLLAPSE IN HOUSING STARTS CONTRIBUTED TO RISING INFLATION

Since this was a contraction focused on housing and residential investment, this was an odd contraction because residential investment represents a unique relationship between consumption and investment. Rising home values can create a wealth effect where homeowners feel more free to increase expenditures. The purchase of a new home is a commitment to consumption of housing. So, both rising prices and rising supply are related to rising consumption. Yet the purchase of a new home is an investment. It is, at its base, a rightward shift in supply.

The tricky part of housing expansion in a Closed Access environment is that most new homes must be built in the less expensive cities. Places where more homes can be built easily are, ipso facto, places that are less expensive. If more homes are built, they will tend to be built where homes are affordable. So, in a country with pockets of Closed Access, new homes still create new supply, but some of the families moving into those homes will have to move away from expensive places to less expensive places. They are reducing their housing expenses while at the same time they are increasing the supply of new homes. In fact, this is all they *could* do. Even in the Contagion cities, where there were features of a bubble in 2004 and 2005, much of the inflow of migrants moved there to *decrease* their housing expenditures, relative to expenditures in Closed Access cities. And increasingly, households were migrating out of the Contagion cities for similar reasons.

Both rising home prices and rising housing starts were treated as stimulative and inflationary. If we understand that we had two different housing markets—one Open and one Closed—then our presumption should be the opposite. Strong housing starts were disinflationary (lowering rents) and were, ironically, part of a downshifting of housing consumption (by facilitating migration out of expensive cities). Consumer price index rent inflation and aggregate rental income during the boom corroborates this reasoning. Rent inflation was declining during the boom in cities that allowed ample building and rental income was declining as a portion of total domestic income.[158]

The collapse of housing starts after the crisis has been associated with rising housing expenditures (in terms of rental expense) as a proportion of total household spending. And it has been associated with rising shelter inflation. The *less* we *invest* in housing (in residential investment), the *more* we *spend* on housing (in rental value).

In March 2006, year-over-year core consumer price index (CPI) inflation was at 2.1 percent. It would top out at 2.9 percent by September and remain above 2 percent throughout 2007. The Fed was aiming to lower inflation. But much of that inflation was from rent inflation which started to rise when housing starts began to decline. The shelter component (which is mostly made up of rent)[159] of the CPI had been 2.5 percent in March 2006 and it would shoot up to as high as 4.3 percent in 2007.[160] Remove the shelter component from core CPI, and the inflation rate for the other components was at 1.8 percent in March 2006. After hanging around 2 percent for a bit, it spent most of 2007 below 1.5 percent. Lowering non-shelter inflation was a contractionary move away from neutral policy of moderate 2 percent inflation.

The Fed was aware of these issues. By the June 2006 meeting, they had taken note of rising rents. The Fed had not yet given in to a sense of inevitability about a deep contraction, but they were set on suppressing the recovery in construction that might have brought those rising rents down. Ben Bernanke told the committee "I'm going to give us a bit of perspective. It is a good thing that housing is cooling. If we could wave a magic wand and reinstate 2005, we wouldn't want to do that because the market has to come back to equilibrium."[161]

What if the Fed had stopped raising rates in 2005, and housing starts had remained relatively strong? Presumably, inflation would have risen for most goods and services as a result of that, but rent inflation would have continued to moderate as housing supply continued to grow. The net effect that would have had on total inflation is not obvious. Inflation remained tame in Canada and Australia, where they avoided housing busts.

Since so much of the early decline in GDP growth was due to the decline in real private investment, the Federal Reserve inadvertently created a contraction with countercyclical inflation. In the case of a negative supply shock, like the oil shocks in the 1970s, monetary policy that targets inflation is not helpful, because the inflation in that case is not a monetary phenomenon. In other words, sudden spikes in something like energy prices already create economic disruptions. Pushing down the prices of other goods by reducing the quantity of money flowing through the economy doesn't help to ameliorate those disruptions. A central bank that targets inflation will react to a negative supply shock (a reduction in the production of real goods) by adding a demand shock (a reduction in money).

In 2005 and 2006, the Fed had continued raising interest rates in order to cool off residential investment. It succeeded. That was associated with rising rents, just like the supply shocks in oil in the 1970s were associated with rising gas prices. Since it has an inflation targeting mandate, it reacted to its own supply shock with a demand shock, which lowered non-shelter inflation. But the economy needed money.

The problem, of course, was that more money would have led to a revival in construction, which Fed officials were, quite explicitly, intent on preventing. Back in 2005, the economy that Bernanke was afraid of recreating had been producing 2.1 million new homes and about 2.1 percent core CPI inflation. That core CPI inflation was the weighted average of 2.6 percent shelter (rent) inflation and about 1.8 percent inflation in all the other goods and services. In other words, inflation indicators in 2005 were signaling that the Fed was doing a really good job hitting its targets but that the country could use more homes to help bring rents down.

PART 4

Marching Hand in Hand to Crisis

CHAPTER 10

NO BAILOUTS!

By the fall of 2007, some markets were experiencing distress. Many observers were worried that rising interest rates would cause borrowers with adjustable rate mortgages to default when rates reset to higher levels. Henry Paulson and the Treasury were working hard to help households who were increasingly in trouble (italics mine):

> The administration's goal was to minimize as much as possible the pain of foreclosure for Americans, without rewarding speculators or those who walked away from their obligations when their mortgages were underwater...
>
> *Surprisingly, the servicers contended that resets were not the critical issue.*
>
> Still, resets remained a concern, and we pushed the industry for faster loan modifications... FDIC chairman Sheila Bair, who deserves credit for identifying the foreclosure debacle early, had proposed freezing rates...
>
> *But after all of our concerns about resets, interest rates ended up not being an issue* once the Fed began to cut rates. By the end of January 2008, the central bank had slashed the Fed funds rate to 3 percent from 5.25 percent in mid-August.[162]

The Treasury had taken on the conventional wisdom by now. Policies that would create universal stability were not acceptable. Stability was unacceptable if it meant "rewarding speculators." The Treasury was furiously trying to accommodate the *right* people. By 2008, the mood in the country had moved from hoping for a soft landing, past accepting a contraction, to requiring economic penance.

When Henry Paulson concluded that the GSEs (Fannie Mae and Freddie Mac) had to be taken over, he insisted that the details would have to be worked out later. When *both* the Republican and Democratic presidential campaigns contacted him for consultation on the matter, the detail they both insisted on knowing was whether Paulson would be tough on the executives and whether the shareholders would be wiped out.[163]

"OLD TESTAMENT" THINKING

The vicious cycle of housing contraction and rising public anger increasingly meant that any stabilizing posture was associated with bailouts. Since stability would help those who had taken the most risk (how could it not?), stability itself was seen as a source of moral hazard.

In October 2002, Bernanke had given a speech on asset prices and monetary policy. He noted that in 1929 the Federal Reserve had been too concerned with high stock prices, and that after Fed leader Benjamin Strong passed away in 1928, "his successors abandoned the hands-off approach and raised rates. The ultimate results of this decision were not only the stock market crash of 1929 (in a tragic sense, the Fed succeeded in its effort to cool the market) but also a too-tight monetary policy that helped cause the Depression."[164]

But later Bernanke wrote in his memoir:

Others derided what they perceived to be a tendency of the Fed to respond too strongly to price declines in stocks and other financial assets, which they dubbed the "Greenspan put." (A put is an options contract that protects the buyer against loss if the price of a stock or other security declines.)...I wanted to avoid the perception of a "Bernanke put" if at all possible.[165]

As the crisis developed, Bernanke—along with others like Don Kohn, Tim Geithner, Janet Yellen, and Frederic Mishkin—had to pull other board members along in order to implement the stabilizing policies. Yet even though Bernanke understood the mistakes of the Great Depression, he still accepted the same perverse idea that had again infected the American psyche eight decades later. Stability—the "Bernanke put"—was a monetary sin.

The New York Federal Reserve has developed a model of the yield curve (interest rates at different maturities) that is widely used in the financial sector as a forward indicator of a coming recession. Even when the Fed was still raising the fed funds rate in early and mid-2006, the slope of the yield curve had moved into territory typically associated with a coming recession.[166] (Long-term rates had fallen below short-term rates.)

Spikes in certain key inflation indicators during this period, mostly from commodity prices, were an important factor that pushed the Federal Reserve and its critics toward tighter policy. So there was some justification for tighter policy at the time. But there was little justification for claiming that the Fed had been pumping up or artificially supporting the housing market. For more than two years they had been raising rates to put the brakes on the housing market. And the brakes worked. Residential investment had taken a hard downward turn. Homeowners were exiting the housing market and shifting their former home equity into other types of investments.

At this point in the cycle, accommodation was already called for, and from this point until the flurry of events that followed the September 2008 meeting, the Fed was under relentless pressure to allow instability. The public intuition to blame creditors for the high prices of houses led to a perverted reaction. The more the Fed erred on the side of contraction, the more distress it caused in housing markets, the more the public was determined to blame that distress on creditors and speculators, and the more the public and the Fed's critics demanded *additional* contraction.

Looking back on these events through this new lens, this is the striking thing about the public conversation of the time: When policymakers or their critics demanded a passive approach to the building crisis or called for policies that would lead to market contractions in order to "discipline" markets, they weren't arguing that more aggressive policies would fail to stabilize the market. They were frequently arguing against stabilization. Since the conventional understanding of the housing boom was wrong, it had been filled in with a parade of villains and scapegoats, whose misbehavior was necessary to explain how prices could be so high. Instability seemed prudent—even righteous—since so many people seemed to deserve punishment and would surely rise again to cause even more financial mayhem if they didn't get it.

Since the conventional wisdom about excess was so universally accepted, demands for outright impairment were often surprisingly explicit. Capital losses and financial panics were not only foreseen but they were also asked for. On August 6, 2007, on the cusp of the first round of panic in mortgage securities markets and some corporate financing markets, the *Wall Street Journal's* editors demanded instability:

[N]aturally the wounded are clamoring for the Federal Reserve to ride to the rescue with easier money when it meets tomorrow, even though the Fed helped create this mess.

Credit panics are never pretty, but their virtue is that they restore some fear and humility to the marketplace.

Adding,

Which brings us to the Fed, and its Open Market Committee meeting tomorrow. As always amid a credit turn, the pleas for easier money are rising. We're even hearing nostalgic cries for the return of Alan Greenspan, who is remembered fondly for supplying liquidity during the credit crises of his era. But what these cries forget is that the Greenspan Fed is one reason for the current mortgage mess....

Current Fed Chairman Ben Bernanke was along for the Greenspan ride, so he's hardly blameless. No doubt he'd love to play the hero role now, signaling easier money this week.[167]

This sort of rhetoric was common during the crisis. Loose money and credit-fueled speculation were blamed for the housing bubble. What they cynically called Bernanke "playing the hero" might more accurately be called "doing his job."

At the same time, Jim Cramer went on a *CNBC* rant, famously screaming about Fed officials that "They know nothing!" He took the opposite position from the *Wall Street Journal* editors.[168] According to Bernanke, he read the *Wall Street Journal* article, but purposefully avoided seeing the Cramer segment.[169] He and the FOMC should have listened to Cramer. The next day, the Federal Reserve held rates steady instead of lowering them. In their press release, they began to refer to sharply dropping home prices as a "correction" and expressed concerns about inflation.[170] That August 2007 meeting was immediately followed by panic in private mortgage markets. The FOMC issued two interim statements in an attempt to calm the market before finally beginning to lower the target fed funds rate at the September meeting.[171]

A year later, in September 2008, the Federal Reserve again held interest rates stable, which again led immediately to market panics. This time the decision was followed by the most jarring collapse in economic activity in generations. The *Wall Street Journal*, for one, remained firm in their resolve:

> These columns have been tough on the Federal Reserve in recent years, so it's only fair to praise the central bank when it does the right thing. And that's what it did yesterday by holding the federal funds rate stable at 2%, despite the turmoil in financial markets and enormous Wall Street pressure to reduce rates further.
>
> Our view is that 90% of central banking is about character. Can a Fed chairman stand up to the inevitable lobbying from business and the political class when the economic moment demands a hard line

for hard money? Any central banker can say yes to easier money. The great ones can also say no.[172]

The following three months saw the worst decline in nominal economic activity since the Great Depression. The housing price collapse worsened, and defaults accelerated. Unemployment started to rise by nearly ½ percent a month.

Timothy Geithner referred to this view as "Old Testament" thinking. As Geithner writes, "The narrative of good-versus-evil was irresistible: We were saving irresponsible bankers while they continued to pay themselves huge bonuses. The conventional wisdom hardened quickly, and with a few honorable exceptions, the media rarely tried to explain that the situation was not so black-and-white."[173]

HELP MAIN STREET IN ORDER TO HELP WALL STREET

The Main Street versus Wall Street meme has been central to critiques of the period. Even the doves had to couch their positions with statements reiterating that their final aim was not to support Wall Street. Bernanke told *60 Minutes* "You know I come from Main Street. That's my background. And I've never been on Wall Street. I care about Wall Street for one reason and one reason only—because what happens on Wall Street matters to Main Street."[174]

Geithner especially was derided as the king of bailouts, and he had to frequently promise that helping Main Street was his ultimate goal. "[N]othing we did during the financial crisis was motivated by sympathy for the banks or the bankers. Our only priority was limiting the damage to ordinary Americans and people around the world."[175]

In the defense of his own record, Geithner writes, "[They] thought we were feckless...But a panic tends to make everyone look feckless in the same way a mania makes everyone look brilliant."[176] If only Geithner's critics had managed some *sympathy*. And, likewise, if only Geithner and his critics could have managed that same sympathy toward the banks. (Here, I might suggest that the most fitting definition of sympathy is the definition relating to persons or objects being in relationship with one another, where they are similarly affected by changing conditions.) One might respond that banks *did this to us* and didn't deserve our sympathy. But what if the idea that the banks were fundamentally the cause of the boom-and-bust is not as strong as we thought? What if they looked feckless, in part, because of the mistakes of federal policymakers? If those mistakes made the crisis worse (And of course they did. Making the crisis worse was *explicitly* the point. "Discipline," "panic," "fear," and "humility" weren't unintended consequences. They were the *stated* goals.) then in the end, marginalized and vulnerable families would be hurt the most. Of course, they were.

"A panic tends to make everyone look feckless in the same way a mania makes everyone look brilliant." This is the central problem of the crisis. Panics were viewed as helpful or necessary, and the more feckless they made everyone look, the more it seemed that those who were beyond the reach of our sympathy deserved to fail.

Tim Geithner argues again and again against that tendency. "There was intense pressure on us to punish the Wall Street gamblers who had gotten us into this mess—to nationalize or liquidate floundering firms or force bondholders to accept 'haircuts' rather than the face value of their bonds. Those get-tough actions would feel resolute and righteous, but in a time of uncertainty, they would damage confidence and accelerate the downward spiral. As we had seen in the panic of the fall, that would hurt Main Street, not just Wall Street."[177]

But even Geithner regarded lending as the fundamental cause of the boom-and-bust. He wrote, "Borrowing frenzies are prerequisites for financial crises, and too many Americans were using credit to finance lifestyles their salaries couldn't support. From 2001 to 2007, the average mortgage debt per household increased 63 percent, while wages remained flat in real terms. The financial system provided this credit with enthusiasm even to individuals with low or undisclosed incomes, then packaged the loans into securities that were also bought on credit."[178] Later, under his tenure as Treasury Secretary, the GSEs would greatly shrink funding for affordable homes for borrowers without pristine credit. The ability to counter "Old Testament" thinking was hamstrung because the belief in the wrong premise about the cause of high prices was universal. In the end, even Geithner was taken in by it.

Bernanke pointed out how odd it was that different critics claimed that both lower interest rates hurt savers and higher asset prices helped the rich. The rich *are* the savers. That's what being rich is. Instead of making these contradictory complaints, he suggested that critics should realize that in a weak economy, easier monetary policy tended to help both labor and capital together, creating jobs and investment opportunities.[179] In other words, Main Street and Wall Street are naturally in sympathy with one another. This is one reason why it makes more sense to think about Fed policy through its effect on incomes and production rather than its effect on interest rates or asset prices.

Whenever an accommodating posture was taken, the Federal Reserve was accused of coddling Wall Street and bailing out speculators. By August 2007, the stock market was already reacting positively when the Fed offered monetary accommodation. For instance, when markets panicked after the Fed's August 2007 meeting, the Fed decided to lower the discount rate, which is somewhat different than the fed funds rate but is another lever they can pull.[180] Within forty-six seconds after the Fed cut the discount rate, the stock market shot up 3.6 percent.[181] These market reactions continued to build up until the aftermath of the September 2008 meeting. During TARP (Troubled Asset Relief Program) negotiations, the AIG bailout, and the various other proposed measures, the market would whip up and down by several percentage points upon daily news of proposals for stabilization. The reason that accommodative policy decisions and statements had such a strong effect on the stock market was because, by now, both Wall Street and Main Street desperately needed it.

The stock market was responding to Fed stimulus because stimulus was the right policy and long overdue. The stock market doesn't really like tight monetary policy or loose monetary policy. It likes *good* monetary policy. The inflationary 1970s are a great example of this. The 1970s weren't a good time for the stock market. In 1965, inflation had been under 2 percent for some time. Then, inflation started rising, and eventually by the late 1970s, it was above 10 percent. Since World War II, stocks have sold, on average, for about eighteen times annual earnings. In other words, if a firm makes one dollar per share, on average, investors have had to pay eighteen dollars to buy a share. The price/earnings ratio of the S&P 500 was nineteen times earnings in 1965. It would decline to less than ten times earnings by 1978 and remain there until the Federal Reserve finally tackled inflation in the early 1980s.[182]

Yet so many critics, such as the *Wall Street Journal* editorialists, reacted to Fed stimulus with cynicism—the Fed was propping up Wall Street. This is why the crisis was inevitable. Their demands were quite explicit. Many Americans would be satisfied with nothing less. The *Wall Street Journal* serves as a valuable historical record of the frame of mind during the moral panic. They reserved their praise for the Federal Reserve for Fed actions that immediately led to the worst moments of the crisis. Crisis was a sign of character.

In chapter 6, I wrote that "once the country was committed to countering wealth-funded consumption with tight monetary policy, it was pragmatically *committed to creating a financial crisis in real estate.*" Maybe that seemed like an overstatement. My point was that by mistakenly trying to deflate the housing market with monetary policy, we could *accidentally* create a financial crisis in real estate. What is strange, in hindsight, is how many Fed critics were *demanding* panic and crisis.

NO BAILOUTS!

At every juncture, the use of the term bailout has been unfortunate because equity holders were generally wiped out in cases where firms were rescued. What are referred to as bailouts for the GSEs, Bear Stearns, and others were more like managed bankruptcies. In addition, other forms of federal capital injections were generally repaid with interest. As Timothy Geithner points out, this has created a public perception that vast quantities of cash were showered on the financial industry and never returned, even though that isn't really the case.

There *were* bailouts that involved simply showering money on people. Those were Main Street bailouts. The Bush tax rebate in February 2008 was an attempt at popular stabilization. About $150 billion was mailed out to American families. Credits to first-time home buyers after 2008 were another example.

There have been debates about whether the government was completely repaid for the bailouts once one accounts for the risks. Has anyone produced a review of the accounting on the tax refund or the home buyer tax credit (or remember "Cash for Clunkers"?[183]) to see if the government recouped its costs for those programs? Of course not. There was no intention of recouping the costs. The idea that the costs would need to be recouped was never part of the proposals. The idea that bailouts were aimed at Wall Street while Main Street was left out is mostly the product of this double standard.[184]

There were some attempts to create special carve-out refinancing programs for homeowners after the crisis, but at the same time there was pressure put on all lenders to retreat from mortgage markets. The shift in lending standards was extreme, and its effect on low-tier home values was extreme. (I will discuss this later.) The Main Street bailout that would have worked—in fact, it is the one policy that might have avoided most of the post-2008 damage—would have been to mimic the Wall Street bailouts: make loans to home buyers with terms similar to what they had been getting for years before 2008 or even before 2003 and expect those loans to be paid back.

For all the complaints about how Wall Street got bailouts but Main Street didn't, did any critics of Wall Street bailouts demand more generous mortgage lending standards? The enforcement of a strict mortgage lending policy may be the most popular policy decision of the crisis. Few actually wanted the equivalent Main Street bailouts that would have helped. In fact, the crisis primarily happened because the country was unanimously opposed to the cure.

The only support for Main Street that was popular were actual bailouts—transfers, straight payments, loan modifications, and "cramdowns."

But a lack of mortgage credit was increasingly causing working-class home values to collapse unnecessarily.

On the other hand, programs to support Wall Street were unpopular, and when that support came, it was generally in the form of loans that were repaid or facilitated bankruptcies and mergers, and yet they would be called "bailouts."

From all of that, we have ended up with the perverse rallying cry "Why did we bail out Wall Street but not Main Street?"

Among other things, the Bernanke, Paulson, and Geithner memoirs are an extended defense of policy decisions at the Fed and the Treasury. Page after page, they discuss the reasons why they had to support policies that had been criticized as Wall Street bailouts. Possibly the most telling part of the books is what isn't in them. The momentous policy shift to very tight mortgage lending is barely noted and is certainly nothing that they feel the need to apologize for.

The lending standards after Fannie and Freddie were taken over in September 2008 are largely treated as a given. The deleveraging of American households is treated as simply the natural unwinding of the bubble. Yet millions of American households wanted to take out mortgages, and they were denied by Fannie, Freddie, and the FHA. The shift was extreme. In 2008, Fannie Mae had guaranteed about $1.2 trillion in loans to borrowers with credit scores over 740. That would increase to $1.7 trillion by 2013. Compare that to mortgages outstanding for borrowers with credit scores less than 740. In 2008, they totaled $1.5 trillion. That *shrank* to $1.1 trillion by 2013. And contrary to conventional wisdom, the portion of their book devoted to sub-740 borrowers had not been unusually high in 2008.

Defending the bailout of Bear Stearns, Bernanke said, "Without access to credit, people would not be able to buy cars or houses, and businesses would not be able to expand, or in some cases, even cover current operating costs. The negative effects on jobs and incomes would be fast and power-ful."[185] How much good does it do to save the investment banks if you kill the mortgage originations they would fund? Most of the foreclosures and bank failures came after 2008, after many homeowners and potential homeowners were prevented from getting new mortgages. One has to wonder how many of the losses on Wall Street ended up being the result of the popular denial of credit to Main Street.

"TOO BIG TO FAIL" WAS A SIDE-EFFECT OF "TOO SMALL TO SAVE"

In early 2008, markets were in turmoil. Securities that had been routinely used as near cash assets were in disarray. At the beginning of March, three minor financial firms were facing failure—Peloton, the Carlyle Fund, and Thornburg Mortgage. Ben Bernanke describes their predicament:

> I called Thornburg. I was sympathetic. He and his company were caught up in a panic not of their own making. But in my heart I knew that use of our emergency authority could only be justified when it served the broad public interest. Whether the firm was in some sense deserving or not was irrelevant. Lending to Thornburg would overturn a six-decade practice of avoiding 13(3) loans—a practice rooted in the recognition of the moral hazard of protecting nonbank firms from the consequences of the risks they took, as well as the understanding that Congress had intended the authority to be used only in the most dire circumstances. The failure of this firm was unlikely to have a broad economic impact, and so we believed a 13(3) loan was not justified. We would not lend to Thornburg, and it would fail.

> [...]

> The Fed used its 13(3) authority during the Depression, but only sparingly. From 1932 to 1936, it made 123 such loans, mostly very small. The largest, $300,000, was made to a typewriter manufacturer; another, for $250,000, was extended to a vegetable grower. As the economy and credit markets improved in the latter part of the 1930s, the Fed stopped making 13(3) loans.[186]

Section 13(3) is a special authority that can be invoked for the Federal Reserve to lend money outside its normal operations. Within the month, 13(3) would be invoked in order to extend credit on a broader range of securities to primary dealers that traded with the Federal Reserve, and it would also be invoked in the arrangement to facilitate the purchase of Bear Stearns.

Notice the strange dissonance in Bernanke's explanation for these early failures. The history of the use of section 13(3), which Bernanke describes himself, was specifically to fund economically unimportant firms who were under duress during a financial crisis. These firms were clearly in that position as Bernanke himself points out. Yet moral hazard and a lack of economic importance are stated as reasons for letting those firms fail without support. Bear Stearns would be supported with the help of section 13(3) because it *was* deemed to be economically important. Eventually, federal funds would be used to rescue AIG and others, and the national discussion would revolve around the problem of letting firms get too big, so that they are "too big to fail."[187]

The actual Federal Reserve policy which Bernanke was inadvertently describing above, was a policy of "too small to save." From the summer of 2007 through early 2008, panics were rolling throughout financial markets, expanding beyond the mortgage markets that were thought to be the problem into markets such as corporate paper and auction-rate securities, which are liquid credit markets generally only used by the most financially stable lenders and borrowers. The fact that markets for these securities were freezing up was clear evidence that circumstances *were* dire.

"Too big to fail" was simply the back side of the coin of the "too small to save" policy. If small firms are routinely left to fail when they are "caught up in a panic not of their own making" precisely because they are "unlikely to have a broad economic impact," and if the primary policy that an economy needs is for the central bank to intervene in order to introduce calm and to stop the panics, then the inevitable final act of that "too small to save" policy will eventually be the imminent failure of a firm that is deemed "too big to fail," which will finally trigger sufficient monetary intervention. And by September 2008, when the Federal Reserve and the Treasury began to routinely engage in "bailouts," the damage from the panics had finally reached firms that weren't too small to save.

Of all the calls for policies that should be prevented in the future, "too big to fail" is not one of them. That wasn't Fed policy. It was only the final option left to them after they watched many other markets and firms fail. Thank goodness for "too big to fail." What would have been left to save if failures and panics had continued? At least they were willing, finally, to stop *something* from failing.

In any case, "too big to fail" is not the policy of a central bank that is too aggressive. It's the policy of a central bank that has not been aggressive enough.

At the April 2008 FOMC meeting, Geithner articulated this policy. "I think the markets now reflect too much confidence in our willingness and ability to prevent large and small financial failures. We are going to disappoint them on the small ones, which may increase the probability they attach to the large. At least I hope we disappoint them on the small ones."[188] Under the premise that the country was curing itself of a period of financial excess, this seemed to make sense. But since the country had mainly been struggling with an economically important lack of housing supply, which it was now inappropriately trying to cure with financial contraction, that comment is a commitment to making sure the financial contraction gets much worse before it gets better.

In his memoir, *Stress Test*, Geithner argues against several causes of the crisis—fraud, deregulation, moral hazard, and so forth. "The fundamental causes of this crisis were familiar and straightforward. It began with a mania—the widespread belief that devastating financial crises were a thing of the past, that future recessions would be mild, that gravity-defying home prices would never crash to earth. This was the optimism of the Great Moderation, the delusion of indefinite stability."

Adding later, "You could say that on the front end, the long period of low interest rates in the United States and worldwide helped fuel the crisis, because it helped fuel the mania that inflated the bubble, encouraging more borrowing, more home building, more risk-taking."[189]

If the *problem* was the perception that crises were a thing of the past and recessions would be mild, then what was the *solution?* Surely avoiding a crisis and a deep recession wouldn't be a solution to *that* problem. If the *problem* was the perception that home prices would never crash, then surely stable home prices wouldn't be a solution to *that* problem. If stability had been a delusion, then what exactly was the Fed's job? And if building more homes was simply part of a mania, then surely the Fed should view construction unemployment and declining residential investment as parts of the solution.

This was the consensus. The heated battles in late 2008 and early 2009 were battles about dealing with the aftermath—a game of macroeconomic chicken about how much damage one could bear before finally reinstating stability.

In 2006 and early 2007, there was a little corner of the American economy that was peculiar—a few locations where a migration event had caused local economic booms, where that event was collapsing and taking local incomes with it, where demand from the migration event had driven home values high, and where new types of lightly regulated mortgage products could be used to tap those homes for cash. That corner of the economy matched *some* of Geithner's description.

But by then, well before the financial crisis, what the economy needed was "more borrowing, more home building, more risk-taking"—exactly what Geithner and essentially all other policymakers were afraid of. The 2005 Fed hadn't been afraid of that. They had expected to stimulate the economy in order to prevent collapsing home prices from creating too much disruption. By 2007, the most dovish members of the Fed were less committed to stability than the Fed consensus had been in 2005.

Former Federal Reserve chairman William McChesney Martin is famous for saying that the Fed's job is "to take away the punch bowl just as the party gets going." The idea that the Fed's job is to disappoint may have some grounding in wisdom, on occasion. But the downside of this thinking is brutal.

In his memoir, Geithner describes an argument he had with Larry Summers about a bank recapitalization program they were contemplating in early 2009. "I remember once while Larry and I were sitting outside the Oval Office, I tried to convince him that this meritocratic form of triage would be brutal to the shareholders of the institutions that most deserved brutality, while avoiding the panic-inducing consequences of nationalization or liquidation." He told Summers, "They're going to be diluted in proportion to their sins."[190]

Even Geithner had to defend his policies by promising they would be hurtful. Not only did he consider this position necessary at the time, but he considered it useful to vocalize it to garner support, and later he relayed this conversation in his book, likely hoping readers would react well to it.

Geithner was pulled to this position by a public that demanded it. To an angry populace, these sorts of statements seem like the least we can do. In his memoir, Geithner is clearly responding to a public that considered him too soft.

How confident should we be about our interpretation of events before we start to govern based on selective brutality? This isn't the way civilized and successful societies approach each other. In the process of demanding comeuppance for those we have blamed, we have created comeuppance for ourselves. We have been brutalizing ourselves.

This sort of language is the product of a moral panic. The moral panic was so profound that the "Bailout King" himself, even in 2009 after the deepest depths of the financial crisis had been experienced, was still trying to gain favor for his attempts at stability by promising that somebody would be harmed by them.

CHAPTER 11

CDOS AND FEAR IN
THE MARKETPLACE

The reckless speculators and lenders that populate the innumerable books on the crisis clearly were engaged in some unprecedented financial activities. Some of their products ended up performing terribly.

According to the FCIC, by 2006, 27 percent of all mortgages originating that year lacked some documentation that would normally be required. Even Fannie and Freddie were starting to accept more loans with incomplete documentation. And as oversight relaxed throughout the industry, cases of outright fraud ballooned.[191]

Some of those products can be blamed for performing poorly in a crisis, but they did not create a housing bubble—certainly not a bubble that necessitated such an economic backlash.

Take St. Louis, just to revisit that premise for a moment. A pretty typical metropolitan area. From 1994 to 2005, the metropolitan area had permitted about six single-family housing units annually, per one thousand residents—about the US average. The vacancy rate from 1994 to 2005 had averaged about 4 percent—also about the same as the US average.[192] The median home price in the St. Louis metropolitan area topped out at a moderate $170,000 in 2006. There was no spike in building activity, no spike in housing vacancies.

There was little in the St. Louis housing market that would throw up a red flag in 2005. Yet, the typical home in St. Louis lost about 18 percent of its value, dropping to $140,000 by 2011. From 2008 on, St. Louis single-family permits have been below three units per one thousand residents every year. Half the pre-crisis level.

St. Louis, like many US cities, didn't have a housing boom, and in 2006 and 2007 when lax underwriting was growing and when increasingly complex financial securities were being created and sold, home building was already slowing down in St. Louis from its previously moderate pace.

Blaming post-crisis troubles on boom-era lenders is like tying concrete blocks to someone's feet before pushing them off the boat, and then complaining, "He never took swimming lessons." The truth of the statement has little bearing on the outcome of the incident. From a supply-side point of view, there was no reason for the typical St. Louis homeowner to lose $30,000 of equity or for half the local residential construction industry to shut down.

It is important to be careful in our thinking here. It is smart to learn how to swim. It is smart to have a stable banking system. Some of the new lending was not socially beneficial, especially the lending that coincided with the early declines in housing markets. But the reason we had a crisis and Canada and Australia didn't isn't that we had subprime mortgage lending, and they didn't. It's that we engineered a crisis, and they didn't. We tied concrete blocks to our economy, and they didn't.

The lesson overwhelmingly to be learned, then, is to not obstruct housing construction in your leading economic centers, and also not to tank spending and building in your own economy. But certainly, one can still say that lending programs that didn't perform well and made the crisis worse should also be reformed. So, maybe we should make the banks hold more capital. Maybe mortgages with a zero-down payment and a teaser rate should be banned. But at some point, this is like engineering a life jacket that can keep someone afloat in spite of the concrete blocks we have tied to their ankles.

The primary question I would like to pose here about the increasingly complicated toxic securities that were accumulating from 2005 to 2007: Why? What was the motivation?

Most of the private mortgage-backed securities (MBSs) from 2003 to 2005 were sold in simple mortgage pools. A number of mortgages were originated, and the funds for those mortgages were collected from investors. The investors were then paid back as the mortgages were paid off. Some investors chose to take on more risk, so that they would be the first to take a loss if some mortgages went bad. Other investors had priority to get paid first. That was less risky, and as a result, they earned a lower return on their investment. In the end though, all of those investors had one thing in common: the money they provided funded a mortgage.

As the private securitization boom aged, engineered Collateralized Debt Obligations (CDOs) became more popular. This was an added layer of complexity. They collected cash from investors and bought MBSs with it instead of just investing directly in mortgages. They had the same setup. Some investors took on more risk, and some took on less risk.

Why weren't those investors just buying MBSs directly instead of the more convoluted CDOs? The motivation was demand for safe securities— securities that were expected to have less risk and that paid lower rates of return. In terms of ratings, the CDOs could buy AA-, A-, and BBB-rated securities, which paid higher returns from MBS pools. They could recombine them and sell much of the new pool off as AAA rated.

In their comprehensive review of the causes of the housing bubble, Adam Levitin and Susan Wachter noted, "This expansion was possible only because CDOs enabled the PLS [private-label securities] market to bypass the constraint of subordinated-debt investors' limited risk appetite... CDOs themselves, however, needed buyers. Again, the investment-grade senior positions in the CDOs were relatively easy to sell, but the junior positions posed a challenge..."[193]

The reason the CDOs found a market was that they could create more securities that appeared to have lower risk. That capital was still finding its way into the housing market indirectly. And the early rise of the basic

CDOs in 2005 coincided with a continuation of active home building and rising home prices. Yet, it doesn't really make sense to see this as another step in a relentless march of recklessness. The reason the funding mechanism moved from MBSs to CDOs was that investors were seeking more safety. Frequently, the popular literature on this topic refers to this trend as Wall Street demanding more "crap" to buy. But the reason the securities were increasingly risky was that there was such strong demand for safe assets that Wall Street had to come up with new innovations to try to make more of them.

In the 1990s, investors were willing to take risks, and so the securities that were invented for them were equities based on business plans. When that risk-seeking became extreme, the quality of the business plans backing new equities decreased in quality. Investors bought stocks of firms that turned out not to be profitable. That's a much different situation than a market constructing low-yielding fixed income of decreasing quality. Rhetoric about replacing an internet bubble with a housing bubble blurs this important distinction.

That rhetoric misses the forest for the trees. Certainly, seeing the range of CDOs that existed within that market, there may have been unsophisticated investors who were "chasing yield" or buying securities without understanding the risks. But the only reason the market as a whole would be reaching for such products is that investors with little appetite for risk had become much more numerous than the universe of pre-existing safe assets could handle. There weren't other forms of ostensibly safe, fixed-income securities sitting out there going unpurchased as investors bought the convoluted CDO securities. Increasingly, the assets that were going unpurchased were the lumber, concrete, and gypsum board that might create new houses.

The housing boom in Phoenix happened because there weren't enough homes in Los Angeles, so home buyers who preferred LA had to pile into what was, for them, a second-best alternative. The CDO boom happened because there weren't enough treasuries, safe corporate bonds, and regular mortgage securities, so savers who were becoming increasingly risk averse had to pile into a second-best alternative. Both of these are examples of booms in inferior goods. Casting them both as simply parts of a "bubble" confuses the motivation for these developments.

By the middle of 2006, all the different parts of the elephant were already starting to tell the same story of decline. GDP growth was slowing. Construction was in steep decline. The migration event was dissipating.

SYNTHETIC CDOS AND THE BUST THAT LOOKED LIKE A BUBBLE

Now, CDOs reached the next phase of crisis. By the second half of 2006, a large portion of the CDOs were CDO-squared, synthetic CDOs, and any number of other exotic securities that turned out to be "crap." These securities were still meeting the unquenchable demand for low-risk assets, but now they weren't even investing in mortgages. Synthetic CDOs were, more or less, agreements between two sets of investors. One set of investors (the longs) was seeking a AAA-rated type of security, similar to the securities that funded real mortgages. The other investors (the shorts) were willing to pay those investors as if they had funded mortgages, and they hoped for a big payoff if the mortgages they pretended to stand in for ended up defaulting. These are the characters in *The Big Short.*

Many have pointed out the role of bank regulations that induced banks into investing in AAA-rated securities that turned out to be toxic, because that rating allowed them to use the cash from bank deposits to buy more of them. That is true. But there was a broad shift in risk appetite, in general, even among savers not affected by banking rules.

By mid-2006, the country had become so afraid of risk that even with lax underwriting and willing investors, it was getting harder and harder to find buyers willing to take a long-term equity position on a house. This was the height of the back-door exodus.

It would get worse for all age groups, but the drop in home ownership rates from 2004 to 2007 for the forty-five- to fifty-four- and fifty-five- to sixty-four-year-old age groups was already the sharpest three-year drop recorded.[194] That drop was accelerating as the use of CDOs and synthetic CDOs increased.[195]

Again, since every round peg of evidence was being pounded into the square hole of a "bubble" explanation, this exodus out of housing was flipped upside down into a story of excess. From 2005 to the first half of 2007, new home sales dropped by 34 percent. The reason the mortgage market looked like it was increasingly catering to risky buyers is that buyers who didn't want to take risks had been fleeing the market. It is impossible to track every dollar moving from one asset to another. Yet, increasingly, that capital in search of safe investments, surely, was capital which had previously been equity in a home.

In 2006 and 2007, cash was piling into money market funds.[196] In mid-2006, about $2.1 trillion was invested in money market mutual funds. It would nearly double by the end of 2008. Even by the end of 2007, it was over $3 trillion, nearly a 50 percent increase in just eighteen months. Savers with hundreds of billions of dollars were seeking safe, fixed income, instead of being invested in home equity, corporate equity, or other forms of real investment.

Midway through 2006, there was a step up in synthetic CDO activity. In the first half of 2006, about $18 billion of synthetic CDOs had been issued. In the second half of 2006, $77 billion were issued. From that point until the CDO market crashed in the summer of 2007, nearly half of all CDO activity was synthetic CDOs.[197]

There are two main sides to a synthetic CDO who, in a nutshell, pretend to buy or sell specific mortgage securities. (1) The investors who expect to earn a relatively low fixed return on their investment and expect the risk of default to be very low, and (2) the shorts. The shorts paid the interest payments to the investors each period. The reason they were willing to do that was that the contract they had with the investors stated that if the contractually referenced mortgage securities defaulted, the shorts would get to keep the investors' cash.

So, we have two parties here. One party is so desperate for a fixed, low-risk way to save that they are willing to put their capital into this toxic contraption rather than invest in assets that might fluctuate in value—like homes or corporate investments. The other party was *speculating* on a *massive* economic collapse and was willing to pay for the privilege of waiting for it. This activity had been a substantial part of the CDO market for more than a year by the time the *Wall Street Journal* was demanding a financial panic, and Federal Reserve and Treasury officials were debating whether lower interest rates or economic growth might let speculators off the hook.

Exactly which one of these parties was drunk on "Fed punch?" Exactly how was slowing down the economy supposed to rein in this market? The shorts wanted nothing more than slower economic growth. They wanted the market to crash. The investors were only there because so many savers were too scared to put their money into any asset that could fluctuate in value. After the August 2007 Fed meeting, the investors panicked. What was left for them to do?

What would have been the only way to kill the synthetic CDO market in a functional way? The only *functional* way to do it would be to convince investors that the economy would be healthy enough for riskier assets to grow, so they would invest in actual houses instead of those contraptions. Or to engage in deficit spending so that more treasuries were available for investors seeking safe returns. Or to convince the shorts that their housing bust wasn't going to happen—that the "soft landing" had been achieved, and now growth and stability would be the goal. Instead, even after CDO markets started to become frozen in panic, the Fed accelerated their forecasts of declining housing starts.

The Fed thought that lowering their target interest rate and injecting some cash into the economy would only boost reckless borrowing even more. It's worth considering that when the Fed finally did stabilize the economy at the beginning of 2009 when interest rates were driven to zero, American households started rebuilding equity.

If the rise in mortgages outstanding in 2006 and 2007 had been primarily the product of aggressive lending and debt-fueled over-consumption, then it should have been associated with rising housing starts, rising home ownership, falling rents, rising non-rent inflation, rising home prices, rising nominal GDP growth, and rising long-term interest rates. Yet all of these indicators pointed in the opposite direction.

YELLING FIRE IN A CROWDED FIXED INCOME MARKET

Eventually, the exotic products themselves became victims of deteriorating expectations. On July 11, 2007, S&P issued a ratings downgrade on 612 sub-prime, residential, mortgage-backed security classes:[198]

> Although property values have decreased slightly, additional declines are expected. David Wyss, Standard & Poor's chief economist, projects that property values will decline 8% on average between 2006 and 2008, and will bottom out in the first quarter of 2008...

> As lenders have tightened underwriting guidelines, fewer refinance options may be available to these borrowers, especially if their loan-to-value (LTV) and combined LTV (CLTV) ratios have risen in the wake of declining home prices.

Notice already the positive feedback loop here. S&P was already projecting future losses that were outside any experienced since World War II. There was poor collateral performance. But the remaining reasons for the downgrades are a sort of self-fulfilling prophecy of contractionary reactions resulting from lower expectations.

S&P recognized that the problem was not caused so much by the rate resets themselves as by the inability to refinance at any rate. The problem wasn't that households couldn't refinance mortgages on favorable terms. The problem was that households couldn't refinance mortgages at all. Lower interest rates weren't going to directly help those homeowners. The value of a stimulative Fed at that point would have been to boost expectations and to increase the amount of cash in the economy.

Ben Bernanke has been criticized for underestimating the effects of the subprime bust. But more fundamentally, Bernanke and the Fed underestimated the effects of the negative turn in expectations. The 2005 Fed had felt confident that they could counter a broad national housing collapse. By 2007, too many Americans on and off the Fed board viewed the prevention of declining prices as a cop-out. This is not to blame the Fed. At every step, they were condemned for doing too much rather than not enough.

By August 2007, home equity was considered so unsafe that even the AAA-rated mortgage securities that had been an alternative safe haven were no longer considered safe. The consensus that the massive housing bust was inevitable happened *before* the bust happened.

More than 80 percent of the standard AAA-rated, private mortgage-backed securities (not CDOs) were downgraded. But only about 10 percent actually failed to make all of their payouts to investors.[199] After all was said and done, losses to AAA securities on standard residential securities were low. The few impairments that happened were later—after 2008 on most investment-grade mortgage securities.[200] Those losses were mostly or wholly due to declining home prices that accumulated in 2008 and 2009. Even so, the lower-rated tranches had mostly done their job, generally protecting the higher-rated tranches. The high-rated tranches generally paid off. The 2007 collapse in prices on those securities reflected a panic, and prices on many securities recovered after the Fed began to stabilize the economy at the beginning of 2009.

In his memoir, Henry Paulson tells of bank executives warning him at a dinner at the New York Fed on June 26, 2007 that credit markets for Wall Street and private equity firms were too hot. Those markets were hot because a lot of money was seeking safety, and those firms were in the business of creating securities that were supposed to be safe. Two weeks later, AAA CDO securities would start selling at less than face value in the first whiffs of panic.[201] That was the first death rattle of an economy that was being managed as if creating safety was a cop-out.

These forces were pushing residential investment down and long-term interest rates down as prices and quantities moved to match the supply and demand for safe capital. But at the time, everything looked like a bubble that had to be tamed. Low interest rates seemed like one more source of unsustainable economic stimulus, but they were really the result of savers willing to accept lower returns in order to avoid risk.

The economist Hyman Minsky has become popular since the financial crisis. His claim to fame is the notion that if speculative booms are allowed to go on too long, they become unstable. The financial crisis was supposedly a "Minsky Moment"—a point where the boom finally collapses in on itself.

There was no Minsky Moment. The Fed had prevented a Minsky Moment from happening in 2006. When the ascendent asset class for more than a year has been an asset where the buyers are those who are afraid of economic contraction and the sellers are those who are banking on it, you are clearly well past the speculative motivations that lead to a Minsky Moment.

Before 2006, borrowing and investment were associated with building and growth. That borrowing was declining by 2006. What made this cycle deceptive was that debt kept growing even after the Minsky Moment had been averted. The reason was that the peculiar migration event that had been set off by the lack of adequate housing in the Closed Access cities left the residents of the Contagion cities in an unusual position. The pendulum was swinging too far in the other direction. Their economies were faltering. And their homes, whose prices had been driven up by the migration surge, were a temporary source of cash. That borrowing was the blinking hazard light indicating that the cycle had turned. The synthetic CDO market was the approaching headlight of a semi-truck blaring its air horn that the cycle had turned.

Rising rents and migration largely explain the housing boom. Since debt-fueled speculation replaced those factors in popular explanations of the boom, the distinction between the pre-2006 debt and the later debt was lost. It all just seemed like one ongoing financial Ponzi scheme. It seemed like debt supported by bubble-inflated collateral was pumping up an overheated economy. But the collateral for the earlier debt wasn't bubble-inflated and the later debt wasn't part of an overheated economy. The Fed had actually done right by Minsky, and it was well past time for stability and growth.

YES, DEBT HAD BEEN FUNDING AMERICAN CONSUMPTION

It was true that growth in debt had been related to growth in spending. From 2002 until the third quarter of 2007, the amount of home equity extracted as new mortgage debt each year was greater than the annual growth in aggregate spending.[202] This is why it seemed so obvious that Americans were spending beyond our means and had to be stopped.

Normally, mortgage growth generally grows along with the investment in new housing. The growth in mortgages beyond that doesn't usually amount to more than a couple percentage points of spending in any given year. But throughout the housing boom, it amounted to more than 5 percent of disposable income every year.

This is one reason why determining the fundamental sources of high home prices is so important. If home prices were high just because lenders were creating a temporary bubble, then that debt-fueled spending should never have been allowed to accumulate. But if home prices were generally high because urban rents were skyrocketing, then there was little anyone could do to stop that debt-fueled spending from happening. A few lucky real estate owners had struck it rich and they were spending some of their spoils either by borrowing against those houses or selling them to new, young buyers.

Reflecting consensus views on the market, the Fed was maintaining a tight posture in order to counteract an overheated housing market and to counteract all the debt-funded spending. The growth of the Fed's monetary base was very slow from 2004 onward. That's why inflation was near their target rate and national income growth was relatively mild even when spending was being funded with new debt. As long as they didn't counteract it too much, that was fine. By 2007, the Fed was pushing back too hard. They pushed so hard that households could no longer tap home equity for cash, and then the Fed stood aside without injecting any new cash into the economy that might have stabilized spending.

One way you can see the Fed was depriving the economy of cash is that the velocity of money increased in 2006 and 2007. The velocity of money is a measure of how many times a dollar gets spent over a given period of time. The velocity of the M1 money stock, which is basically cash and checking accounts, has never been higher than it was at the end of 2007. Americans were playing hot potato with money because there wasn't enough of it out there. Eventually, when there isn't enough money, spending, prices, and wages decline. One way to think about all the capital that was being funneled into money market accounts in 2006 and 2007 is that those accounts are a sort of money.

All those savers desperate for safety were pushing down interest rates. The interest rate the Fed targets when they communicate their policy stance had become a moving target because of the panic. Most people think that the Fed was very aggressive when their target short-term interest rates went from 5.25 percent in September 2007 to 2.25 percent in March 2008. Do you know how much money they printed from September to March to move that interest rate down? Approximately zero. The rate was tumbling down because the economy was in tatters, not because the Fed was printing money. In fact, during the period where the target interest rate was declining, the Fed was printing money to make emergency loans to some banks caught up in the panic. At the same time, they destroyed an equal amount of money to make sure they didn't create any money, on net. They called this sterilization. When the Fed would announce at each meeting that they were lowering their target interest rate, they were chasing down interest rates, not leading them down.

The Fed was playing the role of The Wizard of Oz. Before the panics of late 2007, we had been sort of like Dorothy. We didn't need the Wizard. The cash had been in our homes all along. When the housing market broke down, we needed cash from the Fed, and they weren't willing to produce it until crisis hit.

In the third quarter of 2007, Americans extracted a little more than $100 billion from their homes, and personal consumption increased by a little more than $100 billion. But by now, the tensions in the housing market were too much. The private mortgage securities that had been dominating the market seized up. By the second quarter of 2008, equity extraction was negative. American homes were using up more cash than Americans were able to extract through new home equity loans. This was a huge shift. To prevent a spending collapse, the Fed would have had to flood the economy with cash. They didn't. They weren't creating any currency at all. So by the third quarter of 2008, spending only grew by about $28 billion, and by the fourth quarter, it dropped by a whopping $244 billion.

The development of the mortgage CDO market, then the synthetic CDO market, then the CDO panics, then the big collapse after September 2008—at every step, a recovery in economic growth would have reversed the growing disaster. But recovery strong enough to avoid disaster would have been strong enough to stimulate residential investment. Americans could not believe that building more homes could be part of the solution. For years as the American economy drifted toward crisis, the Fed stopped short because a recovery in housing construction seemed like a return to excess.[203] An arrest of losses on real estate investments, even as a side-effect of economic stability, seemed like a dangerous "get out of jail free" card. Even the tepid economic support they maintained was very unpopular.

 CHAPTER 12

WHY DID BORROWERS DEFAULT?

Expectations are an important aspect of market turns, even though they are hard to identify. The country had been expecting a contraction, and stories of troubled borrowers had been piling up in the newspapers for months. A *BusinessWeek* article from September 2006 described apparent victims of fraud and the dangers of option ARMs (Adjustable-Rate Mortgages)—mortgages with potentially destabilizing payment resets. The article entitled "Nightmare Mortgages," begins:

> For cash-strapped homeowners, it was a pitch they couldn't refuse: Refinance your mortgage at a bargain rate and cut your payments in half. New home buyers, stretching to afford something in a super-heated market, didn't even need to produce documentation, much less a downpayment.
>
> Those who took the bait are in for a nasty surprise...
>
> The bill is coming due. Many of the option ARMs taken out in 2004 and 2005 are resetting at much higher payment schedules -- often to the astonishment of people who thought the low installments were fixed for at least five years. And because home prices have leveled

off, borrowers can't count on rising equity to bail them out. What's more, steep penalties prevent them from refinancing. The most diligent home buyers asked enough questions to know that option ARMs can be fraught with risk. But others, caught up in real estate mania, ignored or failed to appreciate the risk.[204]

By September 2006, delinquency rates were rising, but both prime and subprime delinquency rates were still about what they had been from 1998 to 2003.[205] Articles like this, in 2006, were anticipatory. Just as expectations of collapsing home prices came before the actual collapse, expectations of a wave of mortgage defaults came before the actual wave. And researchers since the crisis have found that the defaults were largely related to collapsing prices.

Using a data set with borrower characteristics, loan characteristics, and home price data, Christopher Palmer at MIT found that declining prices explained 60 percent of rising subprime defaults, loan characteristics (such as payment terms) explained 30 percent, and borrower characteristics had little to do with it.

Palmer found that median loan-to-value ratios among subprime loans climbed from about 90 percent in 2005 to about 98 percent by 2007, making those loans more vulnerable to price declines. Since declining prices began to affect them immediately, the combination of those factors caused defaults to rise immediately when prices started to decline. Then they continued to scale up as declining prices persisted. In ways like this, declining prices and changing loan characteristics jointly affected default rates.

Mortgages originated in different years give a clue about what happened. Mortgages originated in 2006 and 2007 had pretty high default rates early on. Among subprime loans originated in 2005, for the first year or two, defaults were only somewhat higher than defaults on 2004 mortgages. This was a rate similar to those issued in 2001—still in the range of performance from recent years. Then, as home prices began to collapse in 2007, equity started to decline for the 2005 loans. That is when defaults started increasing among those loans. And, as with the 2006 and 2007 loans, as declining prices

MARCHING HAND IN HAND TO CRISIS

persisted, defaults continued to rise. Eventually, by some measures, defaults for 2005 subprime loans would be in the same range as those in 2006 and 2007. This is despite the fact that the beginning loan-to-value ratio for the 2005 loans was similar to those in 2003 and 2004. By 2010, many of those homes were sitting on losses of 50 percent of their value, which made beginning loan-to-value ratios somewhat irrelevant.

Loans originated in 2004 had the same pattern as 2005 loans. Defaults only began to accelerate after prices started to decline. Borrowers didn't suddenly become less qualified two or three years after they took out those loans. The value of their homes had deteriorated.

Palmer shows that the same pattern holds across metro areas. He compares Minneapolis to Pittsburgh, which had similar shares of subprime lending. Price declines, and thus negative equity, were deeper in Minneapolis, and defaults were much higher. [206]

According to an analysis by Yuliya Demyanyk of the Federal Reserve Bank of Cleveland, normally factors like credit scores, mortgage rates, loan-to-value ratio levels, and so forth, all have a marginal effect on default rates. In this housing bust, declining home prices became the overwhelming reason for default.[207] And it turned out that default rates were not particularly sensitive to rate resets. [208]

According to Federal Reserve researchers, in 2007, 62 percent of mortgage defaults were from ARMs, partly because ARMs had been used more in the 2006 to 2007 cohorts that developed negative equity. But among that 62 percent, only 12 percent had any payment increase before defaulting.[209]

The changing landscape was reflected in news of the time. This *CNN* piece from February 2008 is typical of the period. It begins:

Mortgage payments are set to jump. Home prices have plunged. "I'm outta here."

Homeowners are abandoning their homes and, more importantly, their mortgages, rather than trying to keep up with rising payments on deteriorating assets."[210]

Defaults were highly correlated with negative equity. For a number of reasons, most households that can make the payment will continue to do so, even if they have significant negative equity. Homeowners only tend to default when there is a combination of issues like unemployment—which became a factor in 2009—combined with negative equity or when negative equity becomes extremely deep.[211] Homeowners don't tend to default just because of a few percentage points of negative equity. That is why home-builder cancellations shot up to more than 30 percent immediately in 2006, while it took several years for mortgage default rates to build up. It is a lot easier for a family to decline a move into a new home than to move away from their old home.

Notice that the *CNN* article refers to both problems—rising mortgage payments and falling prices. Because lax underwriting and changing rates were predicted as the main sources of the crisis, this continued to be the presumption. The article notes, "And now reports are emerging of home-owners skipping out on mortgages even though they can still afford to pay them. Wachovia CEO Ken Thompson described these people on an earnings call last month. '[These are] people that have otherwise had the capacity to pay, but have basically just decided not to, because they feel like they've lost equity, value in their properties.'"[212]

Two weeks after that article, *CNN* posted another article that began:

For months, we've fretted about the Armageddon that will hit when subprime adjustable-rate mortgages start resetting to much higher interest rates.

What's happening is even worse: Many of these loans are defaulting well before their rates increase.

Defaults for subprime loans issued in 2007—none of which have reset yet—hit 11.2 percent in November. That represents perhaps 300,000 households and is twice the default rate that 2006 loans had 10 months after being issued, according to Friedman, Billings Ramsey analyst Michael Youngblood.

Defaults are spiking well before resets come into play thanks to the lax lending environment of the past few years. Many borrowers were approved for mortgages that they had little chance of affording, even at the low-interest teaser rates.[213]

That article is a confirmation of the findings that rate resets were not particularly important.[214] Yet the focus at *CNN* remained on underwriting. Most indicators suggest that by 2007, lending standards were tightening up.[215] The key factor for defaults was the fall in home prices.[216]

When the facts changed and rate resets ended up not being important, it was one more round peg that needed to be pounded into the square hole of the bubble story. One can see here, in real time, how when canonized presumptions are wrong, each additional fact can't be powerful enough on its own to change the canon. There is no point where some marginal new fact on its own can do that. So, instead, observers in real time are driven to more and more implausible conclusions, like that huge numbers of borrowers couldn't even afford their teaser rate payments after a few months. And the more implausible those conclusions became, the more dastardly the financial villains seemed who must have been responsible for it. Ironically, when the canon is wrong, it can actually fuel the passion for believing it.

Researchers like Yuliya Demyanyk have also found that underwriting had little to do with the rise in delinquencies. Upon concluding that credit scores, for instance, were not a good predictor of defaults, after accounting for other factors like falling prices, she concluded, "The subprime mortgage crisis is still a black box, and it requires more analysis to fully understand how the developments in the subprime mortgage market and a subsequent crisis have 'subprimed' so many issues that used to be considered fundamental, like credit scoring."[217]

What if credit scores didn't correlate well with mortgage performance because poor underwriting wasn't the fundamental cause of the default crisis?

The performance of any given cohort of mortgages depended mostly on how near those mortgage originations were to the collapse in prices.[218] Most subprime loans were paid off within two to three years. Most of the loans that originated before 2006 were paid off already. Most borrowers of 2/28 loans never intended to hold the loans past the date of the rate reset, and in fact, most didn't.[219] Borrowers from 2006 and 2007 were more likely to still hold their loans because the downturn in home prices and in lender sentiment made it more difficult for them to refinance or to sell the homes for more than they owed. [220]

Those mortgages depended on a liquid mortgage market where refinancing was broadly available. That made them systematically dangerous, and this should cause us to be careful about letting that type of mortgage dominate again. Yet this is one more case where the crisis that happened wasn't the crisis that everyone expected. The coming rate reset catastrophe was a big theme in the lead up to the crisis. Fed critics ask why the Fed didn't see the crisis coming. But the crisis that came wasn't the crisis that the bubble doomsayers had expected, either.

In March 2007, Ben Bernanke famously told the Joint Economic Committee (JEC) that "the impact on the broader economy and financial markets of the problems in the subprime market seems likely to be contained." Bernanke, and many others, believed that the subprime market was destined to contract, but that it was a small enough market that the rest of the economy could continue to grow even with some contraction in that market. In *The Courage to Act*, he writes, "Adjustable-rate subprime mortgages, where delinquencies were climbing as introductory teaser interest rates expired, constituted only about 8 percent of all outstanding mortgages. Even if subprime mortgages defaulted at extraordinarily high rates, we calculated, the resulting financial losses would be smaller than those from a single bad day in the global stock markets."[221]

Bernanke *was* correct in March 2007, but unfortunately for him, the committee he chaired in the months after that served to make him *appear* to be incorrect. There wasn't a foreclosure crisis because of rate resets. There was a foreclosure crisis because of an economic meltdown, most of which developed after his March presentation. It is only because the eventual scale of the crisis is imbued with a sense of inevitability that Bernanke's statement seems naive. The coming disaster was largely created by policy choices that happened after March 2007 because of "Old Testament thinking."

The number of mortgage defaults that happened before the broader economic collapse is insignificant compared to the number of defaults that happened after the recession. Those later defaults were the result of popular monetary and credit policies meant to prevent capital from flowing into mortgages and housing for years after the peak of the market in early 2006.

Figure 8[222] gives an indication of the scale of the two phases of the delinquency crisis. Foreclosures were just starting to increase in the Contagion cities when Bernanke told the JEC that the fallout would be contained.

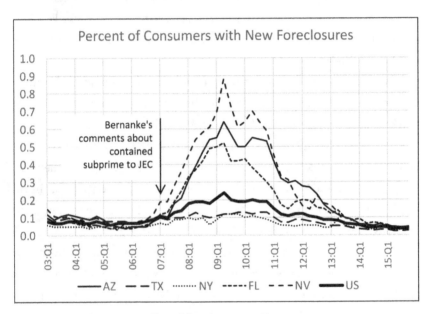

Figure 8 Foreclosures over time

The difference in the scale of the default crisis between the early subprime defaults in 2007 and the mountain of defaults from 2008 to 2012 is massive. Plenty of choices were made after March 2007 that raised that mountain. *Many* more defaults came after the broad economic decline than had come before. As the crisis aged, the defaults became more complicated. They were the result of a combination of problems—negative equity, negative shocks to incomes, unemployment, the inability to refinance, and so forth. It is more accurate to say that economic decline led to a foreclosure crisis than that the foreclosure crisis led to economic decline. Both were largely created by policy choices—choices largely made after March 2007, some of which I will discuss in the next section.

PART 5

Adding Insult to Injury

CHAPTER 13

THE FEDERAL RESERVE'S BIG BLUNDER

In late 2008, many momentous things famously happened. But some of the most momentous things are mostly unknown or misunderstood outside a few economists that study monetary policy. (I apologize to readers who are sophisticated economists if occasionally my language here eschews technical precision in an attempt for conceptual clarity. A lot happened in 2008.)

The Fed tends to talk about interest rates as their method for managing the money supply. The problem is that in a crisis, the right interest rate can move around rapidly. So, interest rates are a confusing way to think about monetary policy, especially in the midst of economic upheaval.

A clearer way to think about it is that the economy needs money to work. The Fed's job is to make enough money for that to happen without making too much. A very simple way to think about it is when they decide that the economy needs some more dollars, they make some dollars and loan them out. Before 2008, they almost always did that by buying treasuries (government debt). So, the Fed basically replaces some public debt with cash. You can think of cash as a form of public debt that pays no interest and can always be redeemed at face value. The Fed buys debt and pays for it with new cash.

In mid-2007, the Fed owned about $900 billion of assets, most all of it Treasury debt. And there was about $800 billion of currency out in the world as a result of it. So, in a nutshell, the Fed makes loans in order to get cash dollars into the world. If it had made more loans, there would have been more dollars, and more dollars chasing the same goods and services would have meant prices were higher. If it had made fewer loans, prices would have been lower. The government, using the Fed, lends the cash it makes to create inflation and takes back its cash to create deflation.

Since cash doesn't earn interest and the loans the Fed makes with it do, this is a profitable system for the government. Instead of buying treasuries, they could make loans to businesses, or even buy stocks. It really doesn't matter that much. In any case, they are exchanging cash for assets that earn a return. In times of need, they have lent cash directly to businesses, but in normal times they usually just buy government debt in order to keep things simple.

Since the economy is generally growing, the need for dollars grows over time. So, the Fed rarely reduces the amount of lending that it does. Generally, it grows the size of its operations by about 5–10 percent annually. That doesn't mean there is 5–10 percent inflation. It is a mixture of an increase in real activity—more things being bought and sold—and inflation, which the Fed has kept at around 2 percent for many years now.

Things got really complicated in 2008. To keep it simple, first, just forget about interest rates. They aren't a reliable indicator of Fed policy. This simple framework is the easiest way to think about each thing the Fed and the Treasury did, and the consequences of it:

The Fed lends dollars to create inflation. The Fed borrows (or reduces lending of) dollars to create deflation.

As we walk through all the complicated events of 2008, just keep those two sentences in mind.

The Fed had been printing cash at an unusually slow pace—less than 5 percent growth per year—since 2005. By 2008, they had practically ground the creation of money to a halt. The Fed had been making emergency loans to banks since mortgage market panics had begun in August 2007. That would be inflationary. (Lend for inflation.) The Fed sold treasuries when it made those loans, so that its total amount of lending stayed the same. Now, on net, it was lending some cash to banks and some cash to the Treasury, but its total lending stayed about the same. The Fed just lent a little less to the government and a little more to some private banks.

They were still just lending. Except for a few small items, they didn't borrow at all before September 2008. The lending was funded with the nearly trillion dollars' worth of cash that the Fed can print whenever they want to. The Fed didn't need to borrow. The point of making loans is to print cash so there is more cash in the economy. Normally, there would be no reason for the Fed to borrow and lend at the same time.

In September 2008, things started to go really badly. On Sunday, September 7, 2008, the Federal Housing Finance Agency (FHFA) determined that the GSEs could not meet their capital requirements and the federal government took them over into what is called conservatorship. The following weekend, Bank of America would be pressed to buy Merrill Lynch, and Lehman Brothers would declare bankruptcy early in the morning of Monday, September 15. On the next day after the Lehman bankruptcy, there was a scheduled meeting of the Federal Reserve's policy board—the FOMC.

Keep in mind the string of events that led up to that meeting. Home prices had dropped 13 percent nationally, but according to the regulators who had just declared the GSEs insolvent, foreclosures had only just begun. Regulators projected such terrible losses for the GSEs that they forced them to write off their tax assets. That was a large part of the hit to their capital, in accounting terms, which led the government to take them over. In layman's terms, the GSEs had already taken some losses, and those losses could be used to reduce taxes from profits earned in future years. But their regulator, the FHFA, expected the GSEs to take so many losses after 2008 from *future* foreclosures that they weren't expected to have any profits to pay taxes on in any foreseeable future. The *reason* the GSEs had been taken over was because the government asserted confidence that the economy was going to get much, much worse.

The decline in the broader economy was also just beginning to be felt. Unemployment had still been at 5.0 percent in April and had risen sharply to 6.1 percent in August. Congress and the president had instituted emergency unemployment insurance at the end of June to address lackluster hiring.

In the midst of these issues, William Dudley, who managed the trading operations for the FOMC, opened the FOMC meeting describing how far the market expected the committee to lower rates that day. He said that on Friday, the market had expected the committee to hold the interest rate at 2 percent but the failure of Lehman Brothers over the weekend had changed those expectations. Many market participants expected a rate cut now, and they were increasingly worried that "the financial system is going to implode in a major way."[223]

The committee's response was to hold the federal funds rate at 2 percent. There was plenty of room to drop interest rates, and markets expected a decrease. That is how the Fed communicates its policy but forget about the interest rate. This was a deflationary decision. By now, fear was strong enough that banks were holding excess cash. The mechanism that the Fed would have to use to target the 2 percent rate would be to suck up cash until banks were willing to pay 2 percent interest to get some.

In their press release, they said, "The downside risks to growth and the upside risks to inflation are both of significant concern to the Committee." And they continued their practice of referring to the "ongoing housing contraction."[224] (Actually, this was an improvement from the late 2007 meetings where they referred to it as an "ongoing housing *correction*." [225] So, while they continued to portray the collapse of the housing market as something they expected to continue, at least they had stopped referring to it as something desirable.) A quick succession of fund, bank, and insurer panics, leading to the emergency TARP[226] legislation, followed the meeting. Yet markets held up remarkably well. The S&P 500 index was at 1,252 the Friday before the Lehman failure and remained at 1,213 two weeks later.

The Fed was unable to keep short-term interest rates at the 2 percent target. Everyone wanted to save. Nobody wanted to borrow and invest. Rates plunged. The Fed would have had to suck more cash out of the economy in order to keep their target rate at 2 percent through normal operations. Even though they had announced a 2 percent rate target, they never sucked enough cash out of the economy to push the rate that high.

A fresh panic had set in. As a result, they started making billions in emergency loans to banks, and again, in order to avoid creating inflation, when they made emergency loans, they sold treasuries so that the total amount of cash they had created didn't increase. So, at the same time, they were lending for inflation (emergency loans to banks) and reducing lending for deflation (getting rid of the Treasury debt they had previously been financing).

According to Bernanke, "Until this point we had been selling Treasury securities we owned to offset the effect of our lending on reserves (the process called sterilization). But as our lending increased, that stopgap response would at some point no longer be possible because we would run out of Treasuries to sell."[227] For some reason, throughout that tumultuous time, the Fed didn't simply lower their target interest rate so they could stop sucking cash back out of the economy to try to hit it. Instead, they requested that the Treasury borrow cash for the Fed by issuing new Treasury bonds. While the country was debating the $700 billion of funding for TARP, in a separate action the Treasury quietly borrowed more than $500 billion and handed the cash over to the Fed. The Fed didn't have enough treasuries to pull more money out of the economy, so the Treasury pulled cash out of the economy by borrowing it and, instead of spending it, handed it over to the Fed.[228]

Up until now, the Fed had never really borrowed cash. Why would they? They had always mainly just printed money for cash. For the first time, using the Treasury, they now had borrowed a significant amount of cash.[229] This is a huge source of confusion regarding the Federal Reserve in 2008 and after. From that point on, most of the money the Fed was injecting into the economy wasn't coming from its magic money vault. It was borrowing money to lend it back out. All the trillions of dollars that the Fed has gotten in the habit of tossing around since then have very little to do with traditional Fed monetary policy.

Since 2007, the Fed had been lending some cash to banks. By early September 2008, about $200 billion of its loans were to banks and the rest was still to the Treasury. After the September 16 meeting, the Fed began making hundreds of billions of dollars' worth of emergency loans to banks. In mid-October, there was still a little less than a trillion dollars' worth of currency in the economy. Currency in circulation did increase a bit, though it probably isn't wrong to say that by that point some of it was literally being stuffed under mattresses for safekeeping.[230] The Fed still owned about $500 billion of Treasury debt but they had also borrowed $500 billion from the Treasury. So, their net position with the Treasury was now about zero. The Fed really would have run out of treasuries to sell if the government hadn't loaned them $500 billion.[231]

The country was in the midst of a deflationary shock—the worst since the Great Depression, by a longshot. The Fed should have been buying more treasuries to increase the amount of cash in the economy, not selling them.

The conventional wisdom about this period is that the Fed was flooding the economy with money to bail out Wall Street. And, indeed, it had shifted its balance sheet away from making loans to the government to making loans to Wall Street. But, in total, these actions constituted extremely tight monetary policy. It was their tight monetary policy that caused the deflationary shock. The technical aspects of this have not been broadly understood. Conventional wisdom has been that the crisis happened in spite of the Fed's loose policies. It has it backward, and we will never learn the right lessons about avoiding crises in the future until we set our understanding right. The crisis happened because the Federal Reserve implemented aggressively *tight* monetary policy. It was so tight that they had to create whole new tools in order to implement it.

The extent of these transfers was so large that the Treasury soon started to worry about running up public debt levels in its effort to keep sucking cash out of the economy to give to the Fed. So, when TARP passed on October 3, it included a provision for the Fed to effectively borrow directly from banks instead of having the Treasury borrow for it. For the first time, the Fed would pay interest on excess cash reserves that the banks deposited at the Fed.[232]

When the Fed announced the implementation of interest on reserves, the press release noted:

> The payment of interest on excess reserve balances will give the Federal Reserve greater scope to use its lending programs to address conditions in credit markets while also maintaining the federal funds rate close to the target established by the Federal Open Market Committee.[233]

It is hard to overstate what a change in policy this was. Before, they just printed cash to lend it. But now they were lending to banks, and in order to fund that lending, they were borrowing it back from banks. When deposits came into the banks now, instead of finding ways to lend those deposits back out to private borrowers, banks could safely lend them to the Fed—and earn interest on them. In October 2008, the Federal Reserve was purposefully competing with private borrowers for bank loans because it was afraid that bank loans would be inflationary.

The Fed did slowly lower its target fed funds rate. From November 6 to December 15, the Fed was paying 1 percent interest on reserves, and it was also targeting a 1 percent federal funds rate. It doesn't just set the Fed funds rate by fiat, though. It creates and destroys cash until banks charge each other the interest rate for very short-term loans that the Fed has targeted. That is the traditional mechanism by which the Fed injected cash into the economy by targeting a certain interest rate that the banks charge each other.

The new interest it was paying to banks to borrow from them was set by Fed policy at an unchanging 1 percent. The problem was the banks didn't want cash. Everyone was in a panic. They were being flooded with cash and they were happy to send it back to the Fed rather than risk lending it to a private borrower, especially if the Fed was willing to pay them for it.

Until both the fed funds rate and interest on reserves were both lowered to 0.25 percent on December 16, interest on reserves was above the *effective* fed funds rate. The Fed was not able to hit its target. In other words, despite the Fed's stated interest rate target of 1 percent, banks could actually borrow at rates much below 1 percent. The interest rate on short term Treasury bills was basically zero. The banks could earn higher returns by giving cash to the Fed than they could earn by lending it to each other, by lending directly to the Treasury, or by lending to private borrowers. In the past, the amount of cash banks held at the Fed in reserves was minimal. Banks preferred to lend cash out to earn interest on it. But now that the Fed was paying them interest, about $800 billion was deposited back at the Fed through the banks over the course of a few weeks.[234]

At the time of the September meeting, the Fed had held about $1 trillion worth of assets. By the end of the year, that was up to $2.2 trillion. But they funded those assets by borrowing $398 billion from the Treasury and $848 billion from banks. Remember, the Fed lends to inflate and borrows to deflate. It is a mistake to see the bloated balance sheet as a cash injection. They were borrowing to lend. The economy needed cash desperately, but the Fed didn't lend enough. It was giving with the right hand and taking with the left. Deflation struck.

By December 15, the day before the fed funds rate and interest on reserves were finally dropped to 0.25 percent, the S&P 500 index was down to 869. For the two epic weeks after the failure of Lehman Brothers, AIG, Washington Mutual, the Primary Reserve Fund, the debate over TARP, and the discretionary tightening of the FOMC, the S&P 500 had been down less than 5 percent. During the following three months when the Fed paid interest to the banks so that they sent nearly a trillion dollars back to the Fed, the stock market fell almost 30 percent. At the same time, expectations of deep deflation developed. By late November, bonds were trading as if investors expected annual average *deflation* of 2 percent for the next five years.[235] Because of the quick succession of these events, the Lehman Brothers failure is given too much weight regarding the cause of the crisis. Even if its failure was as systemically important as it is frequently made out to be, that would make the contractionary policies of the Fed for the three months that followed it even less defensible.[236]

"ZERO INTEREST RATE POLICY" IS NOT A POLICY

Here, I want to take a brief digression from the timeline of events. The habit of describing monetary policy in terms of interest rates is toxic, and we can see why in the events of late 2008. Since 2008, it is very common to hear people talk about the Fed's "Zero Interest Rate Policy." Even Fed officials do. It even has its own acronym—ZIRP. But clearly that isn't the Fed's policy. They drove the economy into the ground at the end of 2008 in an effort to keep interest rates *above zero*. But the market rate by then was zero. The Fed could do nothing about that. There is no way they could have even gotten the rate to 2 percent. They tried. They invented new tools in an effort to do it. If the last few months of 2008 taught us nothing else, surely, they should have put to rest the notion that the Fed controls what the interest rate is. Yet, for a decade, monetary policy has been continuously and falsely described as "loose" because of ZIRP, when in fact, the Fed was dragged kicking and screaming to zero and initiated a financial crisis trying to stop it.

The Fed announced at the end of 2008 that it would begin buying mortgage-backed securities with what was called quantitative easing (QE). After two months of introductory purchases in January and February of about $70 billion, they added about $170 billion in March and finally, began to add to their holdings of Treasury bonds again in March. They also initiated the TALF (Term Asset-Backed Securities Loan Facility) program, which backed private lending. In March, the S&P 500 began to recover.

Much of the cash that the Fed injected with its QE purchases continued to come back to the Fed in the form of excess reserves. When the Fed had initiated interest on bank reserves, it was inducing banks to remove cash from private credit markets and park it at the Fed with an interest rate that was higher than the market rate for short-term cash. When it initiated QE, the intention was reversed. Now the Fed was flooding banks with cash by buying MBSs and treasuries, with the intention of increasing cash in the economy. But in spite of those efforts, the banks continued to send most of that cash back to the Fed as reserves. By the time of quantitative easing, the banks considered a rate of nearly zero to be a better alternative than new private lending. Yet, some cash was able to move into the broader economy in the process, which did finally improve expectations about recovering economic activity and low but positive inflation.

QE is frequently described as unconventional policy, but looked at a certain way, it was more of a return to conventional policy. This was the first time since August 2007 that the Fed increased their holdings of treasuries for the sake of injecting cash into the economy.

In October 2008, there were about $7.1 trillion in deposits at commercial banks and about $7 trillion that the banks had loaned back out. When savers deposited cash at banks, banks loaned that cash back out. By May 2013, there were $9.3 trillion in outstanding deposits, but loans and leases were still at $7 trillion. Instead of making loans to the private sector, the banks held $2 trillion in cash in the form of reserves—essentially loans back to the Fed.[237]

In a recent paper, economist David Beckworth with the Mercatus Center at George Mason University found that the higher the interest rate on reserves was relative to market interbank lending rates, the less banks made private loans, over the period from 2009 to 2018. This suggests that interest on reserves has been inducing banks to decrease their private lending.[238] Economist George Selgin has also shown that interest on reserves was associated with reduced private lending.[239]

The conventional wisdom about 2008 has been that the inevitable collapse of the housing bubble became so overwhelming that, try as it might, the Fed just couldn't do enough to counteract it. William Dudley, who had warned the FOMC in September 2008 that some traders thought the bottom was about to fall out from under the economy, later became President of the New York Federal Reserve Bank. He reflected on that conventional wisdom in a speech in 2014. "[D]uring the financial crisis, especially during the fall of 2008, financial market conditions tightened dramatically even as the FOMC was cutting its federal funds rate target to zero. Monetary accommodation turned out to be insufficient to produce an easing of financial market conditions, and the economy fell into a deep recession."[240]

Even though it is conventional wisdom, this description is inaccurate. The first action the Fed took immediately after the Lehman Brothers failure was to hold the target rate at 2 percent because of inflation fears. Then, over the *three months* that it took them to reduce the rate to zero, the country experienced a deep and sharp collapse in dollar spending. Over those three months, the Fed increased the total assets that they owned from $1 trillion to $2.2 trillion. If they had increased their assets in the traditional way, by simply lending, that would have been wildly inflationary. In fact, if they had lowered their target rate to zero in September, it is plausible that even an increase to $1.1 trillion or $1.2 trillion in the traditional way would have been inflationary. But the reason their balance sheet exploded was not because they were lending to inflate. They were on record as being worried about inflation. Their balance sheet exploded because they were borrowing to deflate.

It could be that any Fed policy board would have made similar mistakes in the heat of the moment. My concern here isn't about blame. But the biggest mistake we could make today would be to believe that an inevitable crash meant that "whatever it takes" monetary policy wasn't enough to stop it. We didn't try "whatever it takes" monetary policy. And, in fact, the Federal Reserve made a huge mistake by implementing radical new procedures meant to prevent inflation while we were in the midst of deflation already. The Fed had all the tools it needed to create inflation in 2008, and instead it constructed new tools that created deflation.

The deflationary shock of late 2008 has generally been treated as just one more step in the inevitable bubble and bust cycle. But the Federal Reserve allowed a deflationary shock to happen that wasn't inevitable at all. The dislocations that followed this shock have also been treated as additional steps in the inevitable bubble and bust cycle. A large majority of foreclosures and unemployment—even most of the construction unemployment—happened after the deflationary shock of late 2008. Those are the tragic consequences that largely fuel our fear of the bubble. But it is more accurate to treat those as consequences of an unfortunate series of errors in monetary policy. The deepest depths of the housing crisis were the result of recessionary monetary policy.

One can see how the presumption of an inevitable housing bust prevented a clear assessment of Fed policy during this crucial time. In the statement that accompanied the September 2008 decision to hold the target rate at 2 percent, in addition to referring to "the ongoing housing contraction," they said, "Over time, the substantial easing of monetary policy, combined with ongoing measures to foster market liquidity, should help to promote moderate economic growth."[241]

Clearly that wasn't even remotely the case. Monetary policy wasn't easy at all. Even by the crude measure of the target interest rate, it had been stuck at 2 percent since the end of April.[242] Inflation expectations, inferred from bond yields, had already started to (accurately, it turned out) collapse before the September meeting. At the time, there were many signs available that policy had become very tight. Consumer prices declined by more than 2 percent in the fourth quarter of 2008. Nominal GDP declined by nearly as much. By definition, it had become disastrously tight.

The expectation of a *future* deluge of foreclosures had been the main motivation for taking over the GSEs. Surely, in the absence of a moral panic that considered those foreclosures inevitable—even just—the Fed would have found something better to focus on in the September meeting than inflation fears.

FATALISM BEGAT OUR FATE

The sense that this was foisted on the Fed prevented them from reacting to their own errors in real time. It seemed like nature running its course. Since this was seen as inevitable, it wasn't their job to fix it. Rather than asking them to be a monetary surgeon, the country was satisfied with a monetary triage nurse.

Richard Fisher, the president of the Dallas Federal Reserve Bank and a voting member of the FOMC at the time, laid out that point of view in a speech given on September 25, 2008, as the financial world was burning down around him:

As I see it, the seizures and convulsions we have experienced in the debt and equity markets have been the consequences of a sustained orgy of excess and reckless behavior, not a too-tight monetary policy.

There is no nice way to say this, so I will be blunt: Our credit markets had contracted a hideous STD—a securitization transmitted disease—for which lowering the funds rate to negative real levels seemed to me to be not only an ineffective treatment, but a palliative and maybe even a stimulus that would only encourage further mischief.

I was and I remain skeptical that lowering the fed funds rate is the most effective antidote for such a pathology, given that, in my book, rates held too low, too long during the previous Fed regime were an accomplice to that reckless behavior....

[B]looms propelled by greed and tomfoolery and busts born of fear,... these underlying forces are deeply rooted in human DNA.

If this is a DNA issue, perhaps no financial system—no matter how enlightened its central bank or sophisticated its regulatory architecture or wise its Congress or executive—can prevent nature from running its course.[243]

Even in the midst of a deflationary debacle, Fisher thought the Fed was being too accommodating. This is why the complicated debates about which factors were most important in creating the crisis are mostly irrelevant. Was the crisis caused by regulatory rules that encouraged banks to hold toxic securities? Was it caused by the failure of Federal Reserve and Treasury officials to save Lehman Brothers? Was it caused by a housing bubble that got too far out of hand? And so on. These are all debates about whether the drowning victim with blocks tied to his ankles should have taken swimming lessons. Both the Fed and its critics, were, to some extent, convinced that nature had to run its course. It doesn't matter what was going to cause a crisis. A crisis was bound to come because a crisis was the only thing that would trigger the Fed to print money. Even when the economy entered a deflationary spiral, Fisher could throw up his hands about the "orgy of excess" supposedly created by low interest rates that, by now, were three years or more in the past. The *Wall Street Journal* editors were praising the Fed for their strong character.[244]

Bernanke and most of the FOMC would finally flinch in the game of chicken, but there were plenty of people who were still speeding straight ahead, not yet sated with the amount of crisis we had already engineered.

Unfortunately, this wasn't the end of tying concrete blocks to the ankles of our housing market, pushing it off the boat, and then "letting nature take its course." Now that the Federal Reserve was committed to stabilization with its QE programs, the conservatorship of the GSEs would begin to play a pivotal role in the continuing crisis. From this point on, the damage would mostly be inflicted on working-class homeowners through a misplaced income- and class-based suppression of mortgage lending.

CHAPTER 14

THE FINANCIAL REGULATORS' BIG BLUNDER

Even though home prices had already fallen by 13 percent from their highs by August 2008, the following six months were the worst of the housing bust, in terms of monthly rates of change, with average home prices now falling by 1 percent to 1.5 percent per month.[245] By then home prices in low-priced neighborhoods were falling more sharply than in higher-priced neighborhoods. The combination of rising unemployment, areas with high and worsening levels of negative home equity, and the collapse of mortgage credit at the low end of the market meant that in almost every city, low-priced homes were especially declining in value. The rise in the number of mortgage delinquencies was sharpest in the fourth quarter of 2008 and the first quarter of 2009.[246]

THE WORST DAMAGE TO WORKING-CLASS HOMEOWNERS WAS INFLICTED AFTER THE CRISIS

When the Federal Reserve finally provided quantitative easing, government regulators prevented that support from making it to the lower tiers of the housing market by tightly regulating lending to marginal borrowers. The effect on working-class homeowners from this late development may be the most damaging policy decision of the entire affair. Because of the widespread false belief that mortgages to underqualified homeowners were the cause of the crisis, there was no public support for mortgage credit to the bottom half of the housing market. Bankers were afraid to extend it, regulators were ready to pounce on them if they did, and the electorate was more than happy to accept that state of affairs. So, only the top half of the housing market stabilized after March 2009 when the Fed finally managed to stabilize the broader economy.

From 2000 to 2007, the average credit score of mortgages guaranteed by Fannie Mae had been relatively stable. In fact, the average had risen slightly over that period. After conservatorship, the average credit score on new issues jumped more than forty points from the long-term norms at Fannie Mae. In 2001, the average credit score for all existing Fannie Mae borrowers was 713. By 2007, it had *risen* to 721. From 2009 through 2012, the average credit score for new mortgages never fell below 760.[247]

At the same time, the average market value of homes with new Fannie Mae mortgages also shows an extreme shift in Fannie Mae activity. Fannie Mae tracks the market values of homes with existing Fannie Mae mortgages as well as homes receiving new mortgages. Every year until 2006, those values were about the same. In other words, in all the years of the housing boom, new Fannie Mae borrowers had similar credit scores as past borrowers, and they were purchasing homes similar to the homes that past borrowers had purchased. This changed after 2006.

In 2006, the average home value in Fannie Mae's book of business was about $246,000, and the average home value in their newly originated mortgages was about $253,000. By 2009, the average home value in their book of business had declined to about $204,000 as home prices across the country collapsed—a drop of about 19 percent. But the average value of homes getting new mortgages through Fannie Mae shot *up* by 33 percent over the same period to about $327,000. That means that in 2009, the average home getting a new mortgage through Fannie Mae had a market value *60 percent* higher than the average home with an existing Fannie Mae mortgage. When private mortgage securitizations dried up, and then when the entire economy went into a tailspin, the federal mortgage agencies could have provided broad support for American homeowners. Instead, they only supported high-end markets. They withdrew support from middle-class, entry-level, and affordable markets.[248]

The private mortgage market was dead, and the federally controlled lenders pulled their support from households that they had successfully serviced for generations. At Fannie, Freddie, and the FHA, the average credit score on *denied* applications after 2008 was higher than the average credit score had been on *accepted* applications before 2008.[249]

According to the "Quarterly Report on Household Debt and Credit" from the New York Fed, credit scores of all borrowers across the country followed a similar pattern as credit scores on Fannie Mae loans. There is no evidence of any systematic shift down in borrower credit scores during the boom, but there was a significant shift to higher credit scores after 2007.[250]

One might quibble about credit scores or argue that some credit scores were inflated during the boom, but this shift was so extreme, quibbles can't begin to bridge the gap. Comparing changes in boom-era borrower qualifications to bust-era qualifications is like comparing a light breeze to a tornado. And the effects on working-class home values were about as devastating as a tornado.

The government had essentially nationalized the remaining functional part of the mortgage market, and used that control to exclude middle- and lower-middle-income households from credit access. The results were devastating.

The Obama administration in October 2016 agreed. A report detailing some of the numbers I laid out above noted:

> While creditworthiness is certainly a critically important factor, this credit selectivity is especially sobering given the fact that more than 40 percent of all FICO scores nationally fall below 700. While a variety of factors contribute to these outcomes, it is clear that the GSEs and the secondary market can do more to reach a

broader swathe of creditworthy households. Constraints on access to affordable credit have ripple effects across the owner-occupied housing market. When a large number of first time homeowners cannot buy a home, established homeowners may face a harder time relocating or moving up in the market.

Behind these statistics are creditworthy families who have not been able to access the wealth-building opportunity of homeownership or enjoy full mobility. This lack of access is particularly acute for minority and low-income families whose homeownership rates are considerably below the national average.[251]

Tracking the most expensive and least expensive neighborhoods from, say, 1999 to the end of 2008, price appreciation had much more to do with which metropolitan area a home was in than whether it was a high-tier or low-tier home. In other words, some cities had become more expensive than others, and that applied to the entire metropolitan area. Over the previous decade, a home in Seattle was likely to have appreciated in value by much more than a home in Atlanta had, regardless of which homes in either city were being compared.[252] After 2008, home values in affordable neighborhoods in each city declined compared to home values in expensive neighborhoods in each city.

High-priced zip codes were generally stabilized after the end of 2008, but low-priced zip codes continued to collapse until late 2011. The Federal Reserve had finally helped to stabilized spending, but between the Federal Reserve encouraging the diversion of credit away from private lending and into excess reserves and federal regulators directing private lending to only the most financially secure borrowers, the stabilization only reached the top end of the housing market. The bottom end was starved of buyer demand.[253]

Outside of the Closed Access and Contagion cities, the worst housing crisis was a crisis mainly for low-tier homes, and it didn't happen from 2006 to 2007. It happened from 2008 to 2011. This wasn't due to a lack of demand for housing or the willingness to pay. After a brief pause, rents have continued to rise. It was due to a lack of credit to fund home purchases.

The Closed Access cities and a few of the other priciest cities were the only cities where low-priced homes had behaved much differently than high-priced homes during the boom. By the time that the Fed began to implement QE1 in the spring of 2009, relative prices of low-tier homes had already dropped back down relative to high-priced homes in those cities. Price reversals that resemble a reversal of bubble price increases had already taken place by September 2008.

The collapse in low-end prices mostly happened in two waves: first, in late 2008 and 2009, when Fannie and Freddie severely tightened their lending standards, and then again in 2010. QE1 ended in March 2010. In July 2010, Dodd-Frank passed, which codified a number of liabilities that banks would have to assume when they lend to households with less than pristine credit or to households in markets with high-housing costs. At the same time, a first-time home buyer credit, which had likely been preventing further collapse in those markets, expired. In 2010, home prices went down another notch, especially at the bottom end of the market.

In the Contagion cities, the average loss to home values in more affordable neighborhoods, *after* the end of 2008, was *34 percent.*[254] The primary effect of new credit regulations was to prevent reasonable buyers from becoming new home owners. But much worse, this wiped out the buyer's market for the homes that were already owned by working-class households and wiped out trillions of dollars of life savings in their home equity. That blow removed an important element of the financial safety net those families would have used when unemployment and other stresses of the recession spread through the economy. This was not a market reaction. The mortgage market was largely defined by the federal lending agencies and regulators at this point. This was a policy choice.

The migration event had pushed prices up in the Contagion cities, and some of the initial decline in those specific places was truly a reversal of temporary price spikes. Even if the early losses in Phoenix were locally devastating, home values in Omaha didn't really need to decline. There were $5 trillion in net losses on residential real estate from 2007 to 2012, much of which may be attributable to the post-crisis crack down on lending.

And those losses were especially hard on households with lower incomes in affordable homes. In most cities, after 2007, affordable homes owned by households with lower incomes declined by more than 10 percent compared to more expensive homes owned by wealthier households.

Exactly which factors in the new mortgage regulatory framework are responsible for these extreme changes in prices? It is difficult to parse out from the web of regulatory mandates. And, the decision process for approval at the FHA, Fannie, and Freddie is not easily publicly reviewable information. Yet, these diverging trends in housing markets happened mainly in two steps that coincidentally fell after the GSEs were taken into conservatorship and after the passage of Dodd-Frank.

Direct action-reaction causality may be difficult to establish here, but one important piece of the conventional wisdom about what happened can surely be set aside. Whatever specifically caused the drop in low-tier home prices after mid-2010, it is highly unlikely that it was caused by the collapse of the subprime mortgage market three years earlier. If the connection of a nationwide low-tier price collapse to conservatorship and to regulations related to Dodd-Frank is merely plausible and not certain, it must still be said that it is *not* plausibly associated with the reversal of bubble-era activity.

In the timeline of events, the Occupy Wall Street movement rose up in September 2011, in the midst of the working-class real estate losses. By the time the movement had arisen, the collapse was well into its late phase. The protestors who were against speculative activity at the banks, "the one percent," the continuing foreclosure crisis, and wealth inequality were engaged in a war of friendly fire. The huge hit to working-class wealth happened when lending was shut off. Ironically, the deep damage caused by years of suppressed lending surely was one of the factors that compelled so many Americans to take to the streets to oppose bankers. By describing a mostly symbiotic relationship as if it could only be exploitative, Occupy Wall Street was a movement passionately engaged in denying working-class homeowners the primary functional solution they had needed—a banking sector able to lend to them as it had for decades.

At the other end of the spectrum was *CNBC* personality Rick Santelli, who is credited with starting the Tea Party movement with a rant on the floor of the Chicago Mercantile Exchange in February 2009. He opposed the new Obama administration's plan to modify mortgages in order to help homeowners avoid foreclosure.

The two ends of the political spectrum held diametrically opposed positions on the topic of how to deal with the aftermath of the housing bust. But they were in agreement in support of the policy decisions that had caused it—that there had been too much money, credit, and housing, and that the aftermath should provide *somebody* with their just deserts.

Henry Paulson sees the clampdown on the GSEs as a component of stabilization and prudence:

> Our decision to put Fannie and Freddie into conservatorship forestalled their collapse and prevented a wider financial system meltdown. Crucially, public backing for the GSEs from Treasury and the Federal Reserve ensured that affordable mortgage financing was available during the worst moments of the financial crisis and beyond. This would prove to be the government's most effective form of economic stimulus, helping to put a bottom on the sharp home-price declines that had so damaged the GSEs and were driving the country into a deep recession. Without such public support, I am convinced, the housing market would have ground to a halt for lack of financing, home prices would have continued their downward spiral, foreclosures would have skyrocketed, and financial institution balance sheets would have suffered much greater losses. All of this would have led to an even more prolonged downturn—and the additional loss of millions of jobs.[255]

Timothy Geithner, who took over at the Treasury during the Obama administration, echoes Paulson. "Even with unemployment rising and defaults increasing, home prices stabilized in mid-2009, and gradually began to rise in the following years. The end of the real estate slump helped avoid further damage to the typical family's largest source of wealth and savings, and was critical to restoring the economy to growth."[256]

But in many neighborhoods, the housing market *did* grind to a halt for lack of financing, home prices *did* spiral down, and foreclosures *did* sky-rocket *after* conservatorship, *because* the GSE mission under conservatorship excluded them.

The GSEs aren't the only source of mortgage funding. But the market for private loans faces many headwinds in reanimating itself, and regulators have formulated liabilities that banks and non-bank originators would take on if mortgages to borrowers with marginal credit go bad. Some of those liabilities are vague. Considering the large drop in prices across cities in the low-tier markets, it would seem that some supplier of credit should rise up to meet a tremendous amount of pent-up demand.[257] But the political, regulatory, and public relations risks faced by banks are preventing that from happening. Post-crisis regulations have contained a carve-out for banks. If Fannie, Freddie, or the FHA buy the mortgage, then it is a "Qualifying Mortgage," and the mortgage originator is protected from various punitive measures on mortgages that default. As a result, banks have originated very few loans that have any risk unless they could sell them to those agencies.

In addition to regulatory limits on lending, extra costs and underwriting requirements have been imposed on lenders while the fees they can charge to cover those expenses have been limited. These costs can especially make it difficult for small banks making small loans in the most affordable markets.[258] Several thousand dollars of additional fees and compliance costs can make a loan for a potential working-class borrower seeking a $100,000 mortgage infeasible.

More than 80 percent of bank failures came after the second quarter of 2009.[259] Mortgage markets for the bottom half of owner-occupiers (and thus demand for the bottom tier of the housing market), had been effectively shut down before most banks failed. Bank failures, just like most homeowner defaults, were a late result of a crippled market.

When a potential borrower who has marginal credit or who needs a smaller loan walks into a bank, the banker that would lend to them now faces a lot of regulatory costs. This has put many households in the strange position of living in homes where the rent is far higher than a mortgage payment would be. Buying the same home with a mortgage would lower their cost of living. This is not an issue of affordability. Yet, in the name of consumer protection, any mortgage that would facilitate that transaction is frequently either illegal or infeasible. The Consumer Financial Protection Bureau and GSE underwriters aren't in the business of declining rental applications. They are only in the business of declining mortgage applications.

AN INTERNATIONAL COMPARISON AND THE FALSE IDEA THAT THE BUST WAS INEVITABLE

The collapse in low-tier home values after 2007 wasn't inevitable or necessary. It didn't undo anything. It was the imposition of a credit shock that was highly focused on low-tier markets in cities of every type. This is clear by comparing low-tier prices to high-tier prices in every city, and it is also clear by comparing economic statistics in the US to those in other countries.

Since 2006, the United States has been the exception among countries like Canada, Australia, and the UK. Home prices and housing starts have collapsed in the US, but not in the others.

From the end of 2006 to the disastrous September 2008, unemployment in the US was already spiking up. It had risen nearly 2 percent already by then. Yet the other three countries remained near cyclical lows. Then, in September 2008, came the global shock, and unemployment spiked in all four countries. But even then, unemployment in the other countries rose only half as sharply as it did in the US.

Those countries had all the kindling for a housing contraction. By the end of 2008, they even had an economic downturn that might have triggered one. Yet declines were relatively brief, and since then their housing markets have generally had stable or rising prices and rates of new building similar to prerecession levels.[260]

The US was alone in experiencing a sharp decline in construction employment during the crisis. To this day, construction employment remains depressed in the US.[261] The drop in US construction activity was cheered. But do policymakers really believe that for more than a decade since 2007, Canada and Australia have been engaging in an unsustainable amount of building? Is their problem that they continued to build too many homes after 2007? If the US had an unsustainable expansion of housing in 2006, then imagine the oversupply these other "bubble" countries must have after another *decade* of construction at that pace. Surely, if the US had an oversupply of homes in 2006, there must be millions of vacant homes by now in Toronto, London, and Sydney.

In late-2007, we were becoming the international outlier. Stabilization by then might have turned the recession into just a bump in the road. But with each passing month and year that followed where capital losses, lower construction employment, and reduced investment were goals to be aimed for rather than problems to be solved, we turned a blip into a generation-defining disaster. This was a double-edged sword. Not only did working-class neighborhoods suffer the worst of the lost housing wealth, but two million construction workers were thrown out of work because potential young and working-class home buyers stopped buying new homes.

SUPPLY AND DEMAND IN THE BUBBLE AND BUST

It's important to carefully keep in mind the difference between consuming housing (an expenditure measured by rent) and owning a home (a capital allocation measured by price) when viewing the housing market after the crisis. There was a severe credit shock imposed on lower-tier housing markets. That was a shock on buyers (capital allocators), not a shock on tenants (consumers). The demand for shelter has not changed. The ability to be an owner has. This has caused rents to rise and prices to fall, especially in low-tier markets that have been most affected.

First, let's consider rent. As I have mentioned elsewhere, contrary to conventional wisdom, the rise in home ownership didn't come from lending to households with lower incomes. According to the Survey of Consumer Finances, the income of the median homeowner in 1995 was 105 percent higher than the income of the median renter. By 2007, it had *risen* to 122 percent higher than the median renter. In 2016, it was still about 125 percent higher.

From 1995 to 2004, rent increased from 21 percent to 23 percent of the average renter's income. By 2016, it had increased to more than 26 percent. Homeowners, on the other hand, were not moving into homes that had higher rental values relative to their incomes. The rental value of the average homeowner's home was about 15 percent of their income in 1995, 2004, and 2016. The past twenty-five years, in both boom and bust, have been characterized by renters getting squeezed, not by insatiable home buyers.

Any analysis that treats home ownership today as if there is an *affordability* problem that is made worse by access to credit or rising prices is simply wrong about what challenges have been inflicted on American families during this time. Certain cities need to allow more homes to be built, and Americans need to have the same tools they had for decades in order to fund the construction of those homes.

Since the housing market is now faced with a supply constraint that raises home prices where incomes are high and a credit market constraint that lowers prices where incomes are low, home building since the crisis has been much more strongly correlated with metropolitan-area incomes.

In the crisis, building slowed down everywhere. But it has only recovered in cities with high incomes. The rich cities—the Closed Access cities— have recovered to the pitifully low rate of building they were allowing in 2005. But most other cities have housing markets that have remained well below 2005 levels.[262]

In a lot of cities where incomes are moderate, where prices had never been extremely high, and where there was not an increase in the rate of home building before the crisis, the rate of building a decade later is still half what it was in 2005. Even in the rich, expensive cities where residential construction has recovered, it has been largely because of institutional multi-unit-building construction rather than a full recovery in the construction of single-family homes.

The same pattern shows up in the prices of new homes sold. The drop in new home building has been mostly in low-priced new homes. New homes selling for $300,000 or more are being built in quantities similar or higher than they were being built before the financial crisis. On the other hand, every year from 1999 to 2004, more than a half million new homes were sold for less than $200,000. In 2018, only seventy-two thousand were sold.[263]

The housing market before 2007 was ruled by supply. Where fewer homes were built, they were more expensive. The housing market since 2007 has been ruled by credit-regulated demand. Where families can't check on the right boxes to meet the new lending standards, fewer homes are built.

I have made many claims and cited a lot of evidence in this book, and the scale and importance of various facts can become lost in the haze. On this topic—the extreme tightening of mortgage credit after 2007—the scale of these effects is especially outrageous.

After a decade, all of these dislocations remain. The sale of new affordable homes under $200,000 dropped more than 80 percent from pre-crisis levels. The rate of new home construction in metropolitan areas with low and moderate incomes is still about half what it had been before the crisis. The average credit score on approved mortgages is forty points higher than pre-crisis norms. The average price of homes receiving new mortgages through Fannie Mae at one point were 60 percent higher than the prices of homes that were on their books from previous years and continue to be higher than the prices of homes that had previously received mortgages.

The scale of each of these measures is staggering. Had anyone thought to survey experts before the crisis about whether these sorts of shifts could ever happen, it is plausible that most would have said "no," or "very unlikely." The regulatory mortgage panic that hardly makes an appearance in memoirs of the crisis and its aftermath is one of the most noteworthy and damaging policy developments since the Great Depression. It's the elephant in the room.

More than a decade after the crisis, home prices are pushing past previous highs, even with tight lending, because a lack of adequate supply continues to push rents relentlessly higher. Loose lending played a role in our housing roller-coaster ride, but it wasn't the root cause of high housing costs.

Appreciating the role of tight supply and rising rents means that we can now say out loud that which previously seemed unspeakable. It's ok—it's imperative—to allow more generous lending again.

PART 6

Where Do We Go from Here?

CHAPTER 15

TURBO CHARGE THE RECOVERY FROM THE COVID-19 RECESSION

The outcome of the housing bust, the Great Recession, and the financial crisis has left the US with several problems of significant scope. None of those problems should have developed. We can reverse those problems. We have an arsenal of economic kinetic energy that can reverse some of the damage of the Covid-19 recession.

Curiously, the early recovery from Covid-19 has had some similarities to the last boom. A mass migration out of the Closed Access cities has created a housing boom in other cities across the country. Because of all the new fetters we have put on housing markets, surges in home prices have been happening even though construction rates of new homes are still much lower than they were before 2006. Unless construction increases, new economic growth will once again lead to rising rents and the stress of inadequate housing. Even more so than in the last boom, rising home prices are fundamentally being driven by a lack of adequate supply, not by rampant lending or speculation.

Because so many households are homeowners, and because homes are frequently owned with leverage, we tend to focus on the dangers of volatile prices and the financial gains of homeowners. But make no mistake. Those rising home prices are a measure of failure. Of distress. Of exclusivity in an asset and access to an essential human need that simply should not and does not have to be so bound up.

There is a ton of low-hanging fruit here: millions of jobs building desperately needed new homes, lower rents especially on properties with tenants who have lower incomes, and a continued rebuilding of household wealth especially for working class homeowners. I'm not talking about escaping the Covid-19 recession by pumping up a bubble. All of these outcomes would be sustainable. This would be the return to normalcy.

We are short millions of units of housing. Before the crisis, there were localized urban housing shortages. Now, we lack adequate housing nationwide. Vacancy rates for both rented and owned homes are at thirty-five-year lows and the trend is fairly uniform across all metropolitan areas.

We have created a new system of housing haves and have-nots, based on who can qualify for the new tight-lending standards. Since the crisis, new single-family homes have gotten larger while new apartments have gotten smaller.[264] Yet, at the same time, since the crisis, the average household of homeowners has fewer members while the average household of renters has more members.[265]

Rent inflation has been high, in general, since 1995. After the crisis, the market for entry-level homes dried up. These homes previously were a release valve where households on the margin between being renters or owners could control their own destinies, fund new homes, and in the process, help keep rents that landlords charge in check. According to inflation data from the BLS (the Bureau of Labor Statistics), rent inflation on rental properties has outpaced the rental value of owned properties by about 8 percent since 2005. Renters are getting squeezed because they're stuck.

Since 2015, rent paid by tenants has taken a higher percentage of American incomes every year than it ever has before—in data that goes back to 1929. This clearly isn't because we are building more housing than ever before. We have created an economy where owners collect royalties on exclusion.

The have-nots that can't be owners have to pay more and more rent for less and less apartment. Landlords keep the proceeds. From 2012 through 2019, inflation, in general, has averaged about 1.9 percent—roughly the Fed's stated target. But using core CPI inflation (consumer inflation without the noisy energy and food categories), that 1.9 percent average is the result of shelter inflation (mostly rent) of 3 percent and inflation on everything else of 1.1 percent. Before the Covid-19 pandemic, this led the Fed to raise interest rates in an attempt to slow down inflation.[266]

This isn't really a monetary issue. Half of the inflation since 2012 has just been an increase in the transfer we are making to homeowners and landlords each year as their properties become more valuable—not because their properties are becoming nicer, but because we have engineered a system where many Americans can't participate.

This has led to a number of articles about how Wall Street investors are turning the screws on hapless tenants.[267] This is the same mistake that was made regarding the CDO market. The idea that Wall Street is this economic powerhouse that can dictate what it wants to do is such a satisfying place-holder for an explanation of how the world works, that it keeps some critics from looking deeper. The idea that Wall Street could conjure up the CDO market as a self-serving, fee-generating machine prevented people from asking the deeper questions. Why this market? Why now? The answers to those questions were important. Investors were desperately seeking securities that seemed safe, and few were willing to take the risk of home equity. Similarly, the idea that Wall Street can buy up a large number of homes and raise rents precludes the deeper question of why those tenants don't go buy their own homes. There is no inherent reason that Wall Street should be able to outbid tenants for homes. Landlords have to put up with many costs that homeowners can avoid. The main advantage Wall Street has is access to funding.

The Closed Access housing problem needs to be solved, and that is a messy, political, long-term project. The post-crisis problem that we imposed on ourselves, on the other hand, could be solved immediately. Fannie Mae, Freddie Mac, and private lenders should be allowed, once again, to make appropriate mortgages to the borrowers who had successfully purchased homes for decades before the crisis. That doesn't mean that all the toxic products of the bubble need to return. Much of the damage to the American homeowner was inflicted by tightened lending at Fannie and Freddie after 2007 that had little to do with those products.

The scale of this change and its reach well into the pool of qualified borrowers has been staggering. Borrowers with credit scores above 760 borrowed 96 percent more in 2019 than they had in 2006. Borrowers with credit scores between 720 and 760 borrowed 58 percent *less*. The average credit score tends to be around 700. These are *above* average borrowers in a country where home ownership rates have been above 60 percent for *decades*, and many can't get funding. Compared to pre-crisis borrowing, the least-credit-constrained borrowers have more than quadrupled the level of borrowing of the merely above-average borrower.[268] And why wouldn't they? The many tenants who are trapped in rentals or are grandfathered into the homes they owned before the crisis can't gather the funds needed to bid up home *prices*, even though rents are rising. This means that the wealthiest borrowers can get mortgages with basement-level interest rates and buy nicer homes with smaller payments. It's a great time to be among the "haves."

This is why homebuilders hardly build any affordable homes. The families that would buy them can't get mortgages, and this has driven the price of existing homes below the cost of building new homes. The most effective way to bring rents down is to allow these borrowers back into the market so that builders can profitably build affordable homes.

In order to do that, we'll need to employ millions of workers in the task of making up for a lost decade in residential investment: more jobs, recovered working-class net worth, and lower rents. It's all there for the taking, but to take it, we have to eschew all the wrong lessons that have soiled the canon about what happened to the US economy in 2008.

One of the reasons that home building seemed overheated before the crisis is that construction employment was relatively high. Since World War II, construction employment has remained between about 4.5 percent and 5.5 percent of all jobs. It had moved to the top of that range during the housing boom, suggesting that a retreat would be a correction to norms. Construction employment then collapsed to a little more than 4 percent of all jobs and has rebounded back to about 5 percent. From peak to trough, about 2.3 million construction jobs were lost.

Canada and Australia also had high home prices in 2005 and their home prices have continued to climb. Their construction employment was high in 2005, and in both countries, it has either stayed high or climbed further since then. There is no reason to expect the proportion of American jobs that are in construction to remain flat. In some industries where productivity hasn't grown as much as in others, employment in those sectors sometimes will grow over time. Housing is a bit like education and healthcare in this way. Grade school education hasn't been automated like television manufacturing has, so as our consumption of both increases with our incomes, we can continue to make televisions with fewer workers, but grade schools require at least as many workers as before, because we expect more out of them just as we expect more from our televisions. Home building has not been automated, and so Canada and Australia are probably more apt examples of normal construction markets. Instead of losing 2.3 million construction jobs only to slowly regain them all over the following decade, construction growth could have continued to climb, even as a percentage of the total labor force. Especially considering that we have a decade's worth of depressed building activity to make up for, there is enough building to occupy millions of additional workers for a long time.

The key for immediate recovery is responsible lending to the sorts of families that could have purchased homes in the 1980s and 1990s, and who have been shut out since the crisis. The effect of the lending crackdown on home ownership has been striking. The year 1994 had been the lowest point in home ownership rates among all age groups under sixty-five since the early 1980s, when the Census Bureau had started tracking home ownership annually by age. By 2016, home ownership rates for all age groups under sixty-five were several percentage points below that previous trough. By 2019, the youngest group had recovered somewhat, but still owned homes at a lower rate than they had in 1994.

For the forty-five to fifty-four age group, from 1982 to 2005, the home ownership rate had tracked a very tight range between 74.8 percent and 77.4 percent. At the end of 2019, it was still well below that range at 70.1 percent.[269] Millions of households that would have been homeowners for generations have been shut out. A building boom of the affordable homes that we haven't built for a decade is there for the taking, but the families that would buy them need mortgages.

Apartments and other multi-unit construction can't make up the difference, probably mostly due to local regulatory hurdles. Since the late 1980s, there just seems to be a hard lid on apartment construction at about four-hundred thousand units per year. This is a long-term problem that needs to be addressed. In the meantime, apartment construction can't make up the difference from the loss of affordable single-family homes.

What we haven't been building are *affordable* homes for homeowners. In order to do that, we simply have to get out of our own way. If we do, benefits will flow in many directions. Millions of new jobs, millions of new homeowners, lower rents for those who remain renters, and a recovery of wealth for the homeowners that have weathered a decade of suppressed demand in affordable neighborhoods. The true return to normalcy and broadly shared economic abundance, growth, and self-sufficiency awaits us if only we choose to allow it.

After having this viral force of nature thrust upon us, at least we can take solace that we have control over our economic recovery from it. Much of that recovery simply entails returning to norms of lending and building that worked for decades. We simply need to do, again, what we know how to do.

CHAPTER 16

CONSIDERATIONS FOR THE LONG TERM

Maybe this prescription seems dangerous. I mean, after all, even if my contention is correct, and we were suffering from a shortage of housing all along, it still led to financial upheaval. What if we loosen up mortgage markets again, and it triggers another migration surge out of the Closed Access cities and another bubble?

All three legs of the stool need to be in place to avoid economic dislocation: ample availability of shelter, broad access to the potential value of ownership, and a stable economy in which to pursue those ends. If America starts building two million units a year and letting a robust mortgage market flourish, an eye needs to be kept on all three legs.

There are some important steps we can take to avoid the same turn of events. Policy issues can be placed in four broad categories. Here, I will review those categories in order of how immediately they can be implemented:

LEND

Extreme shifts in lending standards have created housing haves and have-nots, so that rental costs are rising for households in entry-level markets who are prevented from becoming owners. That is the most important and vital short-term issue that must be corrected in order to create broadly abundant and affordable shelter again.

It is important to differentiate between the three phases of changing lending standards over the past twenty-five years.

From 1994 to 2004, home ownership rates increased substantially, but home ownership rates for working-age households were not higher than they had been in the early 1980s. Borrower characteristics don't appear to have changed much. If anything, lenders, including the GSEs, were using technology to better match mortgages with qualified borrowers. The rise in home ownership was largely among young professionals with college degrees. These cohorts of mortgages didn't have particularly high default rates.

From 2003 to 2007, a variety of new mortgages gained market share that had terms and investment structures that were destabilizing. These mortgages seemed to favor speculators, home flippers, and other short-term oriented buyers more than other mortgage products do. The early mortgages of this type happened during the last spike of migration out of the Closed Access cities. The later mortgages of this type were associated with high default rates in the Contagion cities.

After 2007, credit standards were severely tightened across the board through federal mortgage agencies and regulation of private lenders. This is most clearly visible in the very large shift in the average borrower's credit score. This was an imposition of a new type of credit suppression. Even Ben Bernanke reported being turned down for a mortgage in 2014 after he left the Federal Reserve.[270]

The changes after 2007 simply need to be reversed. Rules and mandates need to be relaxed until they are associated with an average credit score on originated mortgages that is back at pre-crisis norms.

The reintroduction of the types of products that became popular from 2003 to 2007 should be pursued with caution. Those were the products that created havoc. That being said, they mostly wreaked havoc because of the context created by policy failures such as the lack of appropriate housing supply in key cities. One way to think about this is that if all the other policy levers created a stable context, these products might not lead to instability, but they require getting the other things right. That is in contrast to reversing the extreme tightening of lending that happened after 2007. That change would be safe in practically any policy context, and, in fact, will likely make most economic contexts more stable.

The lending activity from 1994 to 2004 has generally been associated with instability because rising Closed Access rents were causing American home prices to increase at the same time. When everything came crashing down, and it was generally blamed on excessive demand, lending in that period was also blamed. There is little reason to fear the lending systems that had helped pull home ownership up to 69 percent in 2004. We shouldn't blindly reimplement every scheme for lending that had ever been tried, but the burden of proof should be flipped. The lending from that period should be treated as benign unless proven otherwise, rather than treated as an inevitable building block to a crisis that happened years later.

Keep in mind the two Americas, though. More generous mortgage lending will mostly be for the good in the cities that have or could have ample housing. But where rents and prices are high because of a lack of supply, any source of demand for housing is stress inducing.

Closed Access begins with exclusion. Until that exclusion is eliminated, policy choices mostly can only change how the gains and losses of that exclusion are dispensed. The high rents on Closed Access housing are oligopoly profits. Those homes are worth more than it should cost to replace them because there aren't enough of them. What they cost, who gets to own them, who gets to live in them—all of those questions have political answers that create tension about who claims that excess value. That will be the case until supply is no longer so constrained, whether lending is loose or tight.

Suppressing lending in the Closed Access markets might help maintain stability, but it has tradeoffs. First, even though the pre-crisis activity was destabilizing for many reasons—higher household debt, a migration spike, volatile prices, and so forth—the fact of the matter is that higher prices and more active lending markets were associated with more housing production in the Closed Access cities. The largest problem in those cities is a lack of housing, and higher prices were associated with more building. It also moved a lot of homeowners out of the Closed Access cities to make room for newcomers.

More generous lending in the Closed Access markets must be more carefully balanced for stability. But if those housing markets are suppressed for the sake of stability, it will come at some other cost.

STABILIZE

Federal Reserve and other central banks appear to be increasingly open to targeting nominal GDP (NGDP) growth instead of targeting inflation and unemployment. Economists that support this approach argue that it is a better tool for minimizing disruptive business cycles. A steady growth of incomes, in dollar terms, is a much better way to minimize cyclical spikes in unemployment and debt defaults than targeting an inflation rate. It is likely that NGDP targeting would have led to more Fed stimulus by 2007 and less chaos in 2008.[271]

Additionally, NGDP targeting would improve the horrible communication tools the Fed uses now. Under the current framework, they imply that they have control over interest rates, which they do not have. When the economy needs a monetary boost, they convey that action as a process of raising prices, which is not politically popular. And they create a never-ending debate between hawks and doves about whether they should slow down the economy or speed it up—whether the economy is "too hot" or not.

In addition to targeting a more useful measure—total dollar incomes—NGDP targeting improves the way monetary policy would be communicated. All the endless debates about whether rising wages cause inflation or not, whether low interest rates are boosting asset prices, what the appropriate unemployment rate is—on and on the debates go—would no longer be tempting.

The answer to all those questions would be the same under an NGDP growth targeting rule. American incomes next year will total 5 percent more dollars than they totaled this year.[272] Are interest rates too low? The answer is these must be the rates that are associated with stable 5 percent growth.

That may be the best part of a NGDP targeting policy. It requires no debate between hawks and doves. The reason there is so much debate now is that the tools and communication devices used now are so imperfect that FOMC members must frequently depend on a large amount of discretion. But if the goal is always and everywhere a 5 percent nominal growth rate, then the goal of the Fed isn't growth versus "pulling away the punch bowl." It is always and everywhere, stability.

This would have greatly simplified Fed actions in 2008. Most of the actions that I have argued were mistakes were the result of the discretion that FOMC members had to depend on because their tools were so imperfect. (Consider their inflation-targeting policy. On the eve of the September 2008 economic collapse, the FOMC was expecting to raise interest rates soon to counteract rising inflation. If they had put more emphasis on market signals of future inflation expectations, they would have voted for more stimulative policy. But the reason forward inflation expectations were collapsing was because forward NGDP growth expectations were collapsing. GDP growth—or, more simply, income growth—is the more straightforward approach.)

NGDP targeting can't fix every problem. It can't get rid of the differences in per capita income that are maintained by housing exclusion. An economy with strong and steady growth may lead to increasing migration pressures into and out of the housing-deprived cities. But it would level out growth and it would diminish the morality-based discretion that led so many FOMC members and critics to associate calamity with character. It is plausible that NGDP targeting would have avoided the excesses on both ends—the extra growth that was associated with the migration surge into the Contagion cities and the steep spending decline in 2008 that precipitated the crisis.

On this and many other issues, it is important to recognize that Closed Access housing makes all good things seem bad. In the Closed Access cities, residents even sometimes complain about local corporate expansion that will bring high-paying jobs because it will just lead to rising rents.[273] If you live in a city that hasn't tied its housing market up in knots, that would be a really odd thing to see. People in some cities really do oppose the local creation of good jobs. That's how screwed up housing has us. Good things can't happen because the populations of those cities are effectively capped. Only tradeoffs can happen. If good things happen to some people, that means other people must pay higher rent or move away.

I would argue that the obsession with monetary policy and asset bubbles that has continued since the crisis is a misdirected version of this pathology. Federal Reserve board members and their critics frequently fret that low-interest rates, or high growth, or stability can be dangerous because it leads to asset bubbles. This is just a subset of "Closed Access makes all good things seem bad." Closed Access makes economic growth seem bad. Where it is at all possible, we should not let this problem lead us to avoid doing good things. Certainly, a strong, stable economy and high-paying jobs are among the things we shouldn't avoid. It is a sign of the damage Closed Access has done to us that this even needs to be a conversation.

TAX

One way that the volatility induced by Closed Access can be targeted is through a more equitable tax policy. This can happen at the federal level through the income tax code and at the state and local level through property taxes.

Income tax benefits to homeowners are highly regressive. This includes the deduction for mortgage interest, and also the fact that homeowners don't claim the rental value of their homes as taxable income. Because of these issues, if two neighbors swapped homes and rented from each other, they would pay more income taxes than they do as homeowners. Tax policy benefits homeowners more than renters, and is highly skewed toward very wealthy mortgage borrowers with expensive homes. The 2017 tax update took steps to reduce this problem. The new tax code limits the tax deductions for wealthy homeowners.

In cities where the rental value of homes is already well above what it should be, those tax benefits just make home ownership more valuable, driving up home prices even further. Income tax benefits to homeowners are destabilizing and worsen income and wealth inequality.

Property taxes can make housing markets more stable. Property taxes are sort of like having the local government as a silent partner in your real estate ownership. If the net rental value of a home after expenses is about 5 percent of its market price, and the local property tax amounts to about 1 percent of its price, then the local government is, effectively, a 20 percent silent owner of the property. However, if things like changing interest rates or supply constraints cause price/rent ratios to rise, as they have, then the rental value becomes a smaller portion of the price. So, maybe, after a price increase, the annual rental value would only be 4 percent of the market price. In that case, taking its 1 percent tax means that the local government is now a 25 percent silent owner.

By capturing some of the changing values of properties for local and public expenditures, property taxes can have a dampening effect on price volatility. And to the extent that someone would have concerns that Americans might overinvest in real estate, taxing it is the most direct way of limiting that investment. Property taxes might be a bit regressive because families with lower incomes tend to spend more of their incomes on housing. But since property taxes are based on home prices, they aren't as regressive as you might think. Price/rent ratios are generally much lower in neighborhoods with low incomes than in neighborhoods with high incomes. In most cities, the prices of homes compared to the incomes of their tenants aren't as acutely different as you might think. And, as a mechanism for moderating price volatility, it's certainly less regressive than the class- and income-based barriers to mortgage lending that we currently have enacted out of fear of stoking a housing bubble. As with any policy, the devil is in the details, and the revenues from property taxes and the expenditures they fund both must be designed with care. Yet, especially if you are worried about volatile housing markets, a healthy and equitable property tax can be a hardy source of local, public capital that both helps fund infrastructure for growing the housing stock and stabilizes home prices.

According to BEA data, property taxes have generally been declining since the 1970s, relative to home prices and rents.[274] The Closed Access cities seem to especially have low and inequitable property taxes. California's Proposition 13 limits tax increases so that homes with similar values frequently pay vastly different property tax rates. This was one reason that the price surge was so strong there. Existing owners are incentivized to stay in their homes because as long as they don't sell them, they can live in very expensive homes with very low tax bills.

At the federal level, some presidential candidates have spoken in favor of wealth taxes. Many wealth taxes pose difficulties in terms of their practicality and their secondary effects on the economy. But the United States has a long history of collecting property taxes effectively. There is a lot of local work that could be done in the Closed Access markets in Boston, New York, Los Angeles, and San Francisco to make the wealth tax that we know can work, work better. In those cities, property taxes are basically a wealth tax on oligarchy. The 2017 tax law (the TCJA) limited the deductibility of property taxes on federal income tax. Reducing that deduction is a tax hike on Closed Access housing oligarchy and was probably a step in the right direction.

BUILD

Solving the local supply problem is the most important issue, but also the most difficult. This will have to be a very long-term project. Fortunately, lately, a burgeoning YIMBY (yes, in my backyard) movement has been rising up to meet the NIMBY (not in my backyard) movement that has created the supply problem.

Expanding housing in Closed Access cities to allow aspirational migration instead of a bidding war and a refugee crisis would have tremendous positive effects on equitable, shared economic growth. This is a difficult political problem that is beyond the scope of this book. Salim Furth and

Emily Hamilton with the Urbanity Project at the Mercatus Center are among the many researchers and advocates who add more value than I can to the discussion of the nuts and bolts of how to affect change in your city.

In a nutshell, the key issue is that cities are living, changing systems. Phoenix makes a good example of this because it has grown so persistently that within a single lifetime, there are homes which were built as greenfield suburban tracts that are now considered adjacent to the central business district. Those neighborhoods were fitting for a city of 500,000 decades ago, but now, it is fitting for downtown Phoenix to host high-rise condo buildings and for most of the surrounding neighborhoods to be filled with duplexes, triplexes, and apartment buildings. In many places, new, more dense housing is either illegal or very difficult to get approved, and this sort of change can't happen.

Innumerable changes happen over the life of a city. Those changes happen naturally. They are pervasive. We can't stop most of them. Homes naturally depreciate. Unless economic and social conditions encourage continual maintenance and upgrading, neighborhoods change even when their residents passively do nothing to affect that change. Sometimes, conditions can become bad enough that units become vacant or condemned. We can't pass a law against depreciation. That is just the natural course of the life of a physical asset.

Sometimes, local demographics change. New residents might have incomes that are higher or lower than the original residents. They may have different types of jobs, be from different ethnic groups, or have different educational backgrounds. New residents can be economically better off or worse off than the original residents. These changes frequently cause social discord. Change is challenging. Yet, again, it is difficult to pass laws to stop this. In fact, laws meant to prevent this can easily become, and frequently have been, basic violations of civil rights.

In all these cases, change is hard. Change creates social friction. But cities must change to match their present socio-economic reality. Cities regularly do stop one type of change—the development of new, more dense housing fitting for a growing city—simply because it is politically possible to stop this sort of change. So, simply because of political expediency, the one type of change that is regularly blocked is the change that accommodates growth and access. The other types of change continue. As a result, our cities are becoming segregated into places in decline and places that are inaccessible and unaffordable. We simply have to find a way for municipal political norms to allow housing growth to be common again. The political path is a complex one, but the end goal is clear.

Recently, even in California, there has been a push at the state level to limit the ways that cities can block new construction, but there are countless bureaucratic mechanisms at the municipality level that will have to be dismantled or streamlined in order for those cities to allow healthy growth again.

WE DIDN'T BUILD THAT

In summary, the housing bubble was created with exclusion, and we have answered it by creating more exclusion and economic uncertainty. Instead, generous means of access to ownership, stable economic conditions, fair taxes, and a commitment to allow more building in our richest cities are the keys to a new century of shared prosperity.

There is a phrase you hear from time to time that markets can be fine, but that we have to protect ourselves from *unfettered* markets. You don't hear about fetters much anymore in other contexts. Fetters are chains or manacles usually put on the wrists or ankles of prisoners or slaves.

We have put fetters on our economy. We know how to build homes affordably, but if you take that knowledge to Los Angeles, the bureaucrats there will place you in fetters. When a tenant goes to the bank to see if they can get a mortgage to lower their housing costs and have more control over their housing, a bureaucrat from the Consumer Financial Protection Bureau will meet them and their bankers at the door and put fetters on them. We are all limping around with fetters on. If you see workers at a construction site in a Closed Access city, imagine them chained at the ankle to a lawyer that they must drag around with them while they hammer together two-by-fours. That is what makes houses expensive there.

On these issues, one can see how a society can devolve—how we can actually, collectively forget how to do things. At a very basic level, capital, and the well-being it creates, depends on fundamental behavioral developments. Broad social trust. The ability to do and build things without seeking permission. The freedom to keep a significant portion of the fruits of your labor and your innovation. Human community has evolved to be capable of these things, but they are not inherent values. Pre-capitalist societies were saddled with many subtle norms that prevented innovation from happening: The notion that being a merchant or a financier was demeaning. The expectation that any unspent wealth would be shared broadly with extended family. A lack of social trust beyond extended family to engage in long-term contracts.[275]

Of course, the broad social trust that allows us to coordinate with so many strangers in economic activity has downsides, too. But on net, the development of the norms that allow it is a bit of a miracle. This abundance is not natural and must be continually cultivated and protected, even while we attempt to ameliorate the downsides and create new sharing norms and new forms of social and financial protection.[276]

In the 2012 presidential campaign, President Obama created a bit of a stir when he said, "If you were successful, somebody along the line gave you some help. There was a great teacher somewhere in your life. Somebody helped to create this unbelievable American system that we have that allowed you to thrive. Somebody invested in roads and bridges. If you've got a business, *you didn't build that.* Somebody else made that happen."[277]

Fundamentally, he was absolutely right. We are all in this together. The economy is a system of coordination, much of it publicly created. The value of everything is tied to everything else. Norms of permission and sharing need to account for that.

Yet, just as "unfettered" capitalism needs to sometimes be tempered, so do norms of social control. In housing, very clearly, we can see the effects of letting those norms become too strong. In the Closed Access cities especially, we have regressed. We have lost some of our miracle. In New York City and Los Angeles, millions of working-class families have been forced away. Millions of others live in subpar housing. Lending regulations since the crisis have expanded this problem out into many other parts of the country. A bureaucratic web of mandates, bans, and permission requirements has placed us in fetters, preventing a massive boom in residential investment which would shower us in shared prosperity and financial relief. President Obama issued his admonition to a country that already frequently makes it literally true. "No, you won't build that," rings daily from municipal daises across the country.

TRUST AND ABUNDANCE: THE CHICKEN AND THE EGG PROBLEM

One of the mysteries of the capitalist miracle is that trust and abundance are inextricably linked. We must have a baseline level of trust among strangers to engage in the complex systems of contract and cooperation that create economic abundance. Yet, it is very difficult to establish trust among strangers when we are in a state of need and deprivation. This is why developed, affluent economies are a bit of a miracle. We have them, but we really don't know how to create them. It's hard to establish trust without a broadly shared sense of economic well-being, and it's hard to establish a shared sense of economic well-being without a broad sense of trust.

Knotted up housing markets may have an even more important effect on communal trust than they have on our pocketbooks. In the chapters above, I highlighted how moral indignation motivated many of the policy preferences that intensified the financial crisis and slowed the recovery from it.

Retrospectives about the boom and the crisis detail the players. Their flaws. The things they did wrong that brought this catastrophe upon us. It seemed like we had a crisis because the country was full of people who couldn't be trusted. Documentaries have titles like *Inside Job* and *American Casino*. Books have titles like *All the Devils Are Here*.

This sense goes much deeper and broader than the major players in the crisis. The documentary *Owned: A Tale of Two Americas* highlights the two extremes of the US housing crisis. It seems that, in the end, there are no winners. There are neighborhoods dealing with decline and struggle, frequently related to a history of racism and classism. There are also neighborhoods not burdened with those problems, but those neighborhoods instead seem to be burdened with price bubbles and affordability problems. High prices in the affluent neighborhoods are generally attributed to loose lending and short-sighted speculation. In *Owned*, Yale finance professor Robert Shiller explains the "Greater Fool" theory. Buyers pay extravagant prices for homes, not because they think they are intrinsically worth that but because they assume that an even greater fool will eventually pay them more.

What leads to this idea of the "Greater Fool"? It is because there is no reasonable benchmark for a moral price on a home in a Closed Access market. In most cities, the price of an existing home will be in the ballpark of what it would cost for the lumber, concrete, and labor to construct a similar home on an empty lot down the road. That gives us a sense of reasonableness. But, in a city like Los Angeles, a house that should cost $200,000 to build might sell for $1,000,000.

If you need to live in Los Angeles, you are faced with an unfair dilemma. Should you pay a million dollars for a $200,000 home? You have little choice. But you feel like a fool for doing it. And, it seems, the reason you are put in this terrible situation is because Los Angeles is filled with even greater fools who keep offering more for homes that shouldn't be worth that much. And, all of them are enabled by fee-hungry lenders getting rich off of this whole dance. It seems like you have to pay an embarrassing price for a home because the city is full of fools and scammers.

That perception is mistaken. Residents in Los Angeles aren't more foolish than residents in Houston or St. Louis. "Fools" aren't why prices are high. People in Los Angeles have been deprived of adequate housing, and they are simply trying to deal with it. It is true that prices are unmoored from what a reasonable cost should be. It is true that prices are more sensitive to forces of demand, like lending standards. But those things are only true because Los Angeles is deprived.

This is a window into the anthropological paradox of trust and abundance. Greater Los Angeles has chosen to deprive itself of abundant housing, and you can see a direct connection between that loss of abundance and the loss of communal trust. As Tim Geithner said, "Panics make everyone look feckless." We have chosen deprivation, and as a result, we have become convinced that our country is full of grifters and dupes. We are eroding essential trust.

In the Closed Access cities, where the housing problem is the worst, literally anything can cause social friction. Locals debate the value of bringing high-paying jobs to the city. People who find opportunity in those cities are scolded as gentrifiers. These reactions really shouldn't be—and don't have to be—normal. In a city that allows ample housing construction, it would be absurd to be angry about some growing industry bringing in high-paying jobs.

One example of this odd duality is the local attitude toward vacant units. The Closed Access cities tend to have very low vacancies in total. But frequently Closed Access residents complain about wealthy outsiders who buy pied-à-terre in prime locations which sit empty most of the year. This seems like a travesty. Units sitting empty while many families can't find a home. It causes anger.

But the problem isn't the vacant unit. The problem is the shortage of other units. The problem is that builders aren't allowed to just build more units in those cities for all types of tenants. Consider other cities that aren't so deprived of housing. Hundreds of thousands of "snowbirds" come to Phoenix each winter from the Pacific Northwest, the Midwest, and Canada. Whole sections of the city are full of seasonally empty homes. Since the Phoenix housing market is not yet tied up into political knots, we are free to welcome our part-time neighbors. Our economy depends on them. It would be absurd of us to, say, impose a vacancy tax, so that they sell their homes to full-time residents and stop coming here. We don't have to be angry because we have not consigned ourselves to a state of deprivation.

There is a lot of anger in this country. There doesn't have to be. We have chosen this path.

There are many avenues for providing adequate urban housing. The family building a backyard rental unit or a unit for their elderly parents. The builder replacing the corner home near a rail station with a six-unit apartment building. The developer putting up the forty-story downtown condo building. They are doing us a favor by deepening the stock of residential capital, yet we have burdened all of them with increasing demands to earn the permission to build.

There are sometimes mitigating factors that may be cause for limiting these developments, but those limits should be the exception rather than the rule. If the opposition to building can become the exception, then we can stop being so angry. We can stop worrying about the next boom and bust. We can stop fuming that the prices on new units are too high for regular working people. We can stop fretting about the devils and the grifters and the dupes. We can stop feeling like fools. We can stop feeling hateful about part-time residents, the families that move to our cities for opportunities, the corporations that determined the location of those opportunities, and the bankers that provided the mortgages. Good things can just be good. Progress can make our cities better and more welcoming rather than simply making them more expensive if we embrace the right to build again.

If we allow abundant building, we can regain the trust that is the magic ingredient in a healthy economy. We would be foolish not to.

ACKNOWLEDGMENTS

The road from idea to research to published manuscript is a long one. At least it is for me. And I briefly want to highlight some help I received from many along the way. Much of that help has been facilitated by the Mercatus Center at George Mason University. I owe thanks to Tyler Cowen, Daniel Rothschild, Eileen Norcross, and Brian Knight for supporting my research even though it is a broad and idiosyncratic project that is difficult to classify.

John Paine, the developmental editor for my first book, *Shut Out*, provided early editorial support again on this manuscript. The narrative structure has changed dramatically from my early drafts, and John's assistance was important in setting me on a good path. Michael Kelley and Austin Fairbanks helped to compile data from various public sources, which has been crucial for continuing to deepen my empirical confirmation of these ideas.

Garrett Brown, the Director of Publications at Mercatus, has been both an indispensable moral and professional support.

Several Mercatus colleagues provided helpful editing input. Scott Sumner has been an inspiration and a writing partner as I have developed the various aspects of this work, and he also provided important feedback on this manuscript. Tracy Miller, Salim Furth, and Emily Hamilton have also provided a lot of valuable input at many points along the way on this specific manuscript as well as on various related research projects that have contributed to the evolution of these ideas.

I want to reserve a special thanks for Stephen Miller, who has engaged deeply with the text, especially on topics like banking regulation and the CDO market. There is an old cliché about how great jazz music comes from the notes that aren't played. You should feel at least as much gratitude toward Steph as I do, because, in addition to the many challenges and corrections that he suggested, which I have attempted to address adequately in the final text, there are surely dozens of pages of unnecessary disquisition which you didn't have to schlep through because Steph's input made me think hard about which elements of the story were crucial and important, and which were not.

Finally, thanks to Krista Mitchell, for coming up with the title and for helping me communicate some complex ideas.

ABOUT THE AUTHOR

Photo by Marie South at South Photography

Kevin Erdmann is the author of *Shut Out: How a Housing Shortage Caused the Great Recession and Crippled Our Economy.* His work has appeared in the *Wall Street Journal*, the *National Review*, US News, Politico, on C-SPAN, and at the Mercatus Center.

ENDNOTES

1   "Santelli's Tea Party Rant, February 19, 2009," CNBC, February 6, 2015, https://www.cnbc.com/video/2015/02/06/santellis-tea-party-rant-february-19-2009.html.

2   You might think an assertion like this on such an important topic would need to overturn a large quantity of existing literature. But even though there are thousands of papers and books on the crisis, on lending, and on home prices, there is scant research on the state of housing supply. One study sometimes cited: Andrew Haughwout et al., *The Supply Side of the Housing Boom and Bust of the 2000s* (Staff Report No. 556, Federal Reserve Bank of New York, March 2012), https://www.newyorkfed.org/medialibrary/media/research/staff_reports/sr556.pdf. The paper's introduction includes the uncited statement: "While it is now clear that too much housing was built in the US in the boom phase, identifying how much and where overbuilding occurred remain important issues." The idea of oversupply became the consensus view with very little effort toward confirmation. I have attempted to remedy the lack of attention to this question in *Shut Out* and the following work:

Kevin Erdmann, *Housing Was Undersupplied during the Great Housing Bubble* (Arlington, VA: The Mercatus Center at George Mason University, April 10, 2018), https://www.mercatus.org/publications/monetary-policy/housing-was-undersupplied-during-great-housing-bubble; Scott Sumner and Kevin Erdmann, *Housing Policy, Monetary Policy, and the Great Recession* (Mercatus

Research Series, Arlington, VA: The Mercatus Center at George Mason University, August 4, 2020), https://ssrn.com/abstract=3667309 or http://dx.doi.org/10.2139/ssrn.3667309; and Kevin Erdmann, *Build More Houses: How an Incorrect Perception of Housing Supply Fueled the Great Recession and Slowed Recovery* (Mercatus Research Series, Arlington, VA: The Mercatus Center at George Mason University, May 3, 2021), https://ssrn.com/abstract=3840450.

3   Bureau of Economic Analysis, "National Data: National Income and Product Accounts: Section 1 – Domestic Product and Income: Table 1.5.3. Real Gross Domestic Product, Expanded Detail, Quantity Indexes," https://www.bea.gov/iTable/iTable.cfm?reqid=19&step=2#reqid=19&step=2&isuri=1&1921=survey. Data were retrieved using the "Housing and Utilities" category.

The gross level of residential investment as a percentage of GDP briefly rose to a level higher than normal during the boom. That statistic is frequently cited as evidence of overbuilding. However, much of the unusual spending in that category was from commissions to real estate brokers, which the BEA includes in the gross measure. Gross residential investment in structures (which doesn't include realtor commissions) was never unusually high. And net investment in structures, after accounting for the depreciation of the existing stock of homes, was lower in 2005, as a percentage of GDP, than it had been in most years between the Great Depression and 1980.

A more straightforward measure is the BEA's estimate of real expenditures on housing, which have been growing more slowly than real incomes for forty years. Robert Shiller noted the lack of growth in real housing expenditures in:

Robert J. Shiller, "Understanding Recent Trends in House Prices and Homeownership," (NBER Working Paper No.w13553, National Bureau of Economic Research, 2007), 89–123, https://www.kansascityfed.org/documents/3224/pdf-Shiller_0415.pdf.

Trends in real housing expenditures track closely with the long-term trends in residential investment, after deducting brokers' commissions and depreciation.

4   Bureau of Economic Analysis, "National Data: National Income and Product Accounts: Section 2 – Personal Income and Outlays: Table 2.5.3. Real Personal

Consumption Expenditures by Function, Quantity Indexes: Line 1 and 19," https://apps.bea.gov/iTable/iTable.cfm?reqid=19&step=2#reqid=19&step=2&isuri=1&1921=survey.

The housing measure is the rental value of all residences, adjusted for rent inflation, which is an estimate in the change of the size, amenities, and quality of the aggregate housing stock.

5 Here, and in general when I refer to rent, I am not referring to a specific transaction where a tenant makes a monetary payment to a landlord. I am referring to the rental value of all homes, both rented and owner-occupied. This may seem odd at first, if you aren't used to thinking of housing in this way, but for the most part, the reason a homeowner has to pay more for a house is that the house has higher rental value.

6 As a point of clarification, anywhere in the text where I refer to a "city," it will usually refer to the metropolitan area rather than to the specific municipal city.

7 For examples of recent research documenting the effect that new housing has on the affordability of existing housing, see:

Liyi Liu, Douglas A. McManus, and Elias Yannopoulos, *Geographic and Temporal Variation in Housing Filtering Rates* (January 27, 2020). https://ssrn.com/abstract=3527800 or http://dx.doi.org/10.2139/ssrn.3527800; Stuart S. Rosenthal, "Are Private Markets and Filtering a Viable Source of Low-Income Housing? Estimates from a "Repeat Income" Model," *American Economic Review*, 104, no. 2 (Feb 2014): 687–706; and Evan Mast, "The Effect of New Market-Rate Housing Construction on the Low-Income Housing Market," (Upjohn Institute Working Paper, Kalamazoo, MI: W.E. Upjohn Institute for Employment Research, 2019), 19-307, https://doi.org/10.17848/wp19-307.

8 According to the Survey of Consumer Finances, conducted every three years by the Federal Reserve, the income of the median homeowner in 1995 was about $59,000 and increased to $72,000 by 2007. The income of the median renter only increased from about $29,000 to $32,000. When homeownership was increasing, new owners were mostly families with the highest incomes. Board

of Governors of the Federal Reserve System, "Survey of Consumer Finances: Table 1," (2019), https://www.federalreserve.gov/econres/scfindex.htm.

For an overview of the debate in defense of the central role of the supply of credit, see: Atif Mian and Amir Sufi, "Household Debt and Defaults from 2000 to 2010: The Credit Supply View," (Kreisman Working Papers Series in Housing and Law Policy No. 28, Chicago: University of Chicago Law School, June 2016), https://ssrn.com/abstract=2606683 or http://dx.doi.org/10.2139/ssrn.2606683.

Examples of research that don't find a significant downward shift in borrower characteristics during the peak boom years include:

Gene Amromin and Anna Paulson, "Default rates on prime and subprime mortgages: differences and similarities," *Profitwise News and Views,* September 2010, Figure 1A & 1B, https://www.chicagofed.org/publications/profitwise-news-and-views/2010/pnv-september2010;   Manuel Adelino, Antoinette Schoar, and Felipe Severino, "Loan Originations and Defaults in the Mortgage Crisis: The Role of the Middle Class," (Tuck School of Business Working Paper No. 2546427, Duke I&E Research Paper No. 15-8, March 2016), http://papers.ssrn.com/sol3/papers.cfm?abstract_id=2546427; Christopher L. Foote, Lara Loewenstein, and Paul Willen, "Cross-Sectional Patterns of Mortgage Debt During the Housing Boom: Evidence and Implications," (NBER Working Paper No. w22985, National Bureau of Economic Research, 2016), https://ssrn.com/abstract=2890109; and Stefania Albanesi, Giacomo De Giorgi, and Jaromir Nosal, "Credit Growth and the Financial Crisis: A New Narrative," (NBER Working Paper No. w23740, National Bureau of Economic Research, August 2017), http://www.nber.org/papers/w23740.

9   Kevin Erdmann, *Shut Out* (London: Rowman & Littlefield, 2019).

10   Mortgage-backed securities are created by originating a large number of mortgages, pooling the cash flows from those mortgages, and selling bonds with various claims on those cash flows. Collateralized debt obligations are created in a similar fashion, using a number of different types of collateral. In this context, mortgage-backed securities were used as collateral for CDOs. Then, as the number of available new mortgages and MBSs to use for collateral declined,

CDOs were recombined to make new CDOs, or credit default swaps (CDSs) were used to mimic the cash flows of MBSs and CDOs where investors funded either the long or the short side of the securities and promised to make or accept payments based on the value of other securities. I will go into a little more detail in chapter 11.

11   Here is an example from Dean Baker, senior economist at The Center for Economic and Policy Research (CEPR), "[T]he housing bubble and its impact on the economy was easy to see. We saw an unprecedented run up in house prices, with no remotely corresponding increase in rents. Vacancy rates were hitting record highs." Dean Baker, "It Was Not 'Flaws in the U.S. Financial System' that Caused the Great Recession, It Was the Collapse of the Housing Bubble," *Beat the Press* (blog), *Center for Economic and Policy Research,* September 7, 2020, https://cepr.net/it-was-not-flaws-in-the-u-s-financial-system-that-caused-the-great-recession-it-was-the-collapse-of-the-housing-bubble/.

This statement is incorrect. It seems true in national data, but high prices and increasing construction at the metropolitan area level were systematically related to rising rents and to low vacancy rates. This error causes Baker to be very confident in his assessment of the bubble. It was "easy to see." Baker is helpful here, by stating the error so explicitly, but he is not an outlier on this issue. This is the conventional position. It goes to show how deeply this error has blocked reasonable inferences about the financial crisis. In fact, Baker is outside the norm, and would agree with some of the position I will stake out here: that there has been too much focus on the financial system as a cause of the deep recession. (See Dean Baker, *The Housing Bubble and the Great Recession: Ten Years Later,* (Washington, DC: Center for Economic and Policy Research, September 2018), https://www.cepr.net/images/stories/reports/housing-bubble-2018-09. pdf.) Yet, because he still shares the deepest error from the conventional story, he retains its worst conclusion—that the deep recession was inevitable.

12   See: Jessica Guynn, "Only in San Francisco: Activists block Google buses with scooters to protest 'techsploitatioin'," *USA Today,* May 31, 2018, https://www.usa-today.com/story/tech/2018/05/31/protesters-block-google-buses-scooters-fight-techsploitation/661076002/; Matthew Yglesias, "Silicon Valley's pro-

found housing crisis, in one sentence," *Vox*, June 7, 2016, https://www.vox.com/2016/6/7/11877378/silicon-valley-housing-crisis; and Casey Newton, "What Amazon got wrong about New York City," *The Verge*, February 15, 2019, https://www.theverge.com/interface/2019/2/15/18225646/amazon-nyc-hq2-collapse-secrecy-incentives-automation.

13 United State Census Bureau, "State-to-State Migration Flows," https://www.census.gov/data/tables/time-series/demo/geographic-mobility/state-to-state-migration.html.

14 Kevin Erdmann, *Build More Houses: How an Incorrect Perception of Housing Supply Fueled the Great Recession and Slowed Recovery* (Mercatus Research Series, Arlington, VA: The Mercatus Center at George Mason University, May 3, 2021), https://ssrn.com/abstract=3840450.

15 Here is one example: "And unlike in the early 2000s, when there were too many homes, housing production has been low for years, plagued by a shortage of skilled labor and rising costs of raw materials." Katy O'Donnell "Soaring home prices are starting to alarm policymakers," *Politico*, March 8, 2021, https://www.politico.com/news/2021/03/08/soaring-home-prices-alarm-policymakers-474433.

16 OECD, "Housing Prices: Housing Prices Indicator," (2021), https://data.oecd.org/price/housing-prices.htm.

17 See: Organization for Economic Co-operation and Development, "Employment by Economic Activity: Construction: All Persons for the United States, Canada, Australia, the United Kingdom, New Zealand, for Q2," https://fred.stlouisfed.org/graph/?g=wi94.

18 Zillow Group, "Mortgage Affordability," Accessed March 28, 2019, https://web.archive.org/web/20190220210045/https://www.zillow.com/research/data. The measure, for each metropolitan area, represents the percentage of the median household income required to make a mortgage payment on the home with the median price at current interest rate on a conventional 30-year fixed rate mortgage.

19 Board of Governors of the Federal Reserve System, "Survey of Consumer Finances,", https://www.federalreserve.gov/econres/scfindex.htm.

20 Len Kiefer, "Forecasting is hard (work)," (blog), August 27, 2017, http://len-kiefer.com/2017/08/27/forecast, using Survey of Professional Forecasters from the Federal Reserve Bank of Philadelphia.

21 See: Karl E. Case, Robert J. Shiller, and Anne Thompson. "What Have They Been Thinking? Home Buyer Behavior in Hot and Cold Markets," (NBER Working Paper No. w18400, National Bureau of Economic Research, 2012), http://www.nber.org/papers/w18400.

22 Greg Ip, "Housing Prices Always Rise," The Worst Ideas of the Decade, Washington Post, 2010, Opinion, https://www.washingtonpost.com/wp-srv/special/opinions/outlook/worst-ideas/housing-bubble.html.

23 Remember the countless articles about how so many borrowers were going to default because their interest rates would reset on adjustable-rate mortgages? See https://www.nbcnews.com/id/wbna22007867 for example. Rate resets ended up not being that important. Mortgages of all types ended up having high foreclosure rates. In many ways, such as this, the bad things that were supposed to happen didn't quite match the bad things that actually happened. This should have created doubt about how inevitable those bad things were, but for the most part it has not.

24 For example: "Paul Krugman, an economist at Princeton University, told the FCIC, 'It's hard to envisage us having had this crisis without considering international monetary capital movements. The U.S. housing bubble was financed by large capital inflows. So were Spanish and Irish and Baltic bubbles. It's a combination of, in the narrow sense, of a less regulated financial system and a world that was increasingly wide open for big international capital movements.' It was an ocean of money." The Financial Crisis Inquiry Commission, *The Financial Crisis Inquiry Report: Final Report of the National Commission on the Causes of the Financial and Economic Crisis in the United States*, (January 2011), 104, https://www.govinfo.gov/content/pkg/GPO-FCIC/pdf/GPO-FCIC.pdf.

25 See: Daniel O. Beltran, Larry Cordell, and Charles P. Thomas, *Asymmetric Information and the Death of ABS CDOs* (Washington, DC: FRB International

Finance Discussion Paper No. 1075, March 2013), https://ssrn.com/abstract=2245216.

26 See: Stephen Matteo Miller, "The Recourse Rule, Regulatory Arbitrage, and the Financial Crisis," *Journal of Regulatory Economics*, 54, no.2, (September 2018): 195–217, https://link.springer.com/article/10.1007/s11149-018-9364-z; Isil Erel, Taylor Nadauld, and René M. Stulz, "Why Did Holdings of Highly Rated Securitization Tranches Differ So Much across Banks?," *The Review of Financial Studies*, 27, no. 2, (February 2014): 404–453, https://academic.oup.com/rfs/article-abstract/27/2/404/1581551; and Craig B. Merrill, Taylor Nadauld, and Philip E. Strahan, "Final Demand for Structured Finance Securities," (August 1, 2014), https://ssrn.com/abstract=2380859 or http://dx.doi.org/10.2139/ssrn.2380859.

27 See: Anat R. Admati et al., "Fallacies, Irrelevant Facts, and Myths in the Discussion of Capital Regulation: Why Bank Equity is Not Socially Expensive," (Max Planck Institute for Research on Collective Goods 2013/23, Rock Center for Corporate Governance at Stanford University Working Paper No. 161, Stanford University Graduate School of Business Research Paper No. 13–7, October 22, 2013), https://ssrn.com/abstract=2349739 or http://dx.doi.org/10.2139/ssrn.2349739; John H. Cochrane, "Toward a Run-free Financial System," in *Across the Great Divide: New Perspectives on the Financial Crisis*, ed. Martin Neil Baily and John B. Taylor (Hoover Institution, Stanford University, number 8, 2014), https://static1.squarespace.com/static/5e6033a4ea02d-801f37e15bb/t/5edab6c52a5b1a69774c0846/1591391943654/across-the-great-divide-ch10.pdf; and Mark Jeffrey Flannery, "No Pain, No Gain? Effecting Market Discipline Via 'Reverse Convertible Debentures'," (November 2002), https://ssrn.com/abstract=352762.

28 Federal Reserve Bank of New York Research and Statistics Group, "Percent of Consumers with New Foreclosures by State" in *Quarterly Report on Household Debt and Credit* (New York, NY: Federal Reserve Bank of New York Center for Microeconomic Data, 2019 Quarter 4), 39, https://www.newyorkfed.org/microeconomics/hhdc.html.

29 See "SEC Filings: Annual Reports, 10-K filings/Quarterly Reports, 10-Q filings," D. R. Horton, https://investor.drhorton.com/financial-information/sec-filings in the "Net Sales Orders and Backlog" section.

30 See: Donghoon Lee and Joseph Tracy "A Better Measure of First-Time Homebuyers," *Liberty Street Economics* (blog), *Federal Reserve Bank of New York*, April 8, 2019, https://libertystreeteconomics.newyorkfed.org/2019/04/a-better-measure-of-first-time-homebuyers/.

31 See: Atif R. Mian and Amir Sufi, "Credit Supply and Housing Speculation," (March 26, 2019), https://ssrn.com/abstract=3209564 or http://dx.doi.org/10.2139/ssrn.3209564.

32 United States Census Bureau, "Housing Vacancies and Homeownership (CPS/HVS)," Table 8, https://www.census.gov/housing/hvs/data/histtabs.html.

Owner households in the fourth quarter of 2005 numbered 75.163 million and in the fourth quarter of 2007 numbered 75.164 million. An increase of one thousand households. The Census Bureau reports a margin of error in the homeownership rate of about 0.5 percent, which amounts to about five-hundred thousand households.

33 Frequently, the national homeownership rate is used as evidence that an unsustainably high homeownership rate inevitably collapsed back to sustainable levels, because the homeownership rate had followed along roughly at 64 percent to 65 percent for many years before peaking at about 69 percent in 2004, then collapsing. But older households are much more likely to be homeowners than younger households. The rise in homeownership was mostly a reflection of aging baby boomers engaged in normal household financial activity. Adjusted for age, homeownership rates were not unprecedented, and after the crisis, when it looked like they returned to normal, in fact, they had retracted to levels far below 20th century norms for Americans under 65 years of age.

34 See: Sonia Gilbukh and Paul Goldsmith-Pinkham, "Quantities and Prices during the Housing Bust," *Liberty Street Economics* (blog), *Federal Reserve Bank of New York*, April 2, 2018, https://libertystreeteconomics.newyorkfed.org/2018/04/quantities-and-prices-during-the-housing-bust.html.

I have referenced three separate measures, which the careful reader may want to make sure to understand clearly. New Inventory are homes that builders have in their construction pipeline and are trying to sell. Vacancies are existing homes that don't have any tenants in them. Existing Inventory is a count of homes listed for sale. Existing Inventory isn't necessarily vacant. Each is slightly different, but in the context of this chapter, an increase in each is a signal of a market failing to find able buyers.

35 Kevin Erdmann, *Build More Houses: How an Incorrect Perception of Housing Supply Fueled the Great Recession and Slowed Recovery* (Mercatus Research Series, Arlington, VA: The Mercatus Center at George Mason University, May 3, 2021), https://ssrn.com/abstract=3840450.

The corollary is not true. Declines in population growth did not always lead to vacancies. Ironically, it was low vacancies from a lack of adequate housing in the Closed Access cities that led to their depopulation during the boom. As a result of this, while it appears at the national level that there was an oversupply of homes if the national inventory of homes is compared to population growth, many of those supposedly excess housing units were in the Closed Access cities, since building increased there during the boom while they were depopulating.

36 Scott Sumner and Kevin Erdmann, *Housing Policy, Monetary Policy, and the Great Recession* (Mercatus Research Series, Arlington, VA: The Mercatus Center at George Mason University, August 4, 2020), https://ssrn.com/abstract=3667309 or http://dx.doi.org/10.2139/ssrn.3667309.

In fact, taking all states with data into account, in a regression with both the 1998 level of construction employment and the change in construction employment from 1998 to 2005, rising construction employment during the boom was still associated with lower vacancy rates, even in 2009.

37 Bureau of Economic Analysis, "Regional Data: GDP and Personal Income: Annual Personal Income and Employment by State: Personal Income, Population, Per Capita Personal Income, Dispensable Personal Income, and Per Capita Disposable Personal Income (SAINC1/SAINC51)," Table SAINC1 -

Personal Income Summary: Personal Income, Population, Per Capita Personal Income, https://apps.bea.gov/iTable/iTable.cfm?reqid=70.

38 Zillow Group, "Housing Data: Median Home Price (ZHVI) by State," ww.zillow. com/research/data/; and New York Federal Reserve Center for Microeconomic Data Household Debt and Credit Report, (2017 Quarter 3) "Total Debt Balance per Capita by State," 20, https://www.newyorkfed.org/microeconomics/hhdc.html.

39 See: Fernando Ferreira and Joseph Gyourko, "Anatomy of the Beginning of the Housing Boom:

US Neighborhoods and Metropolitan Areas, 1993–2009," (NBER Working Paper No. 17374, National Bureau of Economic Research, August 2011), https:// www.nber.org/papers/w17374 for a quantitative examination of this topic.

40 Florida is the primary landing spot for migrants from Boston and New York.

41 In growing cities like Phoenix, an inflow of residents is an economic boon. When they arrive, they need shelter, but shelter is a durable good. Their arrivals trigger local economic production that creates a home which won't just provide shelter this year, but will provide shelter for decades. The inflow of new residents has a multiplicative affect on local incomes. The family moves into town, either with their own capital or they get a mortgage from the bank, and that capital gets spent locally on all the work that is necessary to create a home. So, when migration suddenly dropped local population growth rates by a percentage point or more, it didn't just take a percentage point off local economic activity. It knocked local incomes by many times that amount. Greg Howard at MIT estimates that the unemployment rate in many of the Contagion cities eventually increased by several extra percentage points because of the amplifying effects of migration on the business cycle.

Greg Howard, "The Migration Accelerator: Labor Mobility, Housing, and Demand," *American Economic Journal: Macroeconomics*, 12 no. 4 (October 2020): 147–79, https://economics.mit.edu/files/13670 or https://ideas.repec.org/a/ aea/aejmac/v12y2020i4p147-79.html.

42 Sources for Figure 1: Median Home Price source: Zillow Group, "Housing Data: Median Home Price (ZHVI) by State," www.zillow.com/research/data/;

Debt per Capita source: New York Federal Reserve Center for Microeconomic Data Household Debt and Credit Report (2017 Quarter 3), "Total Debt Balance per Capita by State," 20, https://www.newyorkfed.org/microeconomics/ hhdc.html; Permits per 1000 residents sources: Permits from: Metropolitan Statistical Areas and US Census Building Permits Survey, https://www.census. gov/construction/bps/, retrieved from https://fred.stlouisfed.org/sing codes: AZBPPRIVSA and NVBPPRIVSA; and population from: Bureau of Economic Analysis, "Regional Data: GDP and Personal Income: Annual Personal Income and Employment by State: Personal Income, Population, Per Capita Personal Income, Dispensable Personal Income, and Per Capita Disposable Personal Income (SAINC1/SAINC51)," Table SAINC1 - Personal Income Summary: Personal Income, Population, Per Capita Personal Income, https://apps.bea. gov/iTable/iTable.cfm?reqid=70.

43 National vacancy rates have ranged between about 3.4 percent and 5.6 percent since the mid-1980s.

The population-weighted vacancy rate of New York City, Los Angeles, Boston, San Francisco, and San Diego are from Tables 4 and 5. Rental and Owner Vacancy Rates for the seventy-five Largest Metropolitan Statistical Areas (MSA) are aggregated using homeownership rates and populations for each MSA.

United States Census Bureau, "Housing Vacancies and Homeownership (CPS/ HVS)," https://www.census.gov/housing/hvs/data/histtabs.html.

44 Zillow Group, "Mortgage Affordability," Accessed March 28, 2019, https:// web.archive.org/web/20190220210045/https://www.zillow.com/research/ data/. The measure, for each metropolitan area, represents the percentage of the median household income required to make a mortgage payment on the home with the median price at current interest rate on a conventional 30-year fixed rate mortgage.

45 Alan Cole, *Stable Monetary Policy to Connect More Americans to Work* (SCP Report No. 5–20, Washington, DC: Joint Economic Committee, September 14, 2020), https://www.jec.senate.gov/public/index.cfm/republicans/analysis?ID= 051267FC-0147-4E31-BE80-946E0543AF82.

46 For more discussion on housing affordability, see my series of short posts at the Mercatus Center:https://www.mercatus.org/tags/housing-affordability-series.

47 See Office of Tax Analysis, *Tax Expenditures* (Washington D.C.: U.S. Department of Treasury, October 16, 2017), https://www.treasury.gov/resource-center/tax-policy/Documents/Tax-Expenditures-FY2019.pdf.

48 See Bureau of Economic Analysis, "National Data: National Income and Product Accounts: Section 7 – Supplemental Tables: Table 7.4.5. Housing Sector Output, Gross Value Added, and Net Value Added (A)," https://www.bea.gov/iTable/iTable.cfm?reqid=19&step=2#reqid=19&step=2&isuri=1&1921=survey.

49 Some interest groups prefer more spending on housing, such as the National Association of Realtors. But, to the extent that they lobby to keep brokers' commissions high, their influence likely reduces home prices and homebuying activity.

50 Board of Governors of the Federal Reserve System, "Mortgage Debt Outstanding," (December 2017) https://www.federalreserve.gov/data/mortoutstand/current.htm. (Data is as percentage of all One- to four-family mortgages outstanding.); Ginnie Mae mortgages: Lines 19+55Fannie Mae and Freddie Mac mortgages: Lines 40+46+58+61.

Total mortgages: Line 2.

51 James R. Hagerty, *The Fateful History of Fannie Mae: New Deal Birth to Mortgage Crisis Fall* (Charleston, SC: The History Press, 2012), 122–133.

52 Hagerty, *The Fateful History,* 127–128.

53 The Financial Crisis Inquiry Commission, *The Financial Crisis Inquiry Report: Final Report of the National Commission on the Causes of the Financial and Economic Crisis in the United States,* (January 2011), 122, http://purl.fdlp.gov/GPO/gpo50165.

54 U.S. Securities and Exchange Commission, "Freddie Mac, Four Former Executives Settle SEC Action Relating to Multi-Billion Dollar Accounting Fraud," press release no. 2007-205, September 27, 2007, http://www.sec.gov/news/press/2007/2007-205.htm.

55 Associated Press, "Former Freddie Mac CEO to pay millions." *Los Angeles Times,* November 7, 2007, https://www.latimes.com/archives/la-xpm-2007-nov-07-fi-freddie7-story.html.

56 In this case, Fannie was accused of overstating earnings by $6.3 billion. However, the same adjustments that reduced cumulative earnings by $6.3 billion increased "Accumulated Other Comprehensive Income" by $10.4 billion. This is a category used to account for certain unrealized gains and losses on unsettled securities.

An example of how rhetoric during this period has tended to emphasize recklessness or negativity: In the press releases regarding Fannie and Freddie, Fannie's earnings were reported as "overstated," but Freddie's were not reported as "understated." They were "misreported."

Guide to Fannie Mae's 2004 Annual Report on SEC Form 10-K, (Washington D.C.: Fannie Mae, December 6, 2006, https://www.fanniemae.com/media/26266/display.

57 Hagerty, *The Fateful History,* 132.

58 Hagerty, *The Fateful History,* 139.

59 "Transcript of Motions Hearing Before the Honorable Richard J. Leon United States District Judge," transcript of motions hearing at United States District Court for the District of Columbia, Case 1:04-CV-01639-RJL, June 5, 2012, 88–90, https://www.scribd.com/doc/122392319/Transcript-Fannie-Mae-Hearings.

60 See Federal Housing Finance Agency - Annual Report to Congress 2013, pg. 17-19. https://www.fhfa.gov/AboutUs/Reports/Pages/Annual-Report-to-Congress-2013.aspx.

61 The lawsuits alleging fraud against the new CEOs were also filed on the same day. (See: Nate Raymond, "Ex-Fannie Mae CEO urges U.S. judge to toss SEC fraud case," *Reuters.com,* January 28, 2016. https://www.reuters.com/article/us-sec-fanniemae-mudd-idUSKCN0V52QC.)

62 Paul Solman, "Joseph Stiglitz, Barney Frank Respond to 'Reckless Endangerment' Allegations," *PBS News Hour,* July 1, 2011, https://www.pbs.org/newshour/arts/rep-barney-frank-d-mass.

63 Board of Governors of the Federal Reserve System, "Mortgage Debt Outstanding", (March 2015), https://www.federalreserve.gov/econresdata/releases/mortoutstand/mortoutstand20150331.htm.

Freddie: Lines 45+57; Fannie: Lines 39+60.

64 The Financial Crisis Inquiry Commission, *The Financial Crisis Inquiry Report: Final Report of the National Commission on the Causes of the Financial and Economic Crisis in the United States*, (January 2011), 122, http://purl.fdlp.gov/GPO/gpo50165.

65 United States Securities and Exchange Commission, *Form 10-K Annual Report for Federal National Mortgage Association*, 2004, http://www.fanniemae.com/resources/file/ir/pdf/quarterly-annual-results/2004/2004_form10K.pdf.

For one brief review of the decline of the GSEs and the rise of private securitizations, see Major Coleman IV, Michael LaCour-Little, and Kerry D. Vandell, "Subprime lending and the housing bubble: Tail wags dog?" *Journal of Housing Economics* 17, no.4 (December 2008): 284–287, https://doi.org/10.1016/j.jhe.2008.09.001.

66 A basis point is one-hundredth of a percentage point.

67 Dwight M. Jaffee, "On Limiting the Retained Mortgage Portfolios of Fannie Mae and Freddie Mac," (UC Berkeley: Fisher Center for Real Estate and Urban Economics, June 30, 2005), 17, http://escholarship.org/uc/item/52z4562n.

68 See the graph at Board of Governors of the Federal Reserve System (US) and Moody's, "30-Year Conventional Mortgage Rate (DISCONTINUED)/Moody's Seasoned Aaa Corporate Bond Yield," https://fred.stlouisfed.org/graph/?g=fbwq.

69 Board of Governors of the Federal Reserve System, "Real Estate Loans, All Commercial Banks/Total Assets, All Commercial Banks," https://research.stlouisfed.org/fred2/graph/?g=4wWK.

70 FHAs long-term decline moderated as the GSEs fell back.

71 New York Federal Reserve Center for Microeconomic Data Household Debt and Credit Report, (2019 Quarter 4) "Total Debt Balance per Capita by State," 32, https://www.newyorkfed.org/microeconomics/hhdc.html.

72 Adam J. Levitin and Susan M. Wachter, "Explaining the Housing Bubble," *Georgetown Law Journal*, 100 no. 4 (April 12, 2012): 1221, http://papers.ssrn.com/sol3/papers.cfm?abstract_id=1669401.

73 Average home value of newly originated Fannie Mae homes was estimated using the average loan amount and the average loan-to-market value estimates in Fannie Mae 10-K filings. Average US home values were estimated by dividing Owner-Occupied Real Estate Including Vacant Land and Mobile Homes at Market Value estimated in the Federal Reserve's Z.1 Financial Accounts of the United States report. (Board of Governors of the Federal Reserve System, "Financial Accounts of the United States – Z.1," https://www.federalreserve.gov/releases/z1/) by the number of owner-occupied homes from the Census Bureau HVS Estimate of the Total Housing Inventory (https://www.census.gov/housing/hvs/data/index.html).

74 Xudong An and Raphael W. Bostic, "GSE Activity, FHA Feedback, and Implications for the Efficacy of the Affordable Housing Goals," (University of Southern California: School of Policy, Planning, and Development, Lusk Center for Real Estate, February 13, 2006), 7, https://lusk.usc.edu/research/working-papers/gse-activity-fha-feedback-and-implications-efficacy-affordable-housing-goals.

75 The Financial Crisis Inquiry Commission, *The Financial Crisis Inquiry Report: Final Report of the National Commission on the Causes of the Financial and Economic Crisis in the United States*, (January 2011), 512, http://fcic-static.law.stanford.edu/cdn_media/fcic-reports/fcic_final_report_full.pdf.

76 Board of Governors of the Federal Reserve System, "Mortgage Debt Outstanding," (December 2017) https://www.federalreserve.gov/data/mortoutstand/current.htm. (Data is as percentage of all One- to four-family mortgages outstanding.)

Ginnie Mae mortgages: Lines 19+55.

Fannie Mae and Freddie Mac mortgages: Lines 40+46+58+61.

Total mortgages: Line 2.

77   According to the Urban Institute's Housing Credit Availability Index, aggregate borrower risk remained fairly stable throughout the boom. The rise in risk from 2003 to 2006 was mostly due to changing terms on loans, which the Urban Institute refers to as "Product Risk." Their index shows stable borrower risk at the GSEs from 1998 to 2005, which then briefly increased in 2006 and 2007, before credit standards tightened sharply in all conduits. See: Urban Institute, "Housing Credit Availability Index," http://www.urban.org/policy-centers/ housing-finance-policy-center/projects/housing-credit-availability-index.

78   Adam J. Levitin and Susan M. Wachter, "Explaining the Housing Bubble," *Georgetown Law Journal,* 100 no. 4 (April 12, 2012): 1217–1218, http://papers.ssrn. com/sol3/papers.cfm?abstract_id=1669401.

79   They do note one difference—that since the CRA had been in place for many years, it is unlikely that it suddenly created sharp increases in demand in 2004 and 2005.

80   For one example of analysis of housing market changes resulting from the shift from the GSEs to private securitizations, see KhasadYahu ZarBabal, Michael LaCour-Little, and Kerry D. Vandell, "Subprime Lending and the Housing Bubble: Tail Wags Dog?" (September 2, 2008), https://ssrn.com/ abstract=1262365 or http://dx.doi.org/10.2139/ssrn.1262365.

81   See: Stephen Matteo Miller, "The Recourse Rule, Regulatory Arbitrage, and the Financial Crisis," *Journal of Regulatory Economics,* 54, no.2, (August 21, 2018), https://ssrn.com/abstract=3013133 or http://dx.doi.org/10.2139/ssrn.3013133.

82   Gene Amromin et al., "Complex Mortgages," (NBER Working Paper No. w17315, National Bureau of Economic Research, August 2011), https://www. nber.org/papers/w17315.

83   Stefania Albanesi, Giacomo De Giorgi, and Jaromir Nosal, "Credit Growth and the Financial Crisis: A New Narrative," (NBER Working Paper No. w23740, National Bureau of Economic Research, August 2017), http://www.nber.org/ papers/w23740.

84   Christopher L. Foote, Lara Loewenstein, and Paul S. Willen, *Cross-Sectional Patterns of Mortgage Debt During the Housing Boom: Evidence and Implications*

(Federal Reserve Bank of Boston, July 6,2016), 2–3, http://conference.nber.org/confer/2016/SI2016/ME/Foote_Loewenstein_Willen.pdf.

85   See: Morris A. Davis et al., "A quarter century of mortgage risk" (AEI Economics Working Paper 2019–04, American Enterprise Institute, Updated May 2012), 19–25 and Figures 4–9, https://www.aei.org/wp-content/uploads/2021/05/Mortgage-Risk-WP.pdf?x91208.

86   Christopher L. Foote et al., *Subprime Facts: What (We Think) We Know About the Subprime Crisis and What We Don't* (Public Policy Discussion Papers No. 08-2, Federal Reserve Bank of Boston, May 30, 2008), 4, 30, https://www.bostonfed.org/economic/ppdp/2008/ppdp0802.pdf.

87   John M. Griffin and Gonzalo Maturana, "Did Dubious Mortgage Origination Practices Distort House Prices?" (27th Australasian Finance and Banking Conference 2014 Paper, January 2016), https://ssrn.com/abstract=2485308 or http://dx.doi.org/10.2139/ssrn.2485308.

88   Deborah Fowler and Ann Baddour, *From "Easy Credit" to a Credit Crisis: Subprime Loans and Foreclosures in Texas* (Austin, TX: Texas Appleseed, May 2008), https://www.texasappleseed.org/sites/default/files/96-FinancialService-ReportTxMortgageCrisis.pdf.

89   Marco DiMaggio and Amir Kermani, "Credit-Induced Boom and Bust," *The Review of Financial Studies* (forthcoming), https://ssrn.com/abstract=2463516 or http://dx.doi.org/10.2139/ssrn.2463516.

90   See: Atif R. Mian and Amir Sufi, "Credit Supply and Housing Speculation," (March 26, 2019), 33–37, https://ssrn.com/abstract=3209564 or http://dx.doi.org/10.2139/ssrn.3209564.

91   Source for Figure 2: Zillow Group, "Rent Affordability," "Price to Income," "Median Household Income," Accessed on March 28, 2019, https://web.archive.org/web/20190220210045/https://www.zillow.com/research/data/.

Combined with author's calculations, adjusted for inflation with US GDP deflator.

92 See: Scott Sumner and Kevin Erdmann, *Housing Policy, Monetary Policy, and the Great Recession* (Mercatus Research Series, Arlington, VA: The Mercatus Center at George Mason University, August 4, 2020), https://ssrn.com/abstract=3667309 or http://dx.doi.org/10.2139/ssrn.3667309; and Kevin Erdmann, *Build More Houses: How an Incorrect Perception of Housing Supply Fueled the Great Recession and Slowed Recovery* (Mercatus Research Series, Arlington, VA: The Mercatus Center at George Mason University, May 3, 2021), https://ssrn.com/abstract=3840450.

93 Source for Figure 3: U.S. Bureau of Labor Statistics, "All Employees: Construction and All Employees, Total Non-Farm," https://fred.stlouisfed.org/graph/?g=r1b, for each MSA.

94 Vacancy data is from the Census Bureau's Housing Vacancies and Homeownership (CPS/HVS) report and is a combined estimate of empty homes for sale or rent.

95 Kevin Erdmann, *Build More Houses: How an Incorrect Perception of Housing Supply Fueled the Great Recession and Slowed Recovery* (Mercatus Research Series, Arlington, VA: The Mercatus Center at George Mason University, May 3, 2021), https://ssrn.com/abstract=3840450.

96 Here is one example, from the Griffin and Maturana paper cited earlier in this chapter. (Bold emphasis is mine.)

"In summary, the fact that a high concentration of the worst originators is related to house price crashes in areas of elastic land supply indicates that the relation between dubious origination and crashes is not due to the worse originators solely concentrating in areas of tight land supply. The increase in credit in areas of elastic supply **seemingly** led to unwarranted housing construction and a subsequent crash of house prices.

While each test above may not accomplish identification in its purest form, **it seems extremely difficult to construct a coherent alternative explanation** that is consistent with all the previous results." John M. Griffin and Gonzalo Maturana, "Did Dubious Mortgage Origination Practices Distort House Prices?," *Review of Financial Studies* 29, no. 7 (July 2016): 1692.

Much of that paper is interesting and useful regarding the interaction between lending and the housing boom. I propose that on this particular point, the presumption about supply was wrong, and that there is, now, a coherent alternative explanation for prices collapsing in so many places. Because this sort of conclusion about collapsing housing markets was so widely believed, a tremendous amount of lost wealth and lost jobs from 2008 to 2012 was incorrectly treated as if it was the inevitable consequence of activity that had already taken place.

97 See: Organization for Economic Co-operation and Development and Board of Governors of the Federal Reserve System (US), "Long-Term Government Bond Yields: 10-year: Main (Including Benchmark) for Australia and Canada/10-Year Treasury Constant Maturity Rate," https://fred.stlouisfed.org/graph/?g=wdSX.

98 It isn't quite that simple, but for now we don't need to complicate things.

99 These estimates are based on cross-sectional regressions of the largest fifty metropolitan areas for each period, where the dependent variable is mortgage affordability, and the independent variable is median household income. The two examples are the expected values for metropolitan areas with median household income 15 percent below the US median or 25 percent above the US median for that period.

Source of data for these measures and for Figure 4: Zillow Group, "Mortgage Affordability," "Median Household Income," Accessed March 28, 2019, https://web.archive.org/web/20190220210045/https://www.zillow.com/research/data/. The measure, for each metropolitan area, represents the percentage of the median household income required to make a mortgage payment on the home with the median price at current interest rate on a conventional 30-year fixed rate mortgage.

100 The real interest rate is the interest rate minus the expected inflation rate. If you borrow money with a 6 percent interest rate, but you expect inflation to be 2 percent each year, that means that the dollars you repay the loan with will be worth 2 percent less each year. Therefore, the real interest rate (the interest rate you would pay for the same loan if there was no inflation) is 4 percent.

101 The Fed has made things much more complicated since 2008, but during the boom the Fed mostly only traded in short-term Treasury bills to influence the rate banks charged one another for overnight lending.

102 See: Board of Governors of the Federal Reserve System (US) and Freddie Mac, "30-Year Conventional Mortgage Rate (DISCONTINUED)/ Effective Federal Funds Rate/ 1-Year Adjustable Rate Mortgage Average in the United States (DISCONTINUED)," https://research.stlouisfed.org/fred2/graph/?g=4jpL.

103 There has been some pushback against the notion that the Federal Reserve should tighten monetary policy to avoid asset bubbles. One notable source is Neel Kashkari, President of the Minneapolis Federal Reserve Bank. For example, see Neel Kashkari, "Monetary Policy and Bubbles," *Federal Reserve Bank of Minneapolis,* May 17, 2017, https://www.minneapolisfed.org/news-and-events/messages/monetary-policy-and-bubbles.

104 The Financial Crisis Inquiry Commission, *The Financial Crisis Inquiry Report: Final Report of the National Commission on the Causes of the Financial and Economic Crisis in the United States,* (January 2011), 103, http://purl.fdlp.gov/GPO/gpo50165.

105 If Wikipedia can be taken as a snapshot of broad consensus, the view that the recession was overwhelmingly caused by excesses of the preceding period seems dominant to the exclusion of any other interpretation.

   "Causes of the Great Recession," Wikimedia Foundation, last modified July 25, 2016, http://web.archive.org/web/20160725160941/https://en.wikipedia.org/wiki/Causes_of_the_Great_Recession.

106 See Robert L. Hetzel, "Monetary Policy in the 2008-2009 Recession," *FRB Richmond Economic Quarterly* 95, no. 2 (2009): 201–233, https://ssrn.com/abstract=2188500 for one example. Also see Scott Sumner and Kevin Erdmann, *Housing Policy, Monetary Policy, and the Great Recession* (Mercatus Research Series, Arlington, VA: The Mercatus Center at George Mason University, August 4, 2020), https://ssrn.com/abstract=3667309 or http://dx.doi.org/10.2139/ssrn.3667309.

107 Scott Sumner, *The Money Illusion: Market Monetarism, the Great Recession, and the Future of Monetary Policy* (Chicago: The University of Chicago Press, 2021).

108 Atif Mian and Amir Sufi, "House Price Gains and U.S. Household Spending from 2002 to 2006," (Abstract, Fama-Miller Working Paper Series, Chicago: Chicago Booth Fama-Miller Center for Research in Finance, May 16, 2014), http://ssrn.com/abstract=2412263.

109 See John B. Taylor, "Housing and Monetary Policy," (NBER Working Paper No. w13682, National Bureau of Economic Research, December 2007). 463-476, https://www.nber.org/papers/w13682.

110 J.W. Mason, "Income Distribution, Household Debt, and Aggregate Demand: A Critical Assessment," (Working Paper No. 901, Levy Economics Institute of Bard College, March 2018), http://www.levyinstitute.org/publications/income-distribution-household-debt-and-aggregate-demand-a-critical-assessment.

111 Closed Access metropolitan areas: New York, Los Angeles, Boston, San Francisco, and San Diego

Other High Demand cities: Dallas, Houston, Atlanta, Minneapolis, Seattle, and Denver

BLS CPI Owners' Equivalent Rent. Unweighted averages.

112 See Charles Himmelberg, Christopher Mayer, and Todd Sinai, "Assessing High House Prices: Bubbles, Fundamentals and Misperceptions," *Journal of Economic Perspectives*, 19, no. 4 (Fall 2005): 67-92, https://pubs.aeaweb.org/doi/pdfplus/10.1257/089533005775196769.

113 See Joseph Gyourko, Christopher Mayer, and Todd Sinai, "Superstar Cities," *American Economic Journal: Economic Policy*, 5, no. 4 (November 2013): 167–99, https://ideas.repec.org/a/aea/aejpol/v5y2013i4p167-99.html.

114 See Enrico Moretti, *The New Geography of Jobs* (Boston: Mariner Books, 2013).

115 I have slightly misspoken here. As I have pointed out about the Contagion cities and as several cities have found during the post-Covid housing boom, when migration becomes heavy and unpredictable, it is difficult for any city to avoid a price spike.

116 And abundant residential investment opportunities help to stabilize interest rates by creating outlets for savings.

117 United States Census Bureau, "American Housing Survey: Biennial rates, % of All Households," https://www.census.gov/programs-surveys/ahs.html. Estimates use author calculations comparing current and previous ownership status of survey-takers.

118 Atif Mian and Amir Sufi, "House Prices, Home Equity-Based Borrowing, and the US Household Leverage Crisis," *American Economic Review*, 101, no. 5 (August 2011): 2132-56, https://www.aeaweb.org/articles?id=10.1257/aer.101.5.2132.

119 This is based on their tenure after migration, which is the only measure available from ACS data.

120 Board of Governors of the Federal Reserve System (US), "Households and Nonprofit Organizations; Total Mortgages; Liability, Level/ Households and Nonprofit Organizations; Real Estate at Market Value, Level," https://fred.stlouisfed.org/graph/?g=r9RZ.

121 They suggest that this is the lower bound of their estimate, and the total is likely higher but difficult to pin down.

122 Eventually, mortgages would rise to 54 percent of home value, but after late 2007, it was collapsing home values that caused the increase, not rising mortgages.

123 Bill McBride, "Homebuilder Cancellation Rate," *Calculated Risk* (blog), June 2, 2009, https://www.calculatedriskblog.com/2009/06/homebuilder-cancellation-rate.html.

124 It is unlikely that homebuilders were either (1) overbuilding speculatively or (2) stretching their financing standards if they were turning away potential buyers because they couldn't get new lots approved fast enough. In fact, at the time, builders were trying to weed out speculative buyers.

125 The Bankruptcy Reform Act of 2005 made it more difficult to utilize home equity for protection in a bankruptcy. This might have lowered the demand for home ownership after 2005. This coincides with the top of the housing

market. Is this a coincidence that made the swing from boom to bust sharper in the 2005–2006 time period? It seems like this is a factor. I don't know how strong of a factor it is. Two papers on the topic include: Donald P. Morgan, Benjamin Iverson, and Matthew Botsch, *Seismic Effects of the Bankruptcy Reform* (Staff Report no. 358, New York, NY: Federal Reserve Bank of New York, revised February 2009), https://www.newyorkfed.org/research/staff_reports/sr358.html and Ulf von Lilienfeld-Toal and Dilip Mookherjee, *How Did the US Housing Slump Begin? Role of the 2005 Bankruptcy Reform* (April 19, 2011), http://ssrn.com/abstract=2023224 .

126 "Transcript of the Federal Open Market Committee Meeting of September 18, 2007," transcript of meeting of the FOMC in Washington, D.C. on September 18, 2007, 43, https://www.federalreserve.gov/monetarypolicy/files/FOMC20070918meeting.pdf.

127 Number of foreclosures compared to 2003-2006 average, See: Federal Reserve Bank of New York Research and Statistics Group, *Quarterly Report on Household Debt and Credit* (New York, NY: Federal Reserve Bank of New York Center for Microeconomic Data), "Percent of Consumers with New Foreclosures," (2019 Quarter 4) 39 https://www.newyorkfed.org/microeconomics/hhdc/background.html.

128 Erdmann, *Shut Out*, 135, Fig. 5–14.

129 Zillow Group, "Sales Turnover {Sold in the Past Year (%)}, by ZIP code," Accessed, April 28, 2016. Sales Turnover in December 2006 minus Sales Turnover in December 2004, by Zip Code of twenty largest MSAs, https://web.archive.org/web/20160421031658/, https://www.zillow.com/research/data/.

130 Zillow Group, "ZHVI, by ZIP code," Housing Data: ZHVI: median home price for 16,378 zip codes, www.zillow.com/research/data/.

131 CoStar Group, "CoStar Commercial Repeat-Sale Indices," http://www.costar-group.com/costar-news/ccrsi CCRSI, August 2020 Report, US Multi-family Value Weighted index, and S&P/Case-Shiller data downloaded from S&P Dow Jones Indices LLC, "S&P/Case-Shiller U.S. National Home Price Index," https://fred.stlouisfed.org/series/CSUSHPISA. Indexes set to 100 in December 2000.

132 One of many examples of the effects of mental benchmarking is a January 2018 article at the Intercept, titled "You Think Your Landlord is Bad? Try Renting from Wall Street." The article contains a litany of stories about "Wall Street" landlords raising rents, driving up prices, treating tenants impersonally, etc. It opens with a tenant whose mother has just passed away and whose husband is sick. Her rent in Los Angeles is $3,000 per month, and a "Wall Street rental behemoth" has notified her of a sudden increase to $3,800. The topic of the story is the impropriety of that $800 rent hike, and the pressure on the landlord to keep the rent at $3,000 is a ray of hope in the story.

(Rebecca Burns, "You Think Your Landlord Is Bad? Try Renting From Wall Street," *The Intercept*, January 20 2018, https://theintercept.com/2018/01/20/you-think-your-landlord-is-bad-try-renting-from-wall-street/.)

But why is that a ray of hope? Why is $3,000 per month rent acceptable for a working-class family dealing with challenges? It seems acceptable because that's what the rent was last month. But that's not an acceptable amount of rent for a working-class home. And the reason the rent is that high has nothing to do with "Wall Street." The rent should be half that level, and the reason the rent is that high comes down to one simple fact: City governments in the Los Angeles area block the reasonable expansion of its housing stock.

Furthermore, why should that family be renters? It certainly isn't because "Wall Street" prefers it this way. "Wall Street" was more than happy to create mortgages so that families like this could be owners instead of renters. This home would sell for about $500,000. It also sold for about that much back in 2005 when "Wall Street" was financing homes like this instead of renting them. And, just like "Wall Street" gets the blame for the rising rents today, "Wall Street" got the blame for rising prices in 2005. That's because financial markets facilitate quick changes, which makes them seem culpable for the root causes of change. So, $3,000 in rent is just the way it is, but a sudden jump to $3,800 seems outrageous, and likewise, a $400,000 little house in LA in 2003 was just the way it is, but a sudden jump to $500,000 seemed outrageous. In both cases, the price reflected underlying injustices, and Wall Street's tendency to act on those prices created a sense of agency—of blame.

Mortgage payments on many homes in 2020 are lower than the rental payments for the same house—vastly lower in many cases. So, it seems as though it might make sense for a long-term tenant to be an owner. It's not "Wall Street" that is preventing that from happening. In the article, Senator Elizabeth Warren, the advocate for the Consumer Finance Protection Bureau is quoted, "We need to do much more to provide clean, safe, and affordable housing for working families—and we can start by taking control away from Wall Street and returning it our communities."

Who do you think can more easily qualify for a mortgage under the regulatory framework Senator Warren has championed? A working-class household, a small-scale local landlord, or a Wall Street firm?

133 "Transcript of the Federal Open Market Committee Meeting of June 29–30, 2005," transcript of meeting of the FOMC in Washington, D.C. on June 29 to 30, 2005, 7-14, https://www.federalreserve.gov/monetarypolicy/files/FOMC20050630meeting.pdf.

134 "Transcript of FOMC 2005," 35-36, 62, 64-65.

135 Ben S. Bernanke, *The Courage to Act: A Memoir of a Crisis and Its Aftermath* (New York: W.W. Norton & Company, 2015), 88.

136 "Transcript of the Federal Open Market Committee Meeting of March 27–28, 2006," transcript of meeting of the FOMC in Washington, D.C. on March 27 to 28, 2006, 13, 36, 96, 139, https://www.federalreserve.gov/monetarypolicy/files/FOMC20060328meeting.pdf.

137 One might argue that housing markets aren't a part of the Fed's dual mandate, and that those mandates were quantitatively what drove FOMC decisions. However, in the opaque context of monetary policy, discretion is always involved. Fed critics certainly pointed to housing as a source of discretionary focus, and at least as far back as the June 2005 meeting, it was a focus of the FOMC regarding discretionary considerations and signals regarding expectations. In statements issued after FOMC meetings, individual sectors are mentioned only sparingly. During the important months leading up to the crisis

of September 2008, from May 2006 on, housing was mentioned in every single FOMC statement.

138 References that follow are taken from the Greenbook that is issued with each FOMC meeting. Housing starts are from the "Other Macroeconomic Indicators" Table and home prices are taken from the "Summary and Outlook: Domestic Developments" section. Greenbooks were retrieved from Board of Governors of the Federal Reserve System, "Federal Open Market Committee," https://www.federalreserve.gov/monetarypolicy/fomc_historical_year.htm.

139 John B. Taylor, *Getting Off Track: How Government Actions and Interventions Caused, Prolonged, and Worsened the Financial Crisis* (Stanford, California: Hoover Institution Press, 2009), 1, 5.

140 "Transcript of the Federal Open Market Committee Meeting of March 20–21, 2007," transcript of meeting of the FOMC in Washington, D.C. on March 20 to 21, 2007, 22, https://www.federalreserve.gov/monetarypolicy/files/FOMC20070321meeting.pdf.

141 Karl E. Case and Robert J. Shiller, *Is There a Bubble in the Housing Market?* (Cowles Foundation Paper No. 1089, New Haven, CT: Cowles Foundation for Research in Economics, Yale University, 2004), 340–342, www.econ.yale.edu/~shiller/pubs/p1089.pdf.

142 Brad Setser et al., "How Scary Is the Deficit?" *Foreign Affairs*, 84, no.4, (July/August 2005), http://online.sfsu.edu/jgmoss/PDF/635_pdf/No_52_HowScaryisthe[Twin]Deficit.pdf.

143 Edward E. Leamer, "Housing IS the Business Cycle," (NBER Working Paper No. w13428, National Bureau of Economic Research, 2007), 164, https://www.nber.org/papers/w13428.

144 Leamer, "Housing IS the Business Cycle," 173.

145 Sources for Figure 6: United States Census Bureau, "New Residential Construction," https://www.census.gov/construction/nrc/index.html; US Census Bureau and US Department of Housing and Urban Development, "New Privately Owned Housing Units Started: Total Units," https://fred.stlouisfed.org/graph/?g=MvB; and US Census Bureau, "Housing Vacancies and

Homeownership (CPS/HVS): Historical Tables: Table 7 Annual Estimates of the Total Housing Inventory for the United States: 1965 to Present," https://www.census.gov/housing/hvs/data/histtabs.html.

146 It's a reasonable approximation of the growth rate of the number of homes over time. It's not an exact measure of the growth rate of the housing stock, mostly because (1) some homes are demolished each year, and (2) manufactured homes add to the stock of housing, but they are tracked separately.

147 Leamer, "Housing IS the Business Cycle," 154, 193.

148 Leamer, "Housing IS the Business Cycle," 193.

149 The discussion of the Jackson Hole presentation appeared first in Kevin Erdmann, *Build More Houses: How an Incorrect Perception of Housing Supply Fueled the Great Recession and Slowed Recovery* (Mercatus Research Series, Arlington, VA: The Mercatus Center at George Mason University, May 3, 2021), https://ssrn.com/abstract=3840450.

150 "Transcript of the Federal Open Market Committee Meeting of August 5, 2008," transcript of meeting of the FOMC in Washington, D.C. on August 5, 2008, 30, https://www.federalreserve.gov/monetarypolicy/files/FOMC20080805meeting.pdf.

151 Andrew Ross Sorkin, *Too Big to Fail: The Inside Story of How Wall Street and Washington Fought to Save the Financial System—And Themselves* (New York, New York: Penguin Books, 2009), 190.

152 Ben Bernanke, *The Courage to Act: A Memoir of a Crisis and Its Aftermath* (New York: W.W. Norton & Co., 2017), 503.

153 The measure here is the sum of housing permits issued for on-site structures and shipments of manufactured homes, divided by the previous year's total inventory of homes.

154 Kevin Erdmann, *Build More Houses: How an Incorrect Perception of Housing Supply Fueled the Great Recession and Slowed Recovery* (Mercatus Research Series, Arlington, VA: The Mercatus Center at George Mason University, May 3, 2021), https://ssrn.com/abstract=3840450.

155 Source for Figure 7: U.S. Bureau of Labor Statistics, "Local Area Unemployment Statistics," https://www.bls.gov/lau/. Measures are the aggregate totals for the Miami, Riverside, Phoenix, and Tampa MSAs.

156 For example, see: Chang-Tai Hsieh and Enrico Moretti, "Housing Constraints and Spatial Misallocation," *American Economic Journal: Macroeconomics*, 11, no.2 (April 2019): 1–39; https://www.aeaweb.org/articles?id=10.1257/mac.20170388.

157 Edward E. Leamer, "Housing IS the Business Cycle," (NBER Working Paper No. w13428, National Bureau of Economic Research, 2007), 193, https://www.nber.org/papers/w13428.

158 Unless noted otherwise, rent and rental income represent the rental value of all homes, both owner-occupied and rented. So, a decline in rental income or rent inflation is not due to a shift from renting to owning. It is the shift in the measured rental value of the entire stock of homes.

159 Rent composes most of shelter inflation. Most of shelter inflation is imputed rents of owner-occupiers—an accounting of estimated value that has nothing to do with monetary transactions.

160 Rent inflation temporarily declined after mid-2007, which may be associated with a decline in housing demand as families were forced to downsize as a result of foreclosures.

161 See: "Transcript of the Federal Open Market Committee Meeting of June 28–29, 2006," transcript of meeting of the FOMC in Washington, D.C. on June 28–29, 2006, 92, https://www.federalreserve.gov/monetarypolicy/files/FOMC20060629meeting.pdf.

162 Henry M. Paulson, Jr., *On the Brink: Inside the Race to Stop the Collapse of the Global Financial System* (New York City: Business Plus, 2013), 74–77.

163 Paulson, Jr., *On the Brink*, 2–18.

In a way, this was politics as usual. It is common for the effect of policies toward various groups to be somewhat predetermined, in what Schneider and Ingram refer to as the "social construction of target populations." Public policy can utilize both carrots and sticks, and the use of either is frequently determined by public sentiment toward the group a policy is targeted to. Schneider and Ingram describe four broad groups, in terms of power and public favor: Dependents (weak power, deserving), Advantaged (strong power, deserving), Contenders (strong power, undeserving), and Deviants (weak power, undeserving). Respectively, representative examples of each category might include children, doctors, Wall Street firms, and criminals.

See: Anne Schneider and Helen Ingram. "Social Construction of Target Populations: Implications for Politics and Policy," *The American Political Science Review*, 87, no. 2 (June 1993): 334–347,

https://doi.org/10.2307/2939044 or https://www.jstor.org/stable/2939044; and

Anne Schneider, Helen Ingram, and Peter Deleon, "Democratic Policy Design: Social Construction of Target Populations," in *Theories of the Policy Process*, ed. Paul A. Sabatier and Christopher M. Weible, (Boulder, CO: Westview Press, 2014), 105–150, https://www.researchgate.net/publication/265377853_Democratic_Policy_Design_Social_Construction_of_Target_Populations.

Wall Street tends to be treated with some distrust, and public policies targeted at Wall Street generally must at least be seen as "sticks" to be politically acceptable. "Wall Street," as a term, in practice, does not really have a fixed definition. Its de facto definition is generally something like "the Contenders in a given financial context." So, if capital gains tax rates are lowered, that seems to benefit shareholders, and someone opposed to it might argue that it's a Wall Street giveaway. On the other hand, investment banks taking large profits as underwriters on initial public offerings, or brokers gaming stock market bids and asks would be extracting money from shareholders, so in that case, shareholders would be in opposition to "Wall Street." Likewise, executives taking large salaries and stock options would be extracting money from shareholders, and in that narrative, again, the executives would be likely to be associated with "Wall Street," in opposition to the shareholders. This slippery language is visible in much of the debate about TARP (Troubled Asset Relief Program) and other emergency measures. Much of the concern was about executives and other employees taking bonuses while the government was supporting credit markets. At other times, it was about propping up stock prices. At other times, it was about paying creditors face value for debt securities. "Wall Street" could refer to executives and other well-paid employees, equity holders, or debt holders. The way to be "Wall Street" was to be aesthetically unsympathetic.

So, the phrase "Wall Street got bailouts and Main Street didn't" does not really contain much information. "Wall Street" is a shifting term that generally refers to whatever group is viewed as Contenders—those for whom the public prefers sticks over carrots.

164 Ben S. Bernanke, *The Courage to Act,* (New York: W.W. Norton & Company, 2015), 63.

165 Parentheticals in both quotations are from the original.

Bernanke, *The Courage to Act,* 146–147.

166 Federal Reserve Bank of New York, "The Yield Curve as a Leading Indicator," https://www.newyorkfed.org/research/capital_markets/ycfaq.html. The probability of recession is based on a twelve-month lag, so the probability of recession in mid-2007 is derived from the yield curve in mid-2006.

167 "Bernanke's Bear Market," editorial, *The Wall Street Journal,* August 6, 2007, http://www.wsj.com/articles/SB118636001831688824.

168 Details are available at John Carney, "Jim Cramer Was Right—They Knew Nothing!" *CNBC,* January 18, 2013, http://www.cnbc.com/id/100392107, including video of the rant, which is worth a viewing.

169 Bernanke, *The Courage to Act,* 146.

170 Board of Governors of the Federal Reserve System, "Press Release: FOMC Statement," August 7, 2007, http://www.federalreserve.gov/newsevents/press/monetary/20070807a.htm.

171 FOMC statements can be found here: Board of Governors of the Federal Reserve System, "Historical Materials by Year: 2007," https://www.federalreserve.gov/monetarypolicy/fomchistorical2007.htm.

172 "The Fed Holds," editorial, *The Wall Street Journal,* September 17, 2008, http://www.wsj.com/articles/SB122160976650345605.

173 Timothy F. Geithner, *Stress Test: Reflections on Financial Crises*, (New York: Broadway Books, 2014), 508.

174 Bernanke, *The Courage to Act*, 415.

175 Geithner, *Stress Test*, 16–17.

176 Geithner, *Stress Test*, 144.

177 Geithner, *Stress Test*, 6.

178 Geithner, *Stress Test*, 106.

179 Bernanke, *The Courage to Act*, 522.

180 This is slightly different than the federal funds rate. The federal funds rate is the rate usually targeted by the Fed by injecting cash into the banking system. It is the rate banks charge one another for overnight lending. The discount rate is the rate the Fed charges to lend directly to banks and is usually somewhat higher than the fed funds rate.

181 Bernanke, *The Courage to Act*, 150, 181, 209.

182 P/E Ratios from "S&P 500 PE Ratio," https://www.multpl.com/s-p-500-pe-ratio.

183 In 2009, the federal government paid Americans for trading in certain models of used cars for new cars. The used cars were then scrapped. I suppose you could say this was the automotive version of Greenspan's comment about burning down houses.

184 A report from public interest justice center Texas Appleseed from May 2008 has a broad list of actions that had been taken by that time to address the building crisis. Deborah Fowler and Ann Baddour, *From "Easy Credit" to a Credit Crisis: Subprime Loans and Foreclosures in Texas* (Austin, TX: Texas Appleseed, May 2008), https://www.texasappleseed.org/sites/default/files/96-FinancialService-ReportTxMortgageCrisis.pdf.

At the federal level, they included:

The December 2007 law that allowed homeowners to accept loan modifications and debt forgiveness without claiming the taxable income that would normally be triggered by them

Funding for HUD foreclosure counselors

A program to allow borrowers who have defaulted because of rising interest rates to refinance

A thirty-day foreclosure freeze of several national lenders

At the state and local level:

Caps on mortgage fees and mortgage payment increases

Increased fiduciary requirements for lenders and brokers

Stricter broker and lender licensing

Required financial education for borrowers

Banning prepayment fees on some mortgages

More disclosures

More notifications before foreclosure

More legal avenues to make claims of predatory lending

The report also lists several forms of litigation against lenders, the GSEs, and bankers.

These actions reflect the fairly universal pattern of clamping down on lenders while attempting to provide forms of benevolence for borrowers. But clamping down on lenders prevented the one form of benevolence that could have prevented further declines in home values—widely available new mortgages.

185 Ben Bernanke, *The Courage to Act,* (New York: W.W. Norton & Company, 2015), 224.

186 Bernanke, *The Courage to Act,* 204–205.

187 Notice here, as always, it is the Federal Reserve's attempt to save anyone from failure that earns them the public's ire. Today, even Ben Bernanke himself admits that the Federal Reserve erred in September 2008—a rare step for a former Fed chair. But any public focus on that is drowned out by the complaints about actually trying to stabilize things.

188 See: "Transcript of the Federal Open Market Committee Meeting of April 29–30, 2008," transcript of meeting of the FOMC in Washington, D.C. on April 29 to 30, 2008, 71–72, https://www.federalreserve.gov/monetarypolicy/files/FOMC20080430meeting.pdf.

189 Timothy F. Geithner, *Stress Test: Reflections on Financial Crises*, (New York: Broadway Books, 2014), 389–390.

190 Geithner, *Stress Test*, 320.

191 The Financial Crisis Inquiry Commission, *The Financial Crisis Inquiry Report: Final Report of the National Commission on the Causes of the Financial and Economic Crisis in the United States*, (January 2011), 165–169, http://purl.fdlp.gov/GPO/gpo50165.

192 This is the vacancy rate of homes for sale and for rent, combined. From United States Census Bureau, "Housing Vacancies and Homeownership (CPS/HVS): Annual Statistics: 2019 (Including Historical Data by State and MSA): Table 6. Rental Vacancy Rates for the 75 Largest Metropolitan Statistical Areas: 2015–Present and Table 7 Homeowner Vacancy Rates for the 75 Largest Metropolitan Statistical Areas: 2015–Present," https://www.census.gov/housing/hvs/data/ann19ind.html, and United States Census Bureau, "Building Permits Survey," https://www.census.gov/construction/bps/.

193 Adam J. Levitin and Susan M. Wachter, "Explaining the Housing Bubble," *Georgetown Law Journal*, 100 no. 4 (April 12, 2012): 1239–1242, http://papers.ssrn.com/sol3/papers.cfm?abstract_id=1669401.

194 From the end of 2006 to 2015, the homeownership rate declined by an average of more than a half a percentage point per year, for nine years.

195 United States Census Bureau, "Housing Vacancies and Homeownership (CPS/HVS): Historical Tables: Table 12. Annual Household Estimates of the Housing Inventory by Age of Householder 1982 to Present," http://www.census.gov/housing/hvs/data/histtabs.html. There was a drop in ownership just as that data series was initiated, coming out of the 1980–82 recession, just as the age group data series begins. The 2004–2007 drop was on par with that decline. Over the entire period for which there is annual data, going back to 1982,

homeownership rates of those age groups had each fluctuated within a range of only about 2.5 percent. Over those three years, the homeownership rate dropped by 1.8 percent for forty-five- to fifty-four-year-olds and 1.1 percent for fifty-five- to sixty-four-year-olds.

196 Board of Governors of the Federal Reserve System (US), "Money Market Funds; Total Financial Assets, Level," https://fred.stlouisfed.org/series/MMMFFAQ027S and Board of Governors of the Federal Reserve System (US), "Households; Owners' Equity in Real Estate, Level," https://fred.stlouisfed.org/series/OEHRENWBSHNO.

197 Larry Cordell, Yilin Huang, and Meredith Williams, "Collateral Damage: Sizing and Assessing the Subprime CDO Crisis," (FRB of Philadelphia Working Paper No. 11-30, Philadelphia: Federal Reserve Bank of Philadelphia. May 2012), Table 2, https://citeseerx.ist.psu.edu/viewdoc/download?doi=10.1.1.371.333&rep=rep1&type=pdf.

198 Standard & Poor's Ratings Direct, "S&PCORRECT: 612 U.S. Subprime RMBS Classes Put On Watch Neg; Methodology Revisions Announced," July 11, 2007, https://fraser.stlouisfed.org/docs/historical/fct/standardpoor_pressrelease_20070711.pdf.

199 Christopher L. Foote, Kristopher S. Gerardi, and Paul S. Willen, "Why Did So Many People Make So Many Ex Post Bad Decisions? The Causes of the Foreclosure Crisis," (April 2012), 56, Figure 9, https://www.russellsage.org/sites/all/files/Rethinking-Finance/Willen.rsage_paper_2_11pw.pdf.

200 Juan Ospina and Harald Uhlig, "Mortgage-Backed Securities and the Financial Crisis of 2008: a Post Mortem," (NBER Working Paper No. w24509, National Bureau of Economic Research, April 2018), http://www.nber.org/papers/w24509.

201 Henry M. Paulson, Jr., *On the Brink: Inside the Race to Stop the Collapse of the Global Financial System* (New York City: Business Plus, 2013), 69.

202 To estimate extracted home equity, I subtracted the annualized residential investment on single family homes (U. S. Bureau of Economic Analysis, "Private fixed investment: Residential: Structures: Permanent site: Single family,"

https://fred.stlouisfed.org/series/A944RC1Q027SBEA) from the one-year change in mortgages outstanding (Board of Governors of the Federal Reserve System, "Households and Nonprofit Organizations; One-to-Four-Family Residential Mortgages; Liability, Level/Gross Domestic Product," https://fred. stlouisfed.org/graph/?g=pD5t). Spending is from U. S. Bureau of Economic Analysis, "Personal Consumption Expenditures," https://fred.stlouisfed.org/ series/PCE.

203 Earlier, I referenced examples of presumptions of housing oversupply at the Federal Reserve. For an example of its appearance in mass media, see this for an example in early 2008:

Molly Edmonds "What's the No. 1 reason for foreclosure?" HowStuffWorks. com, April 16, 2008, Accessed July 23, 2021, https://home.howstuffworks.com/ real-estate/selling-home/number-one-reason-for-foreclosure.htm.

The article does an excellent job, considering its timeliness, of expressing doubt about loose lending or resets on adjustable-rate mortgages, as causes of the developing foreclosure crisis, yet the article states, "While California has the country's largest rate of subprime mortgages, it is also suffering from an oversupply of houses due to a popped housing bubble." This notion acted as a hard lock on conventional wisdom. One could consider how to minimize the damage of a contracting mortgage or housing market, but the idea that we had built too many homes removes a recovery in construction from consideration.

This remains the conventional wisdom. A recent example is:

Nicole Friedman "The Pandemic Ignited a Housing Boom—but It's Different From the Last One," *The Wall Street Journal*, March 15, 2021, https://www.wsj. com/articles/the-pandemic-ignited-a-housing-boombut-its-different-from-the-last-one-11615824558.

Again, without citation, the writer asserts about the pre-crisis market, "Too much new construction led to an oversupply of houses."

These are not errors by the writers, per se. They are reflecting the canon—shared wisdom that doesn't require citation.

There are parallels here to the Great Depression, when deflationary monetary policies also threw the economy into a tailspin. Americans lacked the funds to buy basic necessities, which gave the appearance of oversupply. While children were begging in the streets for sustenance, the federal government famously plowed under crops and killed off livestock in order to try to raise prices. It is surprisingly difficult to discern a lack of money from a surplus of goods and services.

204 "Nightmare Mortgages," *BusinessWeek Online*, September 11, 2006, https://web. archive.org/web/20061113160008/http://www.businessweek.com/magazine/ content/06_37/b4000001.htm?.

205 See: Mortgage Bankers Association / Haver Analytics, "U.S. Residential, Virginia, Maryland, North Carolina, South Carolina, Washington, D.C., and West Virginia Mortgage Foreclosure and Delinquency Rates," https://web. archive.org/web/20190718013957/https://www.richmondfed.org/~/media/ richmondfedorg/banking/markets_trends_and_statistics/trends/pdf/delin-quency_and_foreclosure_rates.pdf.

206 Christopher Palmer, "Why Did So Many Subprime Borrowers Default During the Crisis: Loose Credit or Plummeting Prices?" (University of California at Berkeley, September 2015), https://faculty.haas.berkeley.edu/palmer/papers/ cpalmer-subprime.pdf.

207 Yuliya S. Demyanyk, "Quick Exits of Subprime Mortgages," *Federal Reserve Bank of St. Louis Review*, 2, (March/April 2009): 89 and Table 2, https://ssrn. com/abstract=1351845.

208 Paul Willen, "Two Facts about Mortgage Design," (PowerPoint presentation, FRBNY Mortgage Design Conference, New York City, May 21, 2015), https:// www.newyorkfed.org/medialibrary/media/research/conference/2015/mort-gage_design/willen.pdf.

209 Christopher L. Foote, Kristopher S. Gerardi, and Paul S. Willen, "Why Did So Many People Make So Many Ex Post Bad Decisions? The Causes of the Foreclosure Crisis," (April 2012), https://www.russellsage.org/sites/all/files/ Rethinking-Finance/Willen.rsage_paper_2_11pw.pdf.

210 Les Christie,. "Homeowners: Can't pay? Just walk away," *CNN Money*, February 7, 2008, http://money.cnn.com/2008/02/06/real_estate/walking_away/index. htm?postversion=2008020714.

211 Neil Bhutta, Jane Dokko, and Hui Shan, *The Depth of Negative Equity and Mortgage Default Decisions* (Finance and Economics Discussion Series: 2010-25 Screen Reader version, Federal Reserve Board of Governors, May 2010), https://www.federalreserve.gov/pubs/feds/2010/201035/index.html.

212 Christie, "Homeowners: Can't pay?"

213 Les Christie, "Subprime loans defaulting even before resets," *CNN Money*, February 20, 2008, http://money.cnn.com/2008/02/20/real_estate/ loans_failing_pre_resets/.

214 Andreas Fuster and Paul S. Willen, *Payment Size, Negative Equity, and Mortgage Default* (Staff Report No. 582, Federal Reserve Bank of New York Staff Reports, revised January 2015), https://www.newyorkfed.org/medialibrary/media/ research/staff_reports/sr582.pdf.

215 See: Board of Governors of the Federal Reserve System, "Senior Loan Officer Opinion Survey on Bank Lending Practices," last updated January 30, 2020, https://www.federalreserve.gov/data/sloos/sloos-202001-chart-data.htm; and

Urban Institute, "Housing Credit Availability Index: Q4 2020, " https:// www.urban.org/policy-centers/housing-finance-policy-center/projects/ housing-credit-availability-index.

216 As Ferreira and Gyourko conclude in a study of panel data:

The crisis was much less of uniquely subprime event than is recognized by scholars and policy makers. Subprime distress did spike first as previous research has showed. And, it occurred at relatively and absolutely high rates. However, distress and home loss among prime borrowers occurred with a lag and became quite extensive itself. Negative equity and owner illiquidity explain much of this variation, as predicted by the traditional mortgage default literature....

(O)ur results suggest that the high rates of home loss among subprime borrowers can be accounted for by two standard factors suggested by the traditional mortgage default literature—negative equity and borrower illiquidity. These affect all borrowers, not just subprime ones.

(Fernando Ferreira and Joseph Gyourko, "A New Look at the U.S. Foreclosure Crisis: Panel Data Evidence of Prime and Subprime Lending," (The Wharton School, University of Pennsylvania and NBER, February 23, 2015), http://cep. lse.ac.uk/seminarpapers/27-02-15-FF.pdf.)

217 Yuliya Demyanyk, "Did Credit Scores Predict the Subprime Crisis?" *The Regional Economist*, (October 2008): 12–13, https://www.stlouisfed.org/~/media/Files/ PDFs/publications/pub_assets/pdf/re/2008/d/mortgage.pdf.

218 Yuliya Demyanyk, and Otto Van Hemert, *Understanding the Subprime Mortgage Crisis* (December 5, 2008), http://ssrn.com/abstract=1020396.

219 Christopher L. Foote et al., *Subprime Facts: What (We Think) We Know About the Subprime Crisis and What We Don't* (Public Policy Discussion Papers No. 08-2, Federal Reserve Bank of Boston, May 30, 2008), 4, 30, https://www.bostonfed. org/economic/ppdp/2008/ppdp0802.pdf.

220 A potentially important, aggravating factor was introduced in late 2007. President Bush signed the Mortgage Forgiveness Debt Relief Act of 2007 on December 20. Normally, homeowners would owe taxes on forgiven mortgage debt after a foreclosure. This act, which would eventually be extended through 2013, temporarily suspended that tax liability, allowing underwater homeowners to more easily default on their mortgages. In an economy full of homeowners watching their home equity slip further into the red each month, this was like throwing a lit match on a pile of rags. This created selling pressure, and plausibly was a factor as the drop in real estate prices and equity levels accelerated.

221 Ben S. Bernanke, *The Courage to Act*, (New York: W.W. Norton & Company, 2015), 134–135.

222 Federal Reserve Bank of New York: Research and Statistics Group, *Quarterly Report on Household Debt and Credit: 2017: Q3* (New York, NY: Federal Reserve Bank of New York Center for Microeconomic Data, released November 2017),

https://www.newyorkfed.org/medialibrary/interactives/householdcredit/data/pdf/HHDC_2017Q3.pdf.

223 "Transcript of the Federal Open Market Committee Meeting of September 16, 2008," transcript of meeting of the FOMC in Washington, D.C. on September 16, 2008, 27–28, http://www.federalreserve.gov/monetarypolicy/files/FOMC20080916meeting.pdf.

224 Board of Governors of the Federal Reserve System, "Press Release: FOMC Statement," September 16, 2008, http://www.federalreserve.gov/newsevents/press/monetary/20080916a.htm.

225 Board of Governors of the Federal Reserve System, "Press Release: FOMC Statement," August 7, 2007, http://www.federalreserve.gov/newsevents/press/monetary/20070807a.htm.

226 "Troubled Asset Relief Program" that authorized expenditures of $700 billion to buy assets in panicked capital markets.

227 Bernanke, *The Courage To Act,* 325.

228 Board of Governors of the Federal Reserve, "Factors Affecting Reserve Balances – H.4.1: Release Dates," https://www.federalreserve.gov/releases/h41/.

"The Treasury Department announced today the initiation of a temporary Supplementary Financing Program at the request of the Federal Reserve. The program will consist of a series of Treasury bills, apart from Treasury's current borrowing program, which will provide cash for use in the Federal Reserve initiatives." U.S. Department of the Treasury, "Treasury Announces Supplementary Financing Program," press release no. HP-1144, September 17, 2008, https://www.treasury.gov/press-center/press-releases/Pages/hp1144.aspx.

Thanks to Alexander Schibuola, the former Chief Macroeconomist of the Joint Economic Committee of the United States Congress for introducing me to this facet of the story.

229 Normally, when the Treasury issues new debt, it isn't really a monetary activity. The Treasury borrows cash from some Americans, promising to repay it in the future, and uses that cash to purchase goods and services or to transfer it to other Americans to purchase goods and services. So, they are really just taking cash from one American and giving it to another. They aren't creating cash like the Fed does.

230 The recent Covid-19 downturn is a good example of this. When a sharp contraction hits, the demand for cash increases, so that, even using currency outstanding as a measure of monetary policy, during a panic the central bank will need to increase currency outstanding even more than usual in order to meet the heightened demand for holding cash. Currency outstanding has increased during the Covid-19 recession without creating a significant inflationary reaction. In fact, coin shortages are being reported, suggesting that, for various reasons, the economic contraction has led to more demand for physical money. Of course, if after the pandemic, demand for currency declines, inflation could rise later if the Fed doesn't adjust the amount of money outstanding back down.

231 See Board of Governors of the Federal Reserve, "Factors Affecting Reserve Balances – H.4.1: Release Dates," https://www.federalreserve.gov/releases/h41/ for Federal Reserve balance sheet data.

232 U.S. Congress Joint Economic Committee, *The 2018 Joint Economic Report: Report of the Joint Economic Committee Congress of the United States on the 2018 Economic Report of the President* (Union Calendar No. 453, Washington, D.C.: U.S. Government Printing Office, March 13, 2018), 56–57, https://fraser.stlouisfed.org/title/joint-economic-report-1250/2018-joint-economic-report-577514.

233 Board of Governors of the Federal Reserve System, "Press Release: Board announces that it will begin to pay interest on depository institutions' required and excess reserve balances," October 6, 2008, https://www.federalreserve.gov/newsevents/press/monetary/20081006a.htm.

George Selgin has pointed out that the statute granting authority to pay interest on excess reserves states that the rate is "not to exceed the general level of short-term interest rates."

See: George Selgin, "Has the Fed Been Breaking the Law?," *Alt-M*, September 6, 2016, https://www.alt-m.org/2016/09/06/has-fed-been-breaking-law/.

Yet, several other rates, such as the three-month treasury rate and overnight LIBOR rates were also below the interest on reserves rate at the time. Selgin also has a number of nice primers on the evolution of Fed policy through this period, including:

George Selgin, "A Monetary Policy Primer, Part 9: Monetary Control, Now," *Alt-M,* January 10, 2017, https://www.alt-m.org/2017/01/10/monetary-policy-primer-part-9-monetary-control-now/.

234 Sources:

Board of Governors of the Federal Reserve System (US), Effective Federal Funds Rate [DFF], retrieved from FRED, Federal Reserve Bank of St. Louis; https://fred.stlouisfed.org/series/DFF, July 24, 2021.

Board of Governors of the Federal Reserve System (US), Interest Rate on Excess Reserves [IOER], retrieved from FRED, Federal Reserve Bank of St. Louis; https://fred.stlouisfed.org/series/IOER, July 24, 2021.

Board of Governors of the Federal Reserve System (US), Federal Funds Target Rate (DISCONTINUED) [DFEDTAR], retrieved from FRED, Federal Reserve Bank of St. Louis; https://fred.stlouisfed.org/series/DFEDTAR, July 24, 2021.

Federal Reserve Bank of St. Louis, Excess Reserves of Depository Institutions (DISCONTINUED) [EXCSRESNW], retrieved from FRED, Federal Reserve Bank of St. Louis; https://fred.stlouisfed.org/series/EXCSRESNW, July 24, 2021.

Retrieved from: https://fred.stlouisfed.org/graph/?g=FDW6.

235 Federal Reserve Bank of St. Louis, "5-Year Breakeven Inflation Rate," https://fred.stlouisfed.org/series/T5YIE.

236 See Laurence M. Ball, *The Fed and Lehman Brothers: Setting the Record Straight on a Financial Disaster* (Cambridge: Cambridge University Press, 2018) for a review of the Lehman Brothers failure.

237 These figures are from the Board of Governors of the Federal Reserve System, "Assets and Liabilities of Commercial Banks in the United States – H.8," https://www.federalreserve.gov/releases/h8/default.htm. Figures were retrieved from Board of Governors of the Federal Reserve System (US), "Loans and Leases in Bank Credit, All Commercial Banks," https://fred.stlouisfed.org/series/TOTLL; Board of Governors of the Federal Reserve System (US), "Deposits, All Commercial Banks," https://fred.stlouisfed.org/series/DPSACBW027SBOG; and Board of Governors of the Federal Reserve System (US), "Cash Assets, All Commercial Banks https://fred.stlouisfed.org/series/CASACBW027SBOG.

238 David Beckworth, *The Great Divorce: The Federal Reserve's Move to a Floor System and the Implications for Bank Portfolios* (Mercatus Research, Arlington, VA: Mercatus Center at George Mason University, November 2018), https://www.mercatus.org/system/files/beckworth-great-divorce-mercatus-research-v1.pdf.

239 See: George Selgin, *Floored!: How a Misguided Fed Experiment Deepened and Prolonged the Great Recession* (Washington, D.C.: The Cato Institute, 2018) which includes an extensive discussion of interest on reserves.

240 William C. Dudley, "The 2015 Economic Outlook and the Implications for Monetary Policy" (speech at Bernard M. Baruch College, New York City, December 1, 2014), https://www.newyorkfed.org/newsevents/speeches/2014/dud141201.html.

241 Board of Governors of the Federal Reserve System, "Press Release: FOMC Statement," September 16, 2008, http://www.federalreserve.gov/newsevents/press/monetary/20080916a.htm.

242 For an academic discussion of how the late 2008 economic collapse was related to monetary decisions see: Robert L. Hetzel, "Monetary Policy in the 2008-2009 Recession," *FRB Richmond Economic Quarterly*, 95, no. 2 (Spring 2009): 201–233, https://ssrn.com/abstract=2188500.

243 Richard W. Fisher, "Responding to Turbulence (With Reference to Bob Dylan, Alan Brooke, Washington Irving, Anna Fisher, and Marcus Nadler)," (speech before the Money Marketers of New York University, New York City,

September 25, 2008), https://www.dallasfed.org/news/speeches/fisher/2008/fs080925.cfm.

244 "The Fed Holds," editorial, *The Wall Street Journal*, September 17, 2008, http://www.wsj.com/articles/SB122160976650345605.

245 S&P Dow Jones Indices LLC, "S&P/Case-Shiller U.S. National Home Price Index," https://fred.stlouisfed.org/graph/?g=5i27.

246 Board of Governors of the Federal Reserve System (US), "Delinquency Rate on Single Family Residential Mortgages, booked in Domestic Offices, All Commercial Banks," https://fred.stlouisfed.org/series/DRSFRMACBS.

247 "Annual Reports on Form 10-K," Fannie Mae, updated February 12, 2021, https://www.fanniemae.com/about-us/investor-relations/annual-reports.

248 "Annual Reports on Form 10-K," Fannie Mae, https://fanniemae.gcs-web.com/annual-filings and author's calculations.

249 Ken Fears, "Green Shoots of Credit?," *Economists' Outlook* (blog), *National Association of Realtors*, June 3, 2014, http://economistsoutlook.blogs.realtor.org/2014/06/03/green-shoots-of-credit/.

250 Federal Reserve Bank of New York Research and Statistics Group, *Quarterly Report on Household Debt and Credit* (New York, NY: Federal Reserve Bank of New York Center for Microeconomic Data), https://www.newyorkfed.org/microeconomics/hhdc/background.html.

251 Antonio Weiss and Karen Dynan, "Housing Finance Reform: Access and Affordability in Focus," *Treasury Department*, October 26, 2016, https://medium.com/@USTreasury/housing-finance-reform-access-and-affordability-in-focus-d559541a4cdc#.lzr6vky7n.

There is a mitigating factor here. In the housing boom, when the GSEs were capturing market share from FHA, this caused the credit standards in each conduit to look worse even though the combined credit standards were relatively stable. Now, this compositional bias is happening in the opposite direction so that the FHA has been capturing market share back from the GSEs, causing credit standards for both to appear tighter than they are. In other words, there may be more borrowers rejected by the GSEs, but some of those borrowers are getting loans through the FHA conduit. Borrowers at the FHA tend to have more credit risk, so if the riskier borrowers move from the GSEs to the FHA, this will increase the average credit standard at both.

The Kansas City Federal Reserve issued a bulletin regarding this effect. Jordan Rappaport and Paul Willen, "Tight Credit Conditions Continue to Constrain the Housing Recovery," (Current Policy Perspectives No. 2014-1, Federal Reserve Bank of Boston, July 7, 2014), https://www.bostonfed.org/publications/current-policy-perspectives/2014/tight-credit-conditions-continue-to-constrain-the-housing-recovery.aspx. However, if we expand our view to the entire market, there has still been significant tightening. The flow of borrowers back to the FHA and away from the GSEs was not enough to counteract the extreme tightening that happened in every conduit—the banks, the FHA, the GSEs, and the private securitization market. Mortgage originators are offered a reprieve from some of the onerous new regulations and liabilities if they sell their mortgages to the government agencies. If they can do that, it is called a "Qualified Mortgage." So, today banks try to sell off mortgages that have any substantial default risk to the government agencies, and they mainly only keep the safest mortgages on their own balance sheets in order to avoid future regulatory penalties. The net result of all of these developments has been a sharp reduction in credit access for relatively qualified, but not perfect, borrowers.

252 By high-tier and low-tier, I mean, within a metropolitan area, higher-priced areas versus lower-priced areas.

253 In some preliminary research, I have found evidence that the effect of credit on home prices was much stronger during this bust period than it had been during the boom. For instance, in the Phoenix market, I identified ten neighborhoods tracked by Zillow that are retirement communities. The homeowners in those neighborhoods tend to be equity owners that are not as reliant on mortgage funding. Those neighborhoods boomed just as other Phoenix neighborhoods did. Both retirement communities and other neighborhoods in Phoenix increased in value by an average of 47 percent from the end of 2003 to the end

of 2005. Average price changes were similar for homes in both more expensive and less expensive neighborhoods. Per capita debt ticked up in Arizona at the end of 2005 and peaked by the third quarter of 2007. Over that span, homes in retirement communities lost about 9 percent of their value and homes in other neighborhoods lost an average of about 7 percent. However, among the least expensive 20 percent of neighborhoods, home prices over that period roughly remained stable. Then, after the third quarter of 2007, the average home in retirement communities lost 49 percent. Home prices in non-retirement neighborhoods lost more, and their losses then were highly sensitive to the economic profile of the neighborhood. Homes in the most expensive 20 percent of neighborhoods lost 57 percent of their value, on average, and homes in the least expensive 20 percent of neighborhoods lost 73 percent. (All figures on a natural log scale.) The comparison of retirement homes to non-retirement homes in Phoenix corroborates other evidence that the pattern of price appreciation within the metro area didn't appear to be sensitive to credit constraints during the boom. Mortgage access during the CDO boom may have briefly prevented prices in neighborhoods more dependent on credit from declining as much as prices in other neighborhoods. Then, Contagion markets like Phoenix took a tremendous hit after 2007, across the board, and the tremendous tightening of credit after 2007 left a huge and telling scar on the most credit-constrained neighborhoods.

254 The 34 percent loss was for homes in zip codes in the second quintile, arranged by price. Zip codes more expensive than the bottom 20 percent and less expensive than the top 60 percent.

255 Henry M. Paulson, Jr., *On the Brink: Inside the Race to Stop the Collapse of the Global Financial System* (New York City: Business Plus, 2013), 437.

256 Timothy F. Geithner, *Stress Test: Reflections on Financial Crises*, (New York: Broadway Books, 2014), 378.

257 Frequently, a lack of demand from low-priced home buyers is cited as the source of the decline. But, these households are spending as much as ever on rent, mortgage affordability has never been better, and mortgage applications

of borrowers who would have previously qualified are now denied. Supply of credit is the main constraint.

258 "Testimony of Jack Hartings President and CEO of Peoples Bank Co. Coldwater, OH on behalf of the Independent Community Bankers of America," testimony before the US House of Representatives Committee of Financial Services Subcommittee on Financial Institutions and Consumer Credit hearing on "How Prospective and Current Homeowners Will Be Affected by the CFPBs Qualified Mortgage Rule," Washington D.C., January 14, 2014, https://docs. house.gov/meetings/BA/BA15/20140114/101654/HHRG-113-BA15-Wstate-HartingsJ-20140114.pdf;Daniel Weickenand CEO of Orion Federal Credit Union on behalf of the National Association of Federal Credit Unions," testimony before the US House of Representatives Committee of Financial Services Subcommittee on Financial Institutions and Consumer Credit hearing on "How Prospective and Current Homeowners Will Be Affected by the CFPBs Qualified Mortgage Rule," Washington D.C., January 14, 2014, https://docs. house.gov/meetings/BA/BA15/20140114/101654/HHRG-113-BA15-Wstate-WeickenandD-20140114.pdf; and Lane, "Here's clear evidence of how much more complicated mortgage lending is now," *Housing Wire*, November 3, 2016, https://www.housingwire.com/articles/38449-heres-clear-evidence-of-how-much-more-complicated-mortgage-lending-is-now.

259 Adonis Antoniades, "Commercial bank failures during the Great Recession: the real (estate) story," (Working Paper Series No. 1779, European Central Bank, April 2015), https://www.ecb.europa.eu/pub/pdf/scpwps/ecbwp1779. en.pdf?7edad23ab5613b9693606b94616231eb.

260 Building in the UK has declined, but not as sharply as the US. Organization for Economic Co-operation, "Total Dwelling and Residential Buildings by Stage of Construction, Started for the United States, Australia, United Kingdom, and Canada," https://fred.stlouisfed.org/graph/?g=cK8W.

261 Construction employment in the UK has been somewhat stagnant. Real GDP growth in the UK has also been low—only about 12 percent since 2007 compared to 18 percent or more for the other countries.

262 Bureau of Economic Analysis, "Personal Income, Population, Per Capita Personal Income (CAINC1)," https://apps.bea.gov/iTable/iTable.cfm?reqid=70&step=1&acrdn=6; and United States Census Bureau, "Building Permits Survey," https://www.census.gov/construction/bps/. Analysis includes largest 34 MSAs. This includes all Closed Access cities, including San Jose.

263 United States Census Bureau, "New Residential Sales: Historical Data," https://www.census.gov/construction/nrs/historical_data/index.html.

264 Maria Gatae, "Average Home Size in the US: New Homes Bigger Than 10 years Ago but Apartments Trail Behind," *StorageCafé*, October 2, 2020, https://www.storagecafe.com/blog/average-home-size-in-the-us-new-homes-bigger-than-10-years-ago-but-apartments-trail-behind/.

265 United States Census Bureau, "American Housing Survey," https://www.census.gov/programs-surveys/ahs.html. Author calculations, compiled from survey responses of renters' and owners' household size in biennial survey, 2001-2013.

266 Using BLS measures for Consumer Price Index for All Urban Consumers: Shelter; All Items Less Food and Energy; and All Items Less Food, Energy, and Shelter in U.S. City Average.

267 Example: Alana Semuels, "When Wall Street is Your Landlord," *The Atlantic*, February 13, 2019, https://www.theatlantic.com/technology/archive/2019/02/single-family-landlords-wall-street/582394/.

268 One nearly doubling while the other halved.

269 US Census Bureau, "Housing Vacancies and Homeownership (CPS/HVS): Historical Tables: Table 12. Annual Estimates of the Housing Inventory by Age of Householder 1982 Present and Table 19. Quarterly Homeownership Rates by Age of Householder: 1994 to Present," https://www.census.gov/housing/hvs/data/histtabs.html.

For more detail on demographic shifts in homeownership, see Laurie S. Goodman and Christopher Mayer, "Homeownership and the American

Dream," *Journal of Economic Perspectives*, 32, no. 1 (Winter 2018): Tables 2 and 3, https://www.urban.org/sites/default/files/publication/96221/homeownership_and_the_american_dream_0.pdf.

They control for age, income, education, and marital status. They find that after accounting for all of those demographic changes, the national homeownership rate was 2.5 percent higher in 1995 and 5.8 percent higher in 2005 than it would have been in 1985 with the same demographics. This makes it tempting to conclude that more aggressive lending to marginal borrowers led to higher homeownership, but the data tells a more complex story. The rise in homeownership in 2005 compared to either 1985 or 1995 was greater among households with more education. Then, when homeownership collapsed between 2005 and 2015, the collapse was larger among less-educated households and smaller among more-educated households. In other words, their data shows that (1) the rise in homeownership before 2005 was focused on households that were more likely to be qualified and that (2) the collapse in homeownership after 2005 was not a reversal of the pre-2005 trends.

270 Bloomberg News, "Former Fed chairman Bernanke turned down for mortgage refinance," October 10, 2014, https://www.chicagotribune.com/business/chi-bernanke-mortgage-refinance-20141003-story.html.

271 Scott Sumner and Kevin Erdmann, *Housing Policy, Monetary Policy, and the Great Recession* (Mercatus Research Series, Arlington, VA: The Mercatus Center at George Mason University, August 4, 2020), https://ssrn.com/abstract=3667309 or http://dx.doi.org/10.2139/ssrn.3667309.

272 The rate of growth is somewhat arbitrary. A 5 percent growth level is probably closest to the growth Americans are used to, with around 2 percent inflation over time.

273 See: Casey Newton, "What Amazon got wrong about New York City," *The Verge*, February 15, 2019, https://www.theverge.com/interface/2019/2/15/18225646/amazon-nyc-hq2-collapse-secrecy-incentives-automation; and Matthew Yglesias, "Silicon Valley's profound housing crisis, in one sentence,"

Vox, June 7, 2016, https://www.vox.com/2016/6/7/11877378/silicon-valley-housing-crisis.

274 Bureau of Economic Analysis, "National Data: National Income and Product Accounts: Section 7 – Supplemental Tables: Table 7.12. Imputations in the National Income and Product Accounts: Line 158 - Taxes on production and imports on Owner-Occupied Housing," https://apps.bea.gov/iTable/iTable.cfm?reqid=19&step=2#reqid=19&step=2&isuri=1&1921=survey.

275 See: Nicolas Peterson, "Demand Sharing: Reciprocity and the Pressure for Generosity among Foragers," *American Anthropologist*, 95, no. 4, (Dec 1993): 860-874, https://www.jstor.org/stable/683021.

276 See Adam Thierer, *Permissionless Innovation: The Continuing Case for Comprehensive Technological Freedom* (Arlington, VA: The Mercatus Center at George Mason University, 2016), https://www.merca-tus.org/publications/technology-and-innovation/permissionless-innovation-continuing-case-comprehensive.

277 *Eugene Kiely, "'You Didn't Build That,' Uncut and Unedited," The Fact Check Wire, Annenberg Public Policy Center of the University of Pennsylvania,* https://www.factcheck.org/2012/07/you-didnt-build-that-uncut-and-unedited.